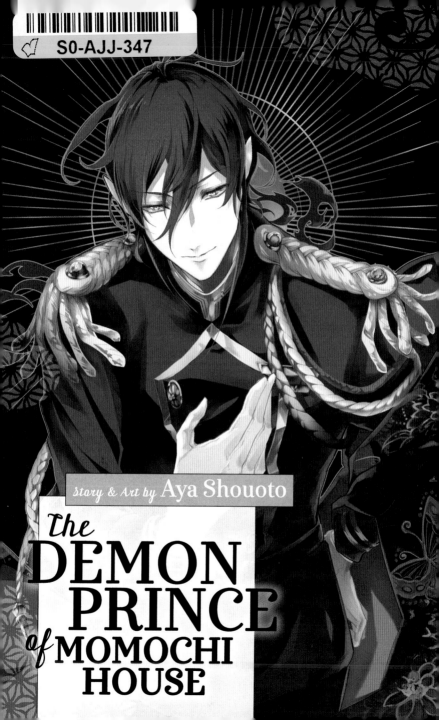

story & Art by Aya Shouoto

The
DEMON
PRINCE
of MOMOCHI
HOUSE

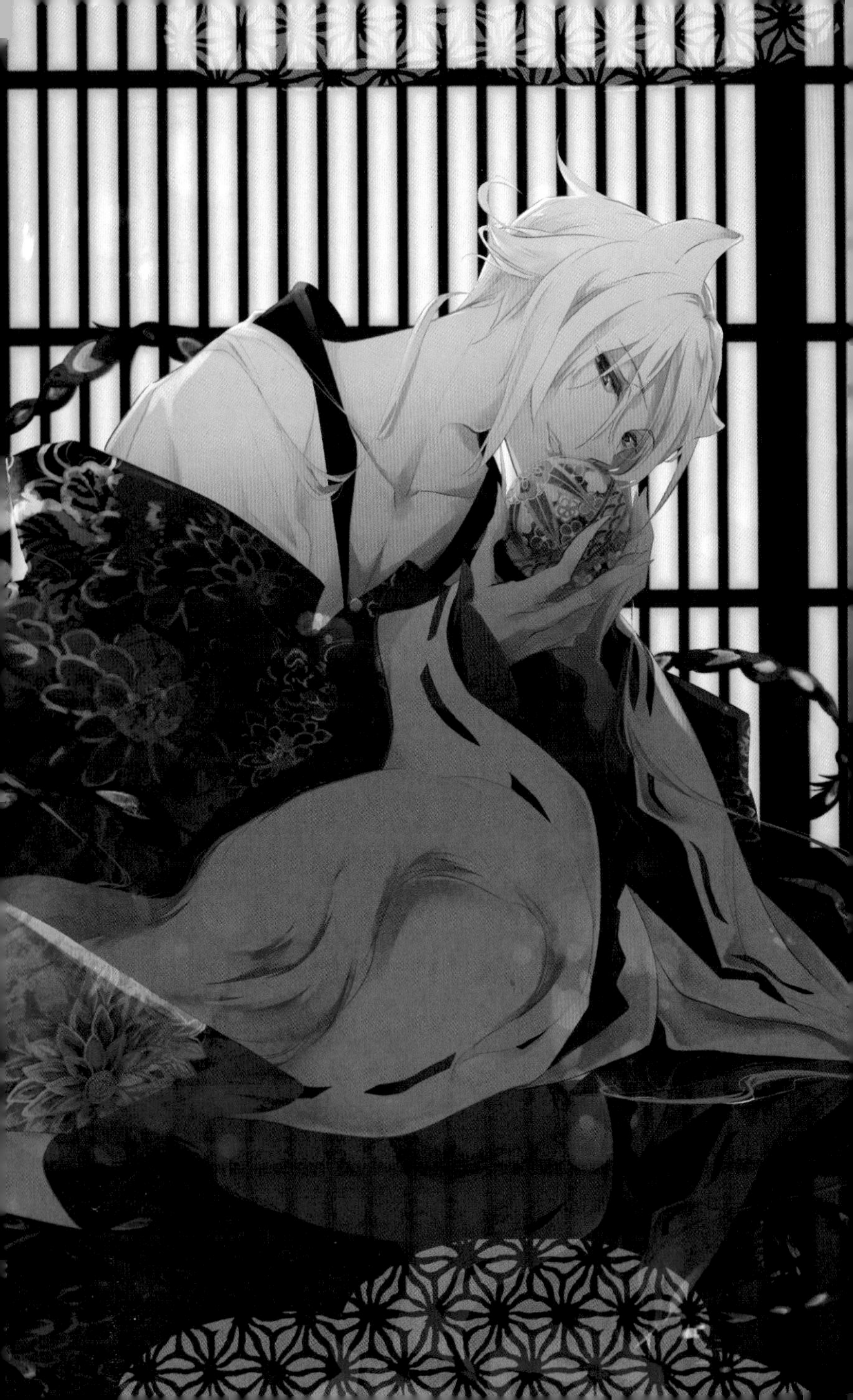

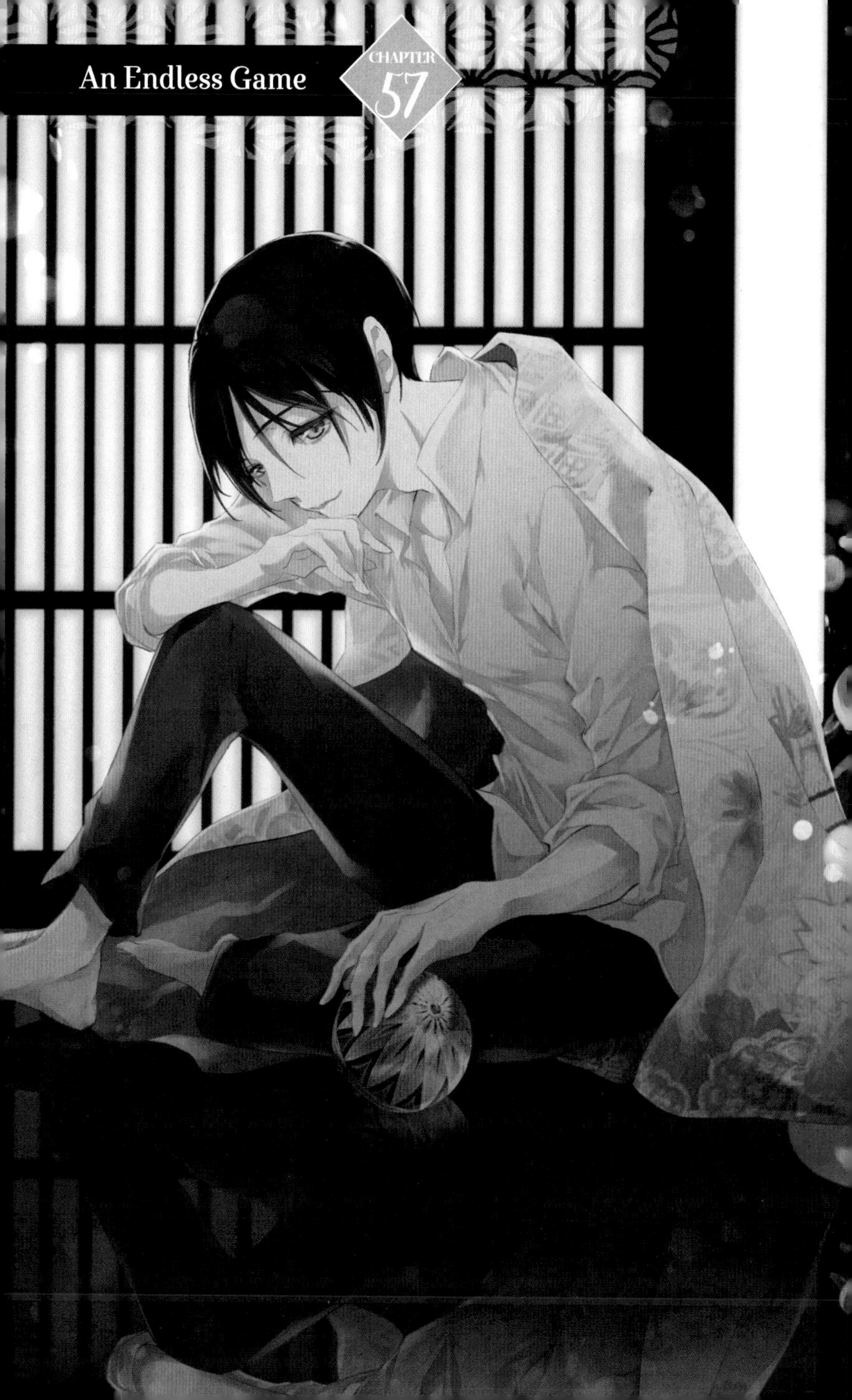
An Endless Game
CHAPTER
57

The DEMON PRINCE of MOMOCHI HOUSE

15

Contents

The Mysterious Residents of Momochi House

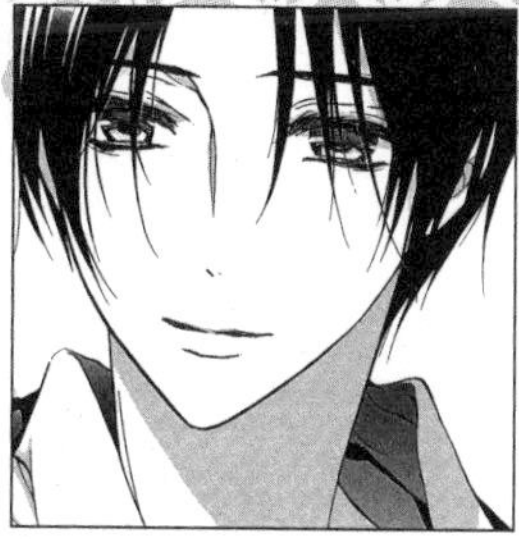

Aoi Nanamori

When he was 7 years old, he wandered into Momochi House and was chosen as the Omamori-sama. He transforms into a nue to perform his duties, but it seems this role was meant for Himari.

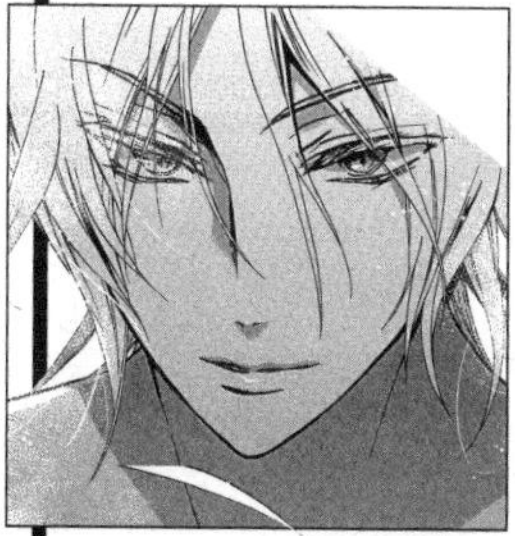

Omamori-sama (Nue)

An ayakashi, or demon, with the ears of a cat, the wings of a bird, and the tail of a fox. As the Omamori-sama, the nue protects Momochi House and eliminates demons who make their way in from the spiritual realm.

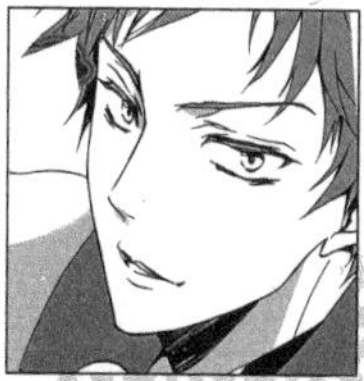

Ise

One of Omamori-sama's shikigami. He's an orangutan.

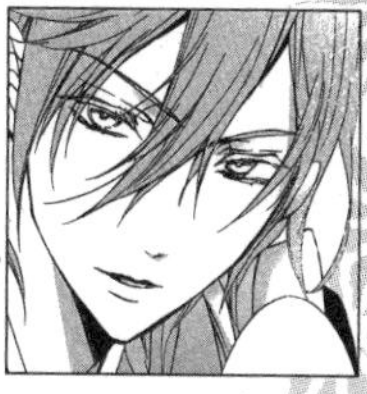

Yukari

One of Omamori-sama's shikigami. He's a water serpent.

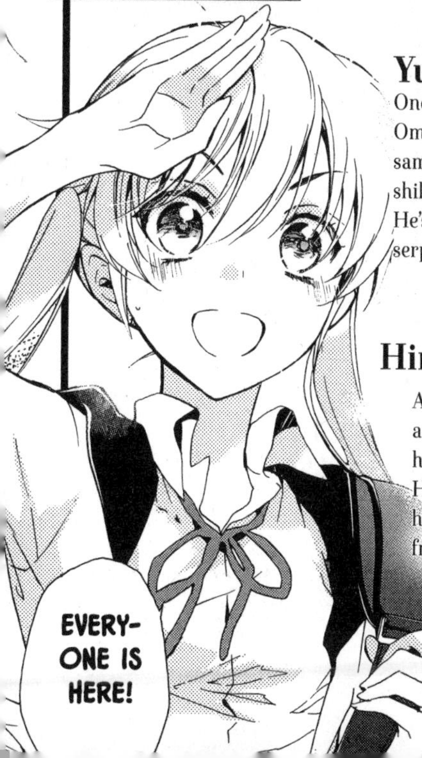
EVERY-ONE IS HERE!

Himari Momochi

A 16-year-old orphan who, according to a certain will, has inherited Momochi House. As rightful owner, she has the ability to expel beings from the house.

Lesser Yokai

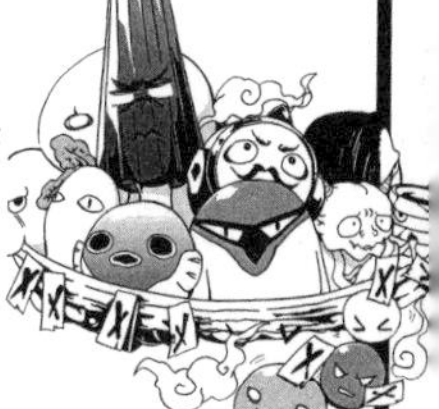

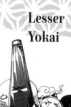

Momochi House: Story Thus Far

Kasha and Aoi battle in the spiritual realm. Aoi's shikigami try to save him, but when Kasha presents their sins to them, the overwhelmed shikigami enter their own personal battles. The bond between everyone on Aoi's side is strong...or at least that's how it appears until Kasha tells the truth about Aoi. It is enough to sink Himari into despair. Aoi was born connected to a vein of human sin, and this is the source of his ayakashi powers. Because Aoi's powers are unlimited, he cannot escape from Momochi House. Aoi reveals he's now half ayakashi and can't return to being human anymore. As Himari tries to cling to the last shred of hope, Nue appears! Meanwhile, Kasha's flames of sin are closing in on Himari. Just what sin has Himari committed?!

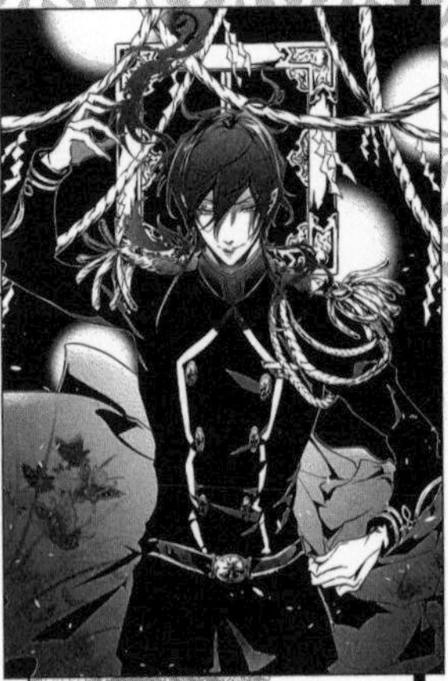

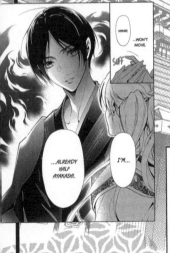

Kasha

The highest level of ayakashi. He reigns over all others. He constantly gives Nue (Aoi) a hard time.

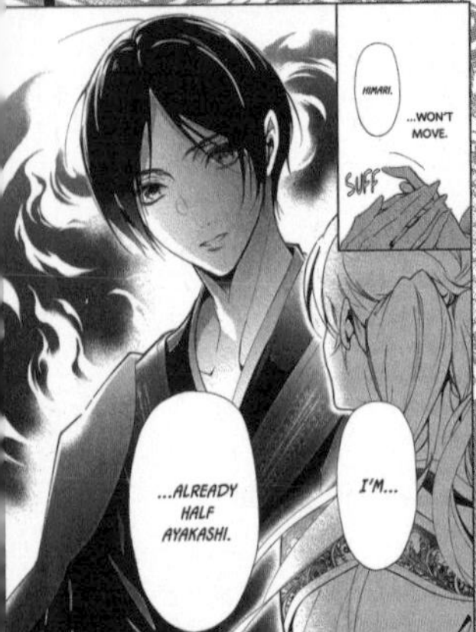
HIMARI.
...WON'T MOVE.
SUFF
I'M...
...ALREADY HALF AYAKASHI.

Hakka

Omamori-sama's newest shikigami. His identity is Shuten Douji.

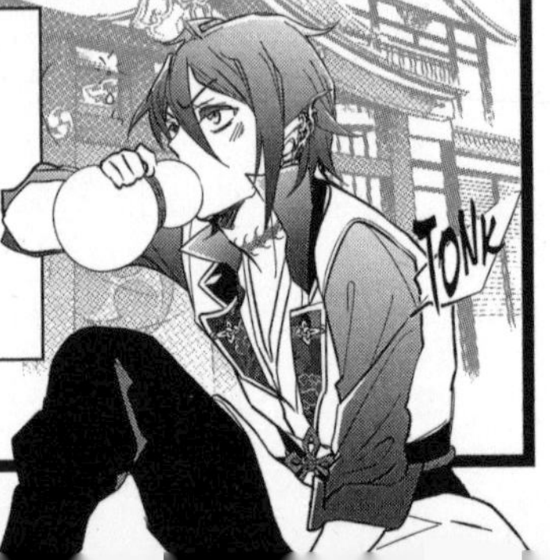
TONK

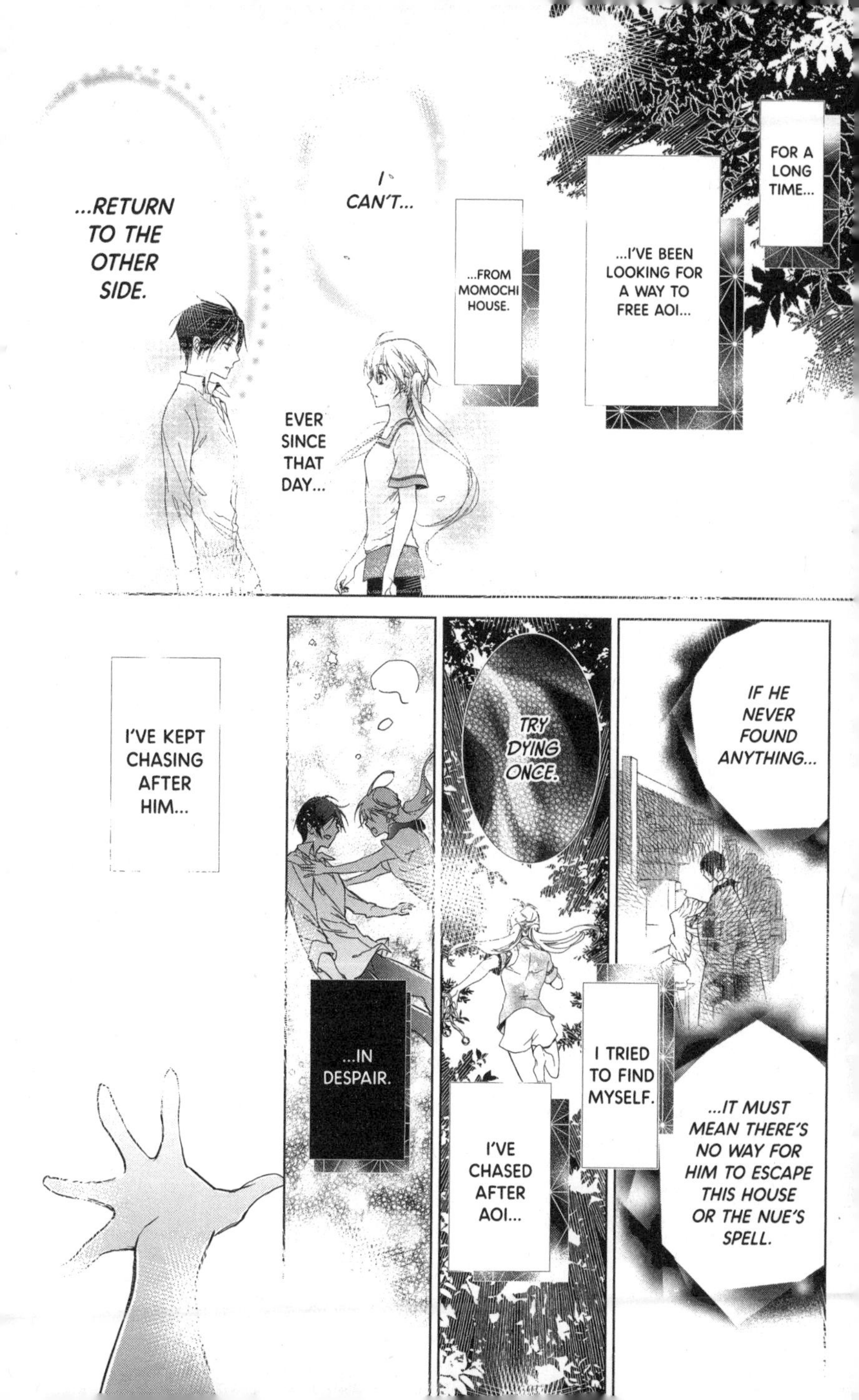
FOR A LONG TIME...
...I'VE BEEN LOOKING FOR A WAY TO FREE AOI...
...FROM MOMOCHI HOUSE.
I CAN'T...
...RETURN TO THE OTHER SIDE.
EVER SINCE THAT DAY...
IF HE NEVER FOUND ANYTHING...
...IT MUST MEAN THERE'S NO WAY FOR HIM TO ESCAPE THIS HOUSE OR THE NUE'S SPELL.
I TRIED TO FIND MYSELF.
TRY DYING ONCE.
I'VE CHASED AFTER AOI...
...IN DESPAIR.
I'VE KEPT CHASING AFTER HIM...

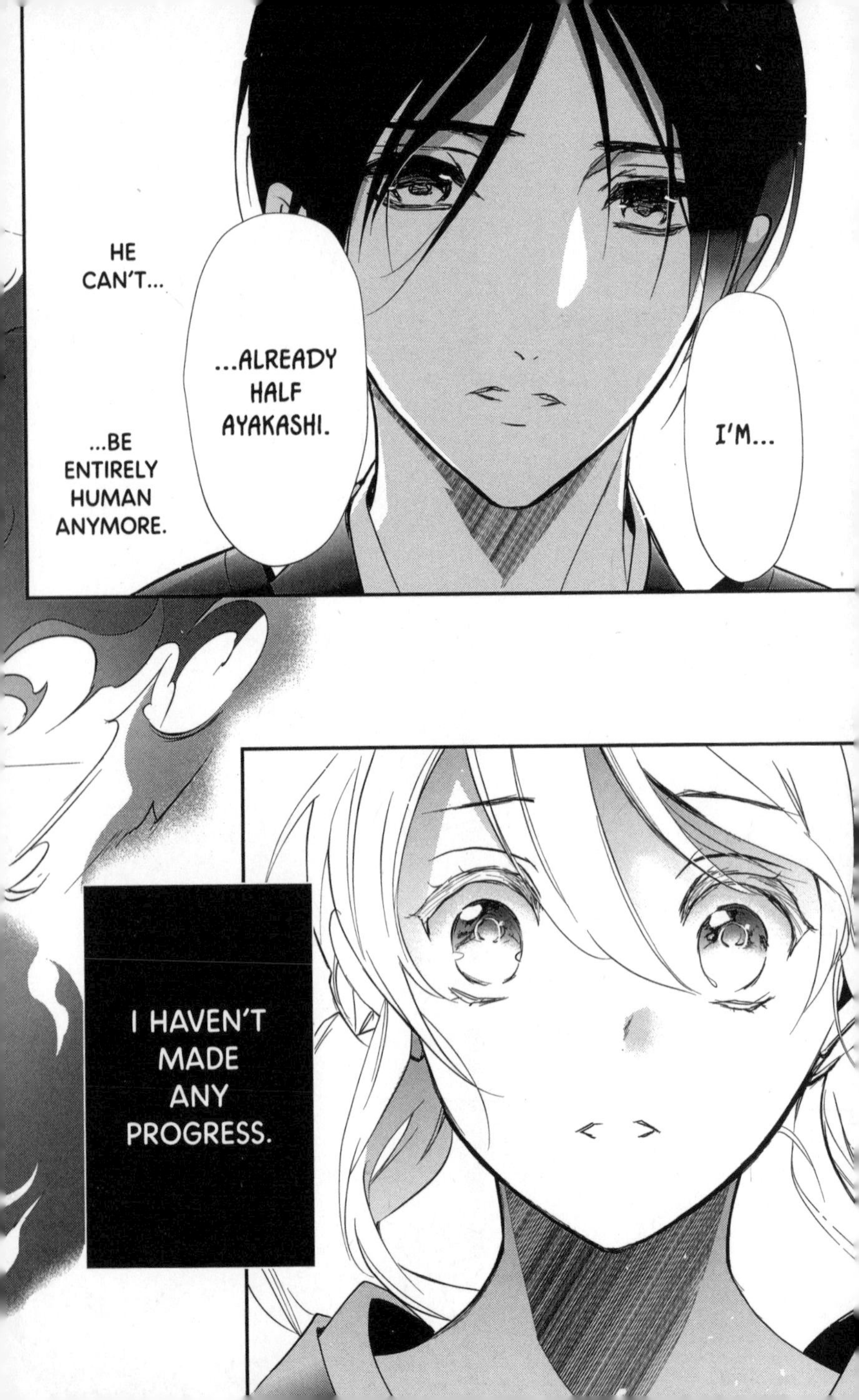
I'M...
...ALREADY HALF AYAKASHI.
HE CAN'T...
...BE ENTIRELY HUMAN ANYMORE.
I HAVEN'T MADE ANY PROGRESS.

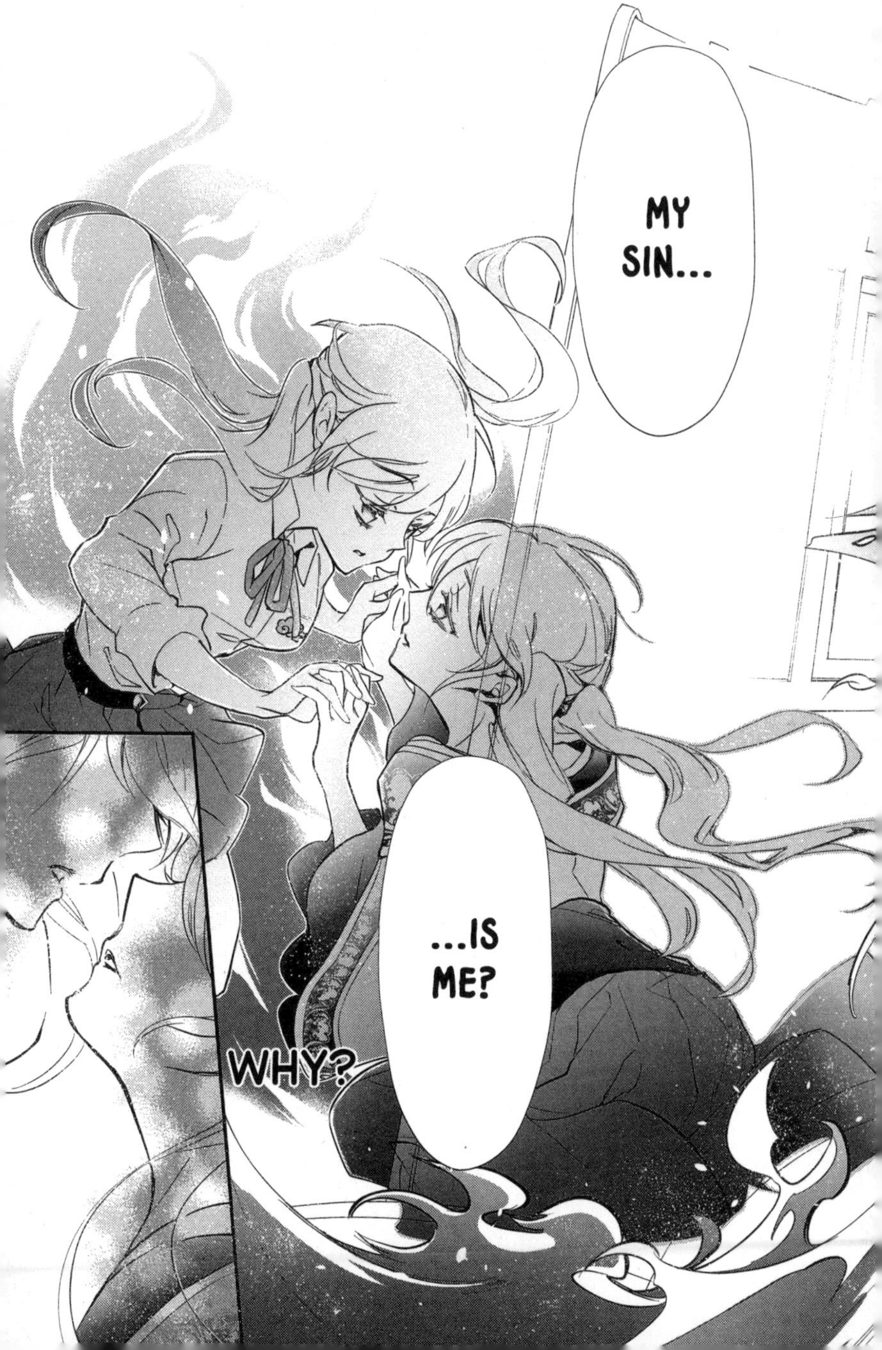
MY SIN...
...IS ME?
WHY?

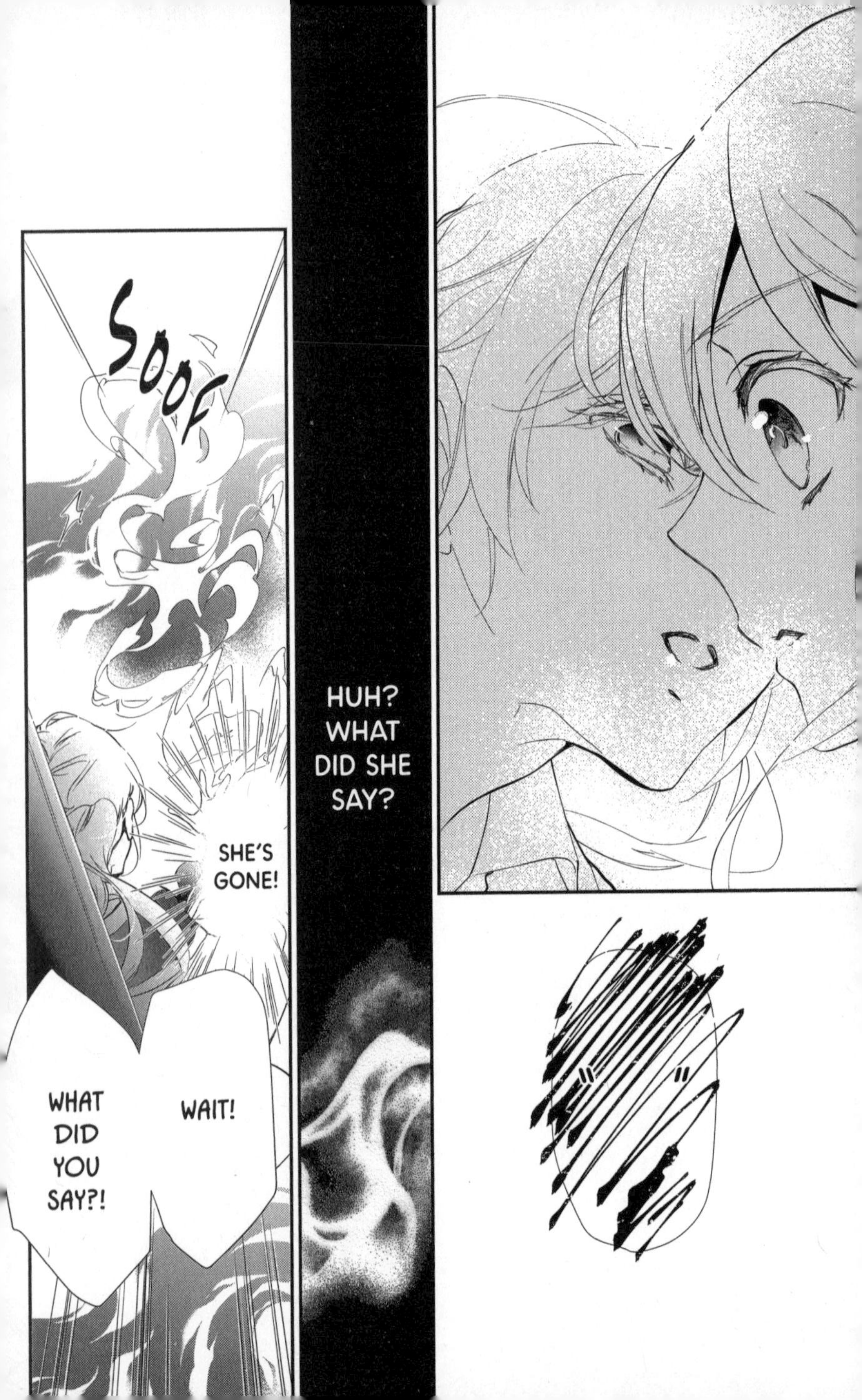
HUH? WHAT DID SHE SAY?
SOOF
SHE'S GONE!
WAIT!
WHAT DID YOU SAY?!

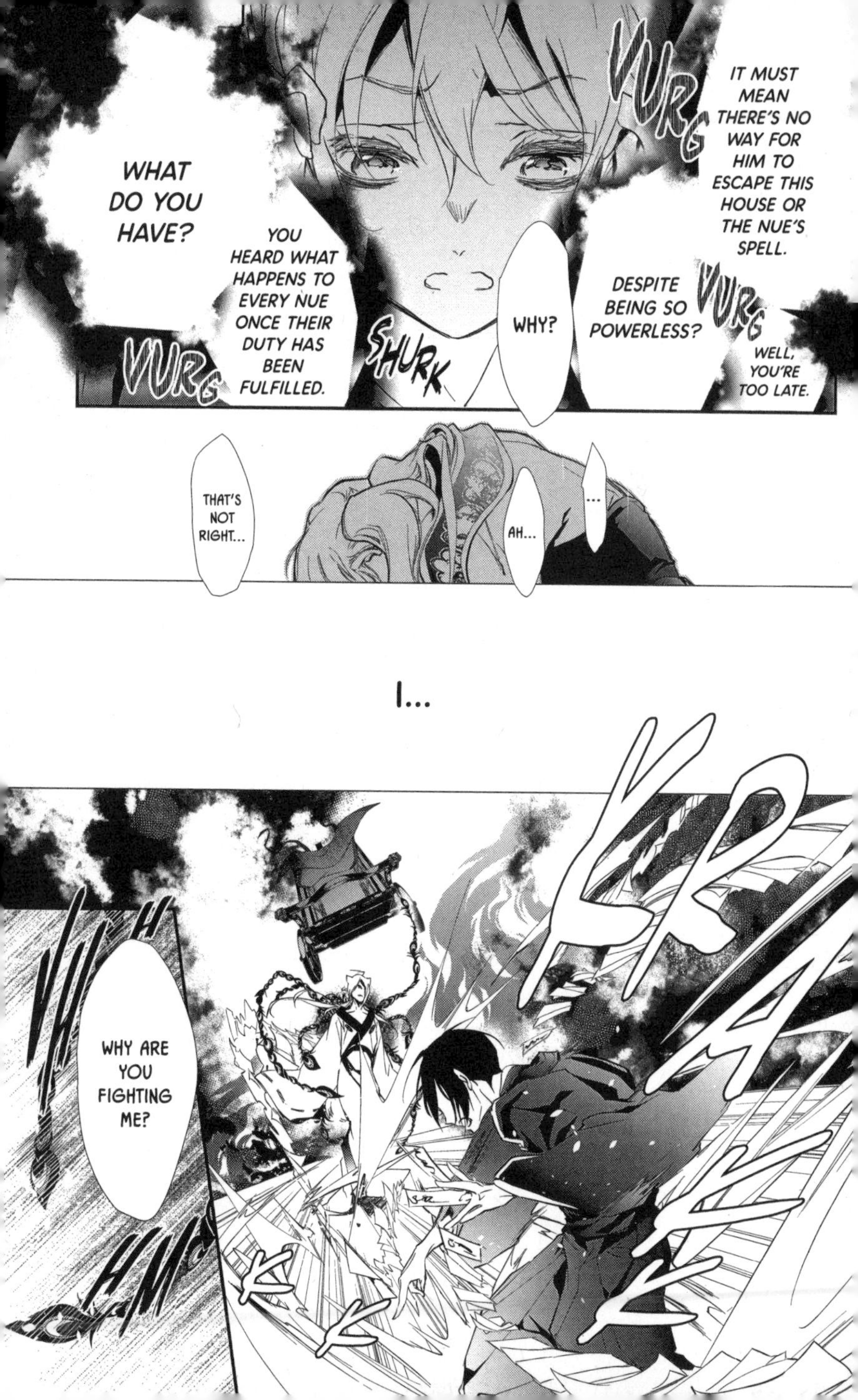

IT MUST MEAN THERE'S NO WAY FOR HIM TO ESCAPE THIS HOUSE OR THE NUE'S SPELL.
VURG
DESPITE BEING SO POWERLESS?
VURG
WELL, YOU'RE TOO LATE.
WHY?
SHURK
YOU HEARD WHAT HAPPENS TO EVERY NUE ONCE THEIR DUTY HAS BEEN FULFILLED.
WHAT DO YOU HAVE?
VURG
...
AH...
THAT'S NOT RIGHT...
I...
KRAK
WHY ARE YOU FIGHTING ME?

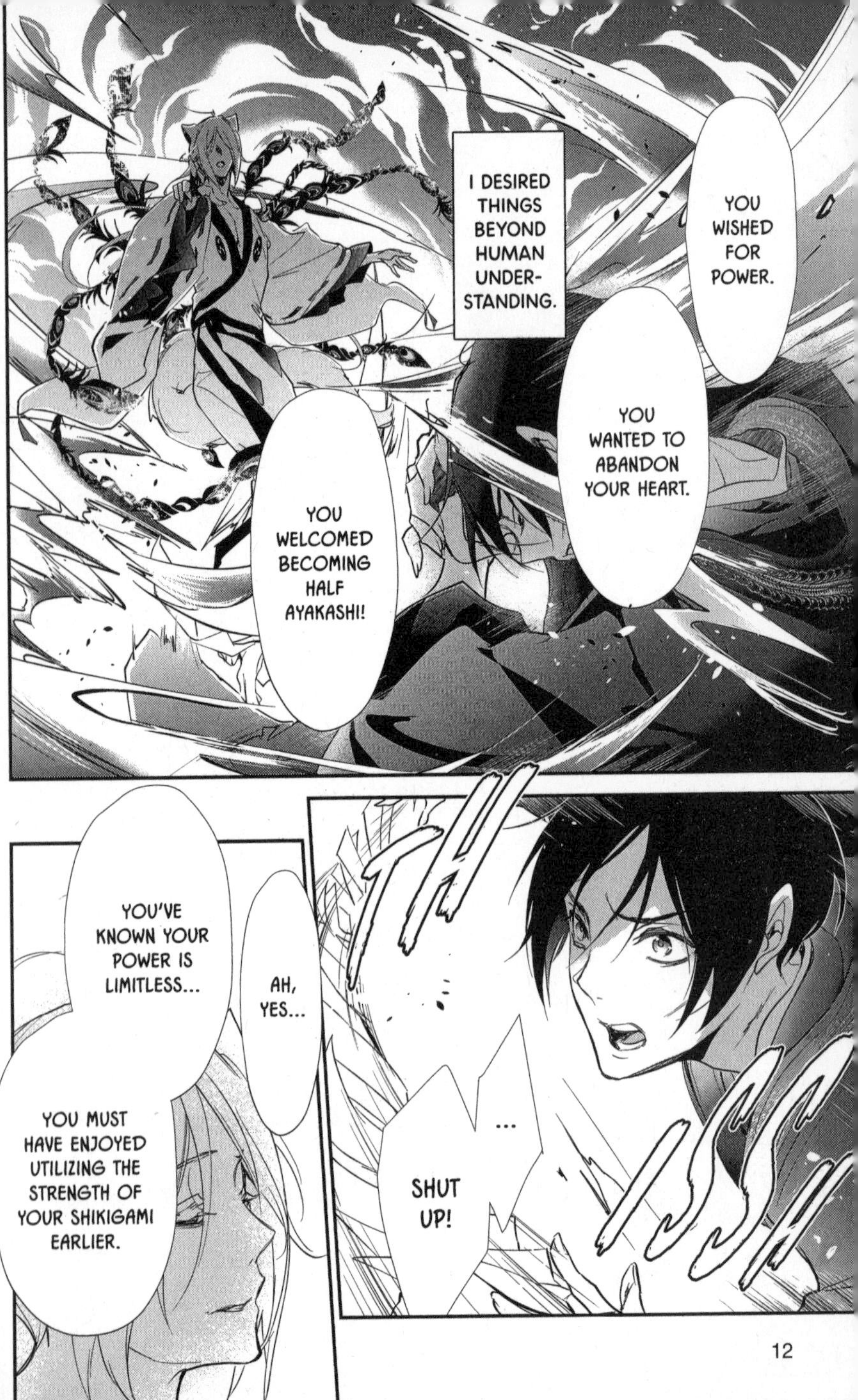

YOU WISHED FOR POWER.
I DESIRED THINGS BEYOND HUMAN UNDER-STANDING.
YOU WANTED TO ABANDON YOUR HEART.
YOU WELCOMED BECOMING HALF AYAKASHI!
TH
ISSH
...
SHUT UP!
AH, YES...
YOU'VE KNOWN YOUR POWER IS LIMITLESS...
YOU MUST HAVE ENJOYED UTILIZING THE STRENGTH OF YOUR SHIKIGAMI EARLIER.

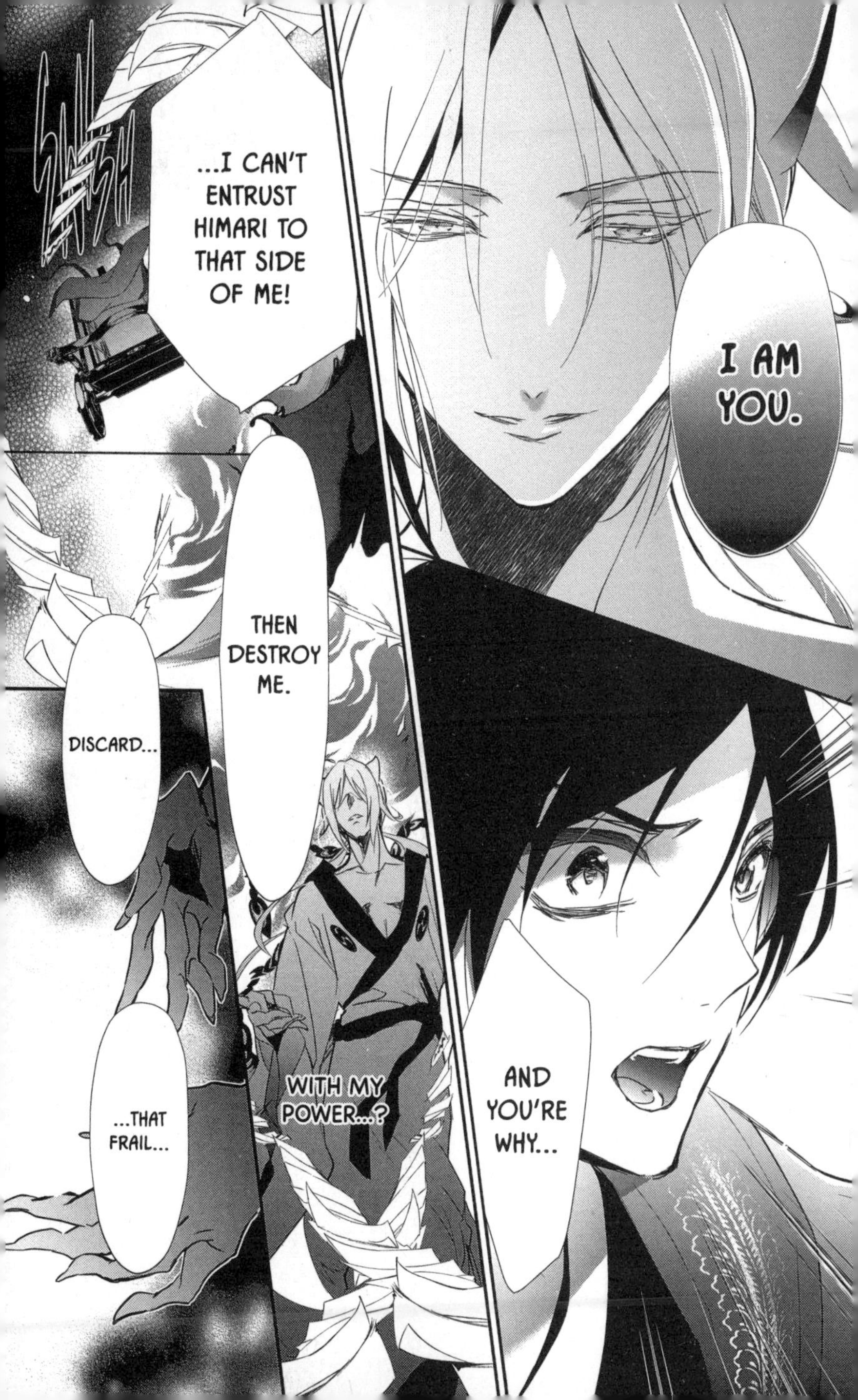
I AM YOU.
AND YOU'RE WHY...
...I CAN'T ENTRUST HIMARI TO THAT SIDE OF ME!
SWISH
THEN DESTROY ME.
WITH MY POWER...?
DISCARD...
...THAT FRAIL...

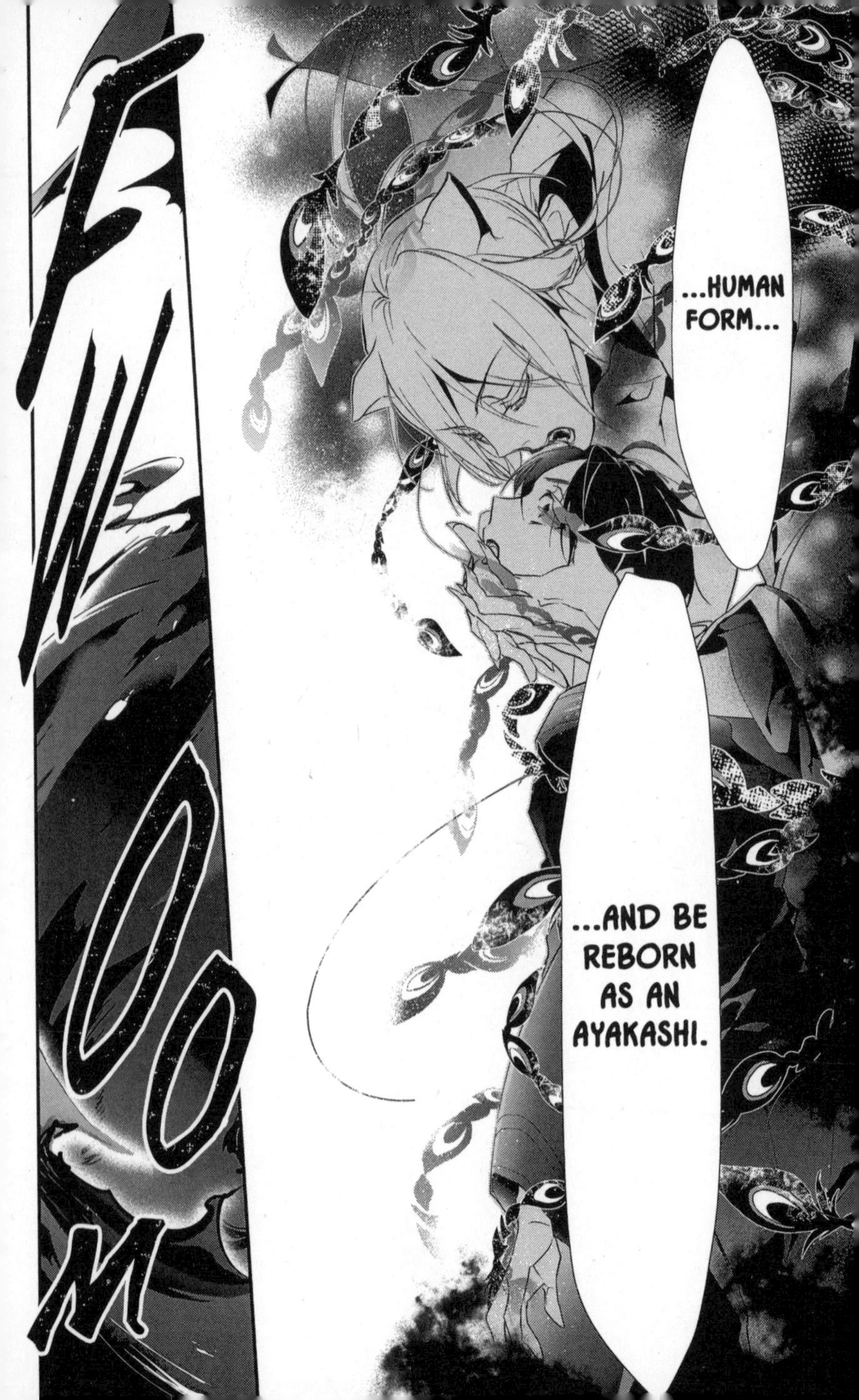
...HUMAN FORM...
...AND BE REBORN AS AN AYAKASHI.
FWOOM

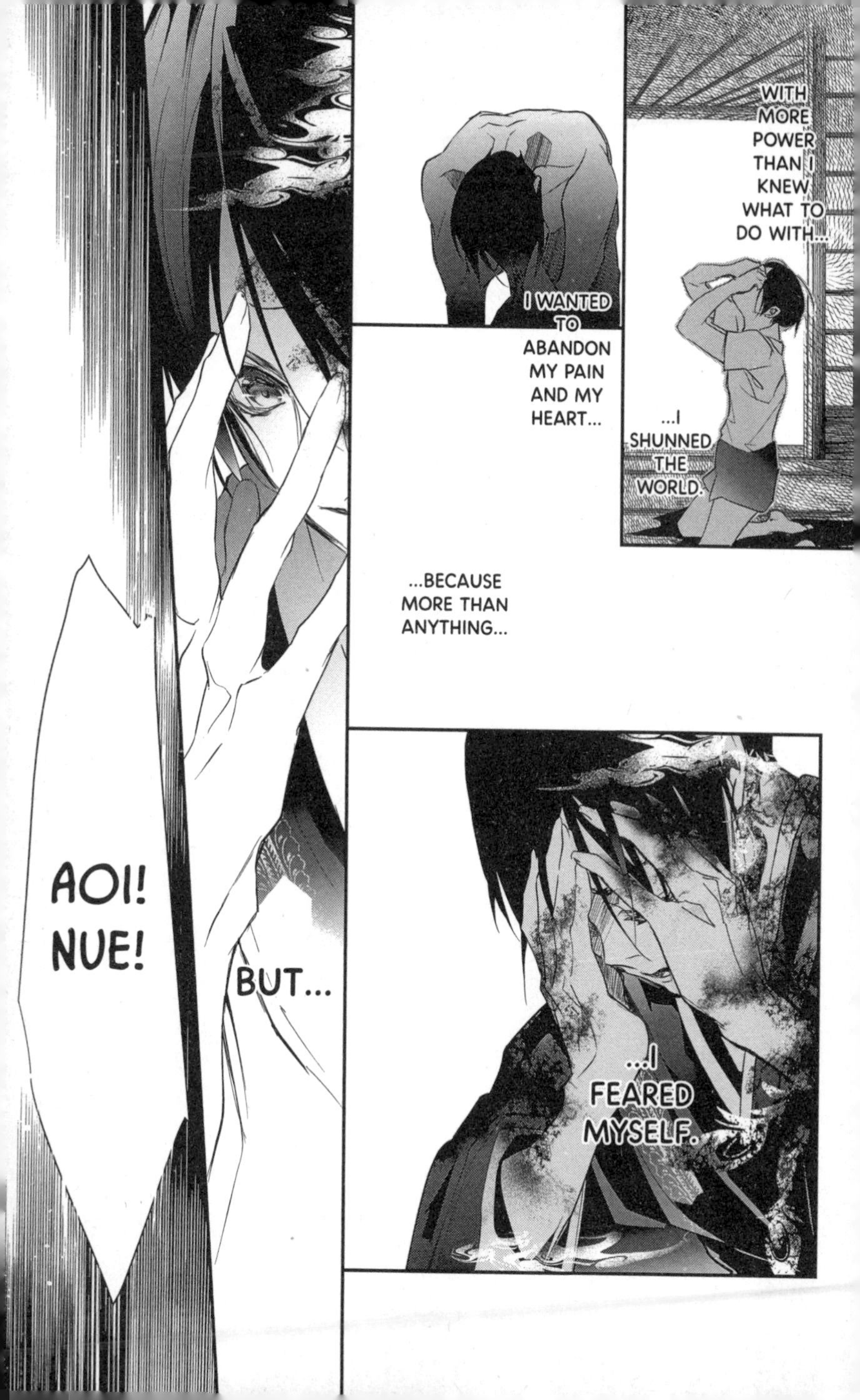
WITH MORE POWER THAN I KNEW WHAT TO DO WITH...
...I SHUNNED THE WORLD.
I WANTED TO ABANDON MY PAIN AND MY HEART...
...BECAUSE MORE THAN ANYTHING...
...I FEARED MYSELF.
BUT...
AOI! NUE!

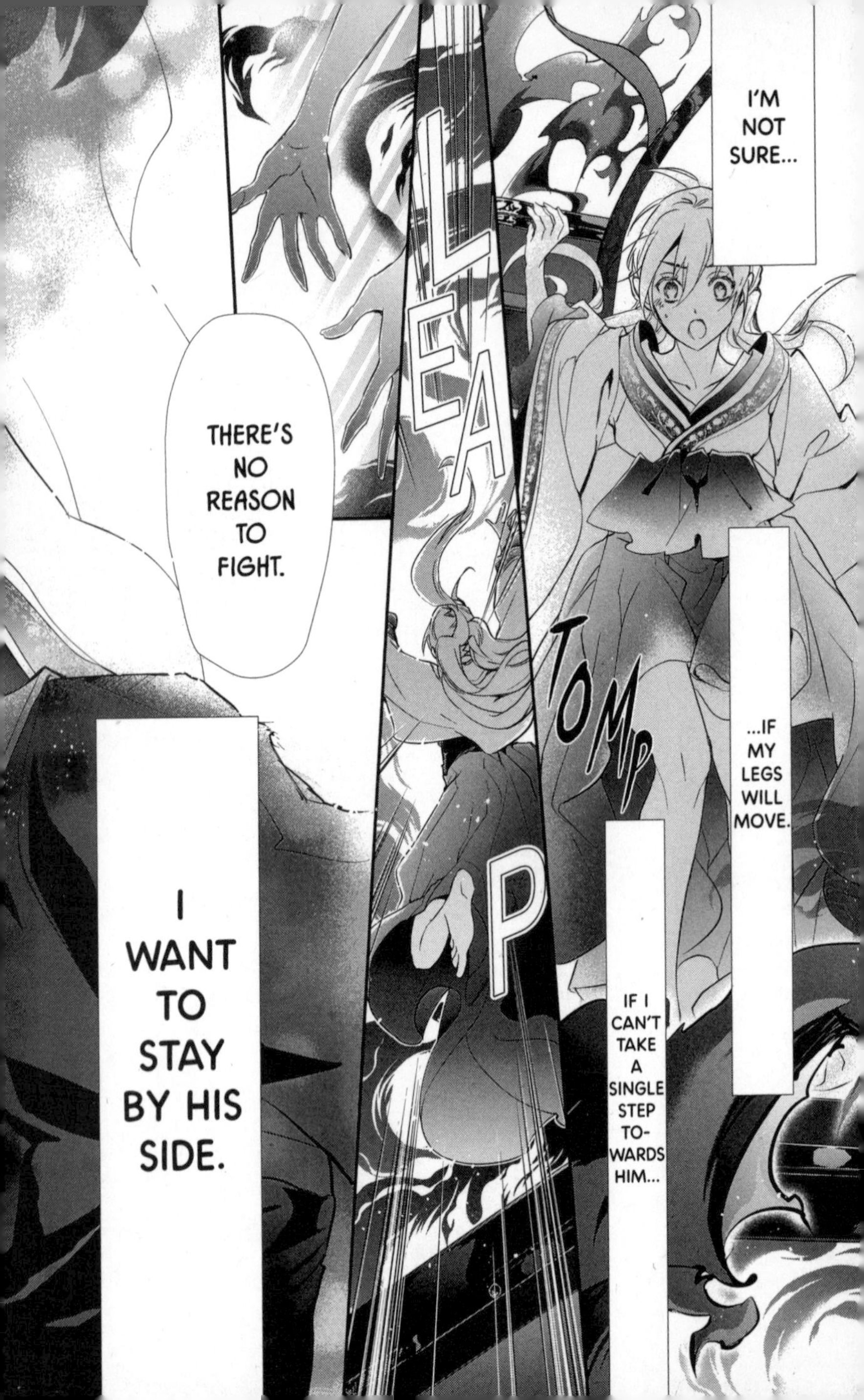
I'M NOT SURE...
...IF MY LEGS WILL MOVE.
IF I CAN'T TAKE A SINGLE STEP TO-WARDS HIM...
LEAP
TOMP
P
THERE'S NO REASON TO FIGHT.
I WANT TO STAY BY HIS SIDE.

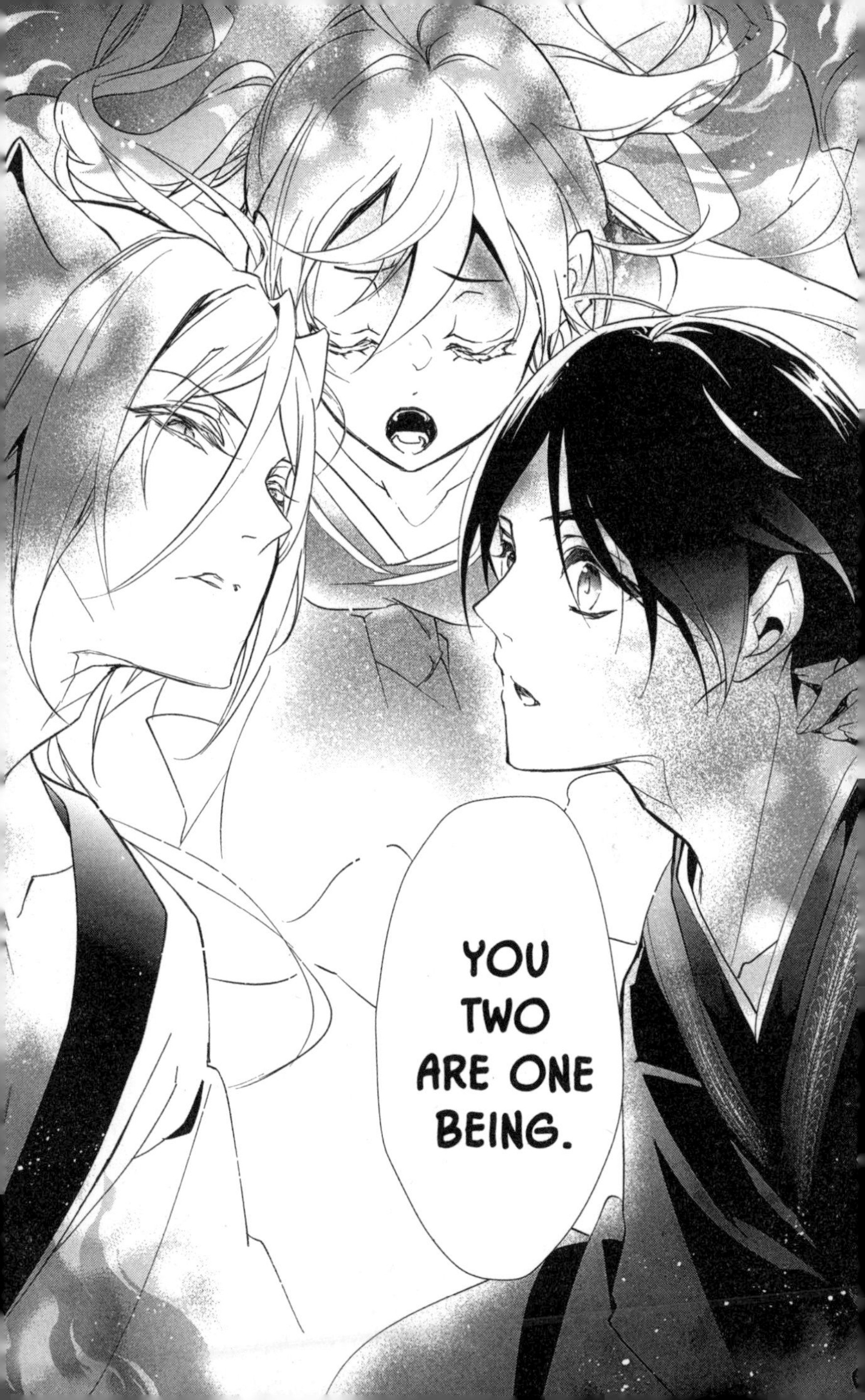
YOU TWO ARE ONE BEING.

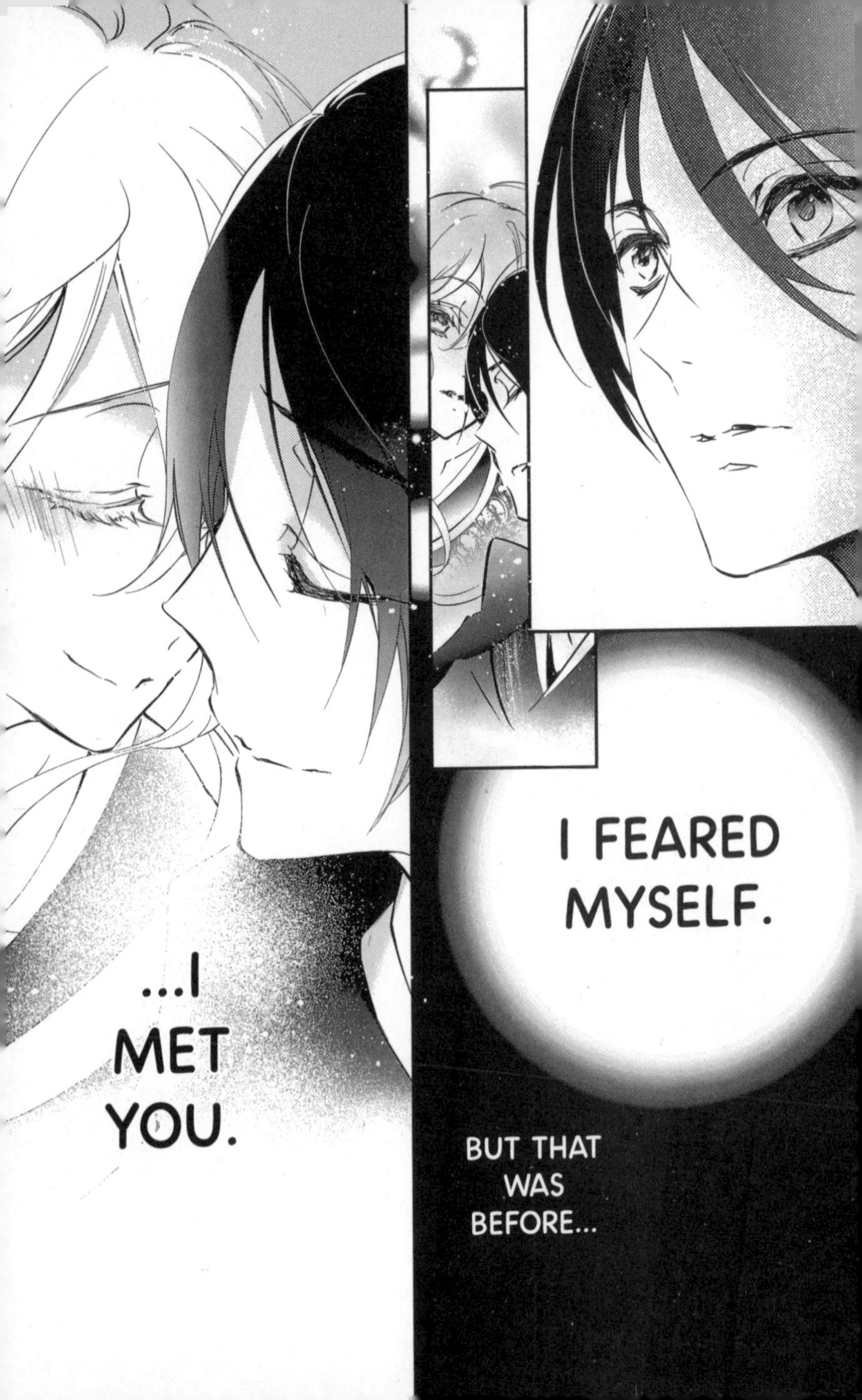
I FEARED MYSELF.
BUT THAT WAS BEFORE...
...I MET YOU.

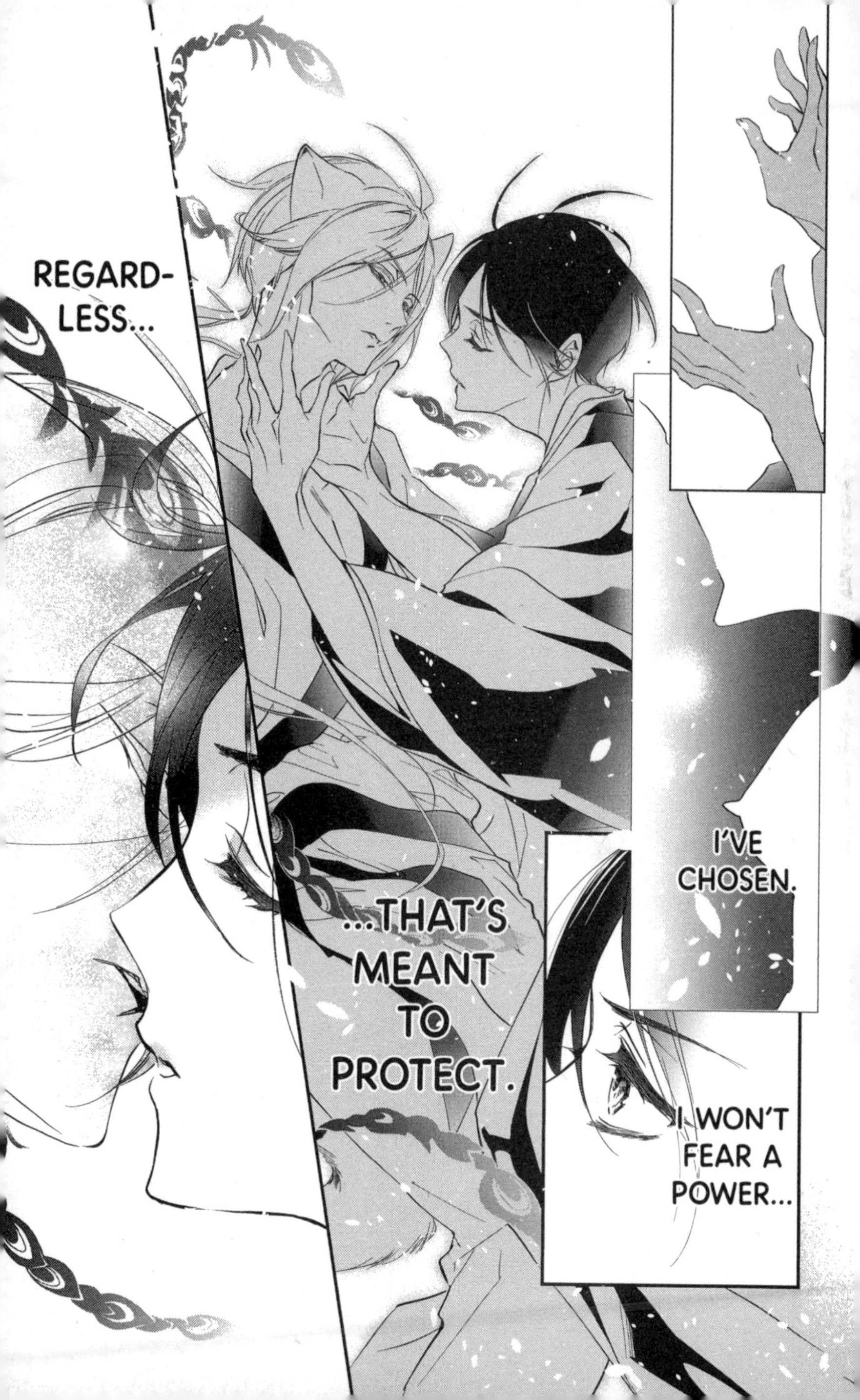
I'VE CHOSEN.
I WON'T FEAR A POWER...
...THAT'S MEANT TO PROTECT.
REGARDLESS...

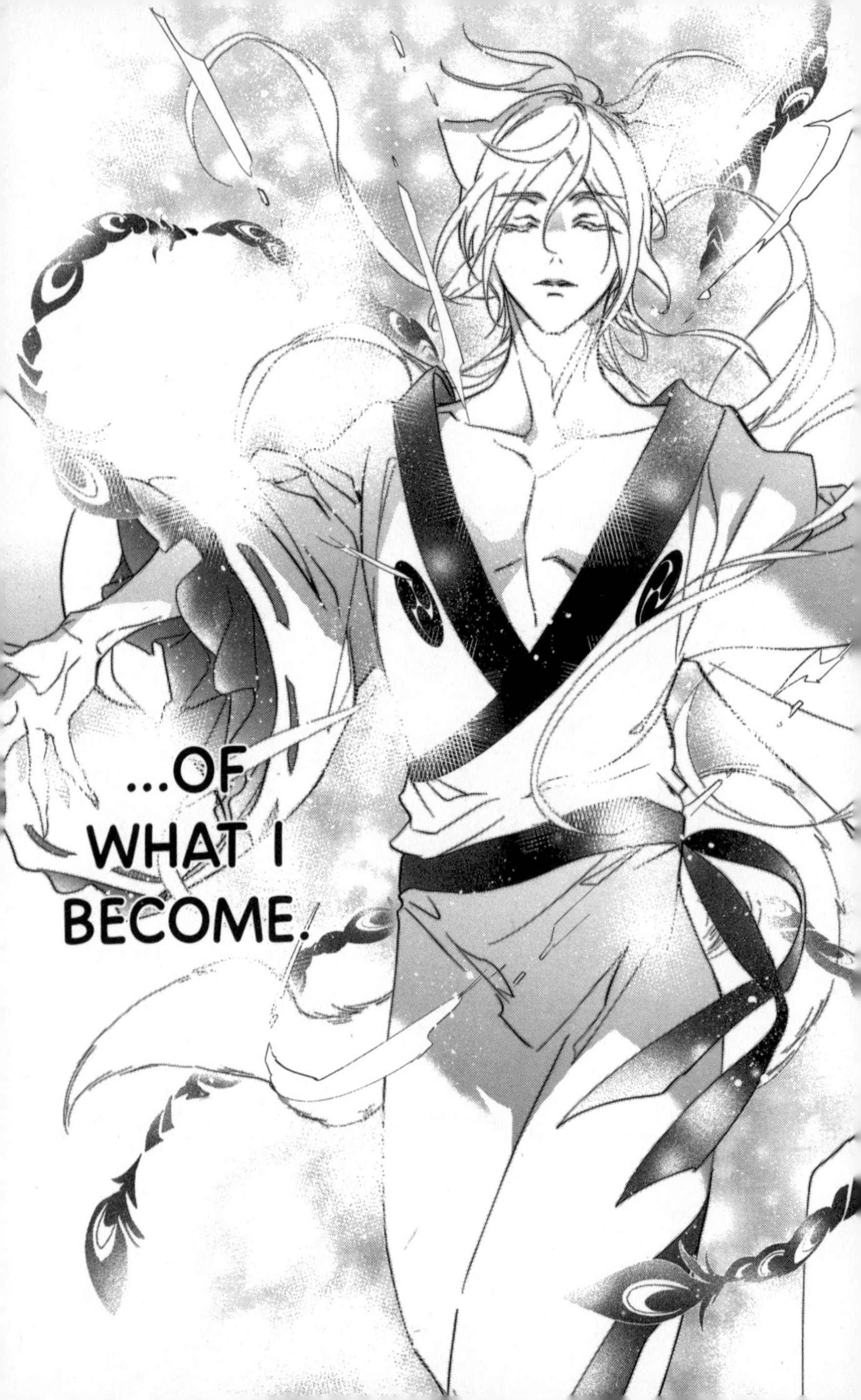
...OF
WHAT I
BECOME.

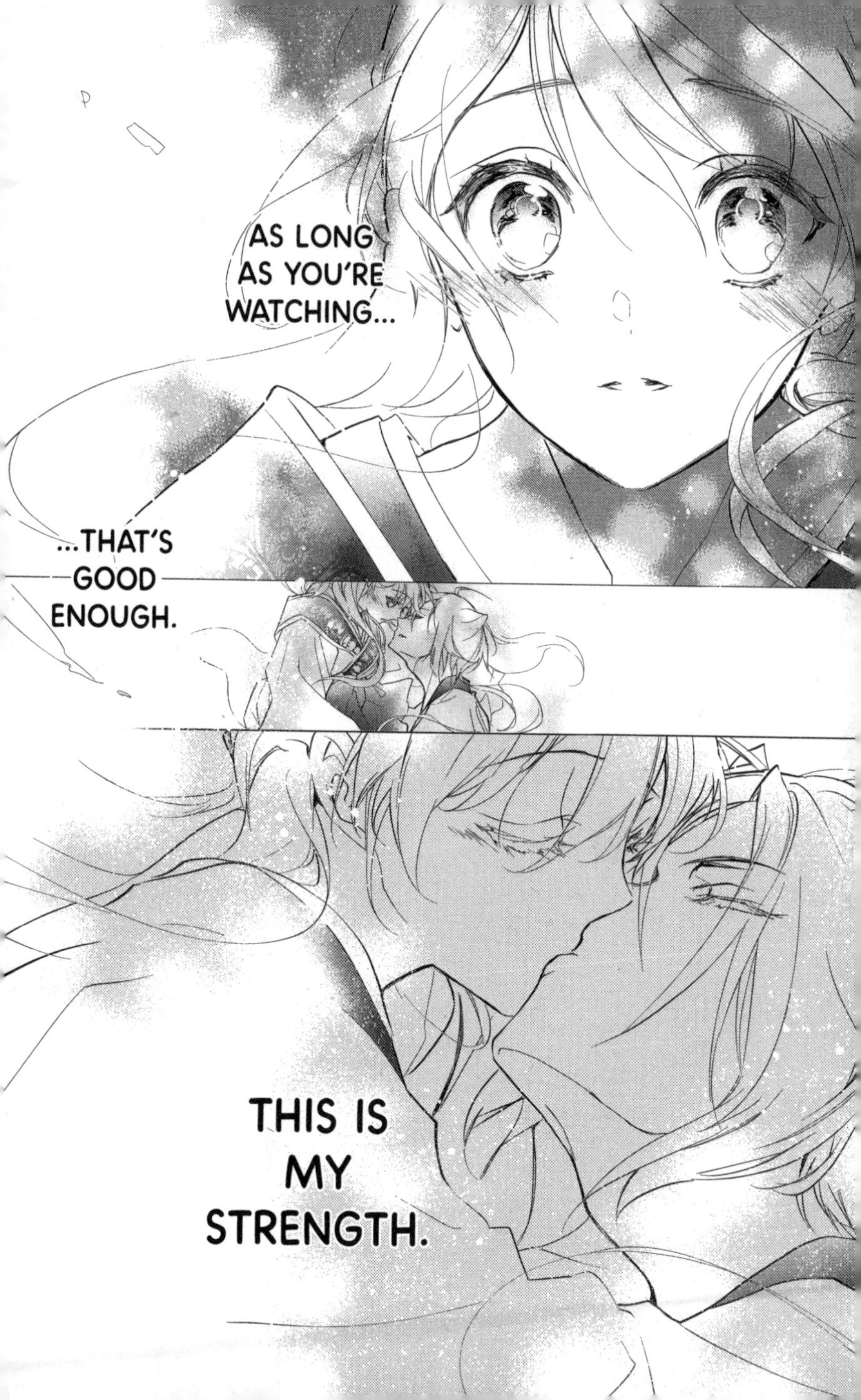
AS LONG AS YOU'RE WATCHING...
...THAT'S GOOD ENOUGH.
THIS IS MY STRENGTH.

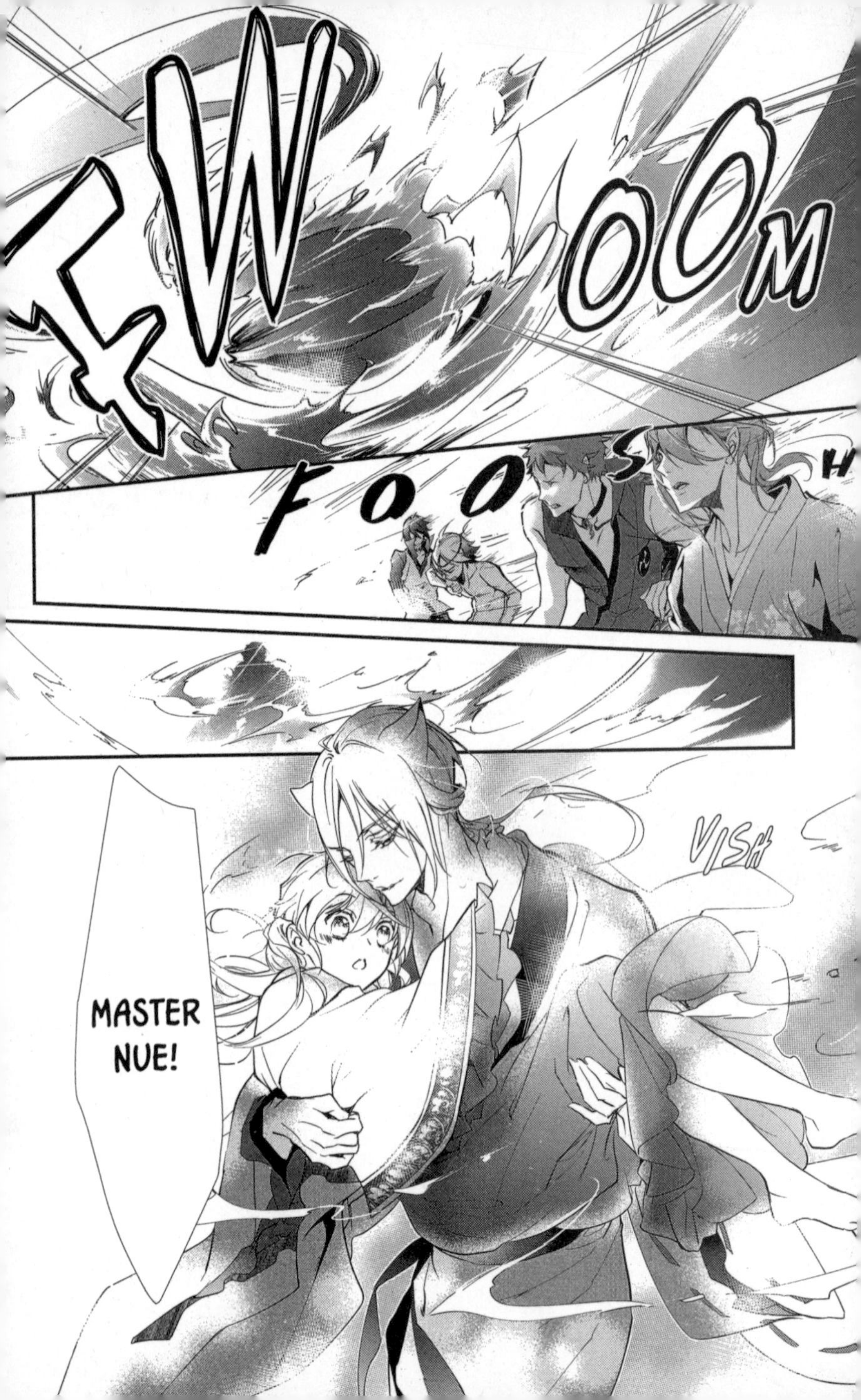
FWOOM
FOOOSH
VISH
MASTER NUE!

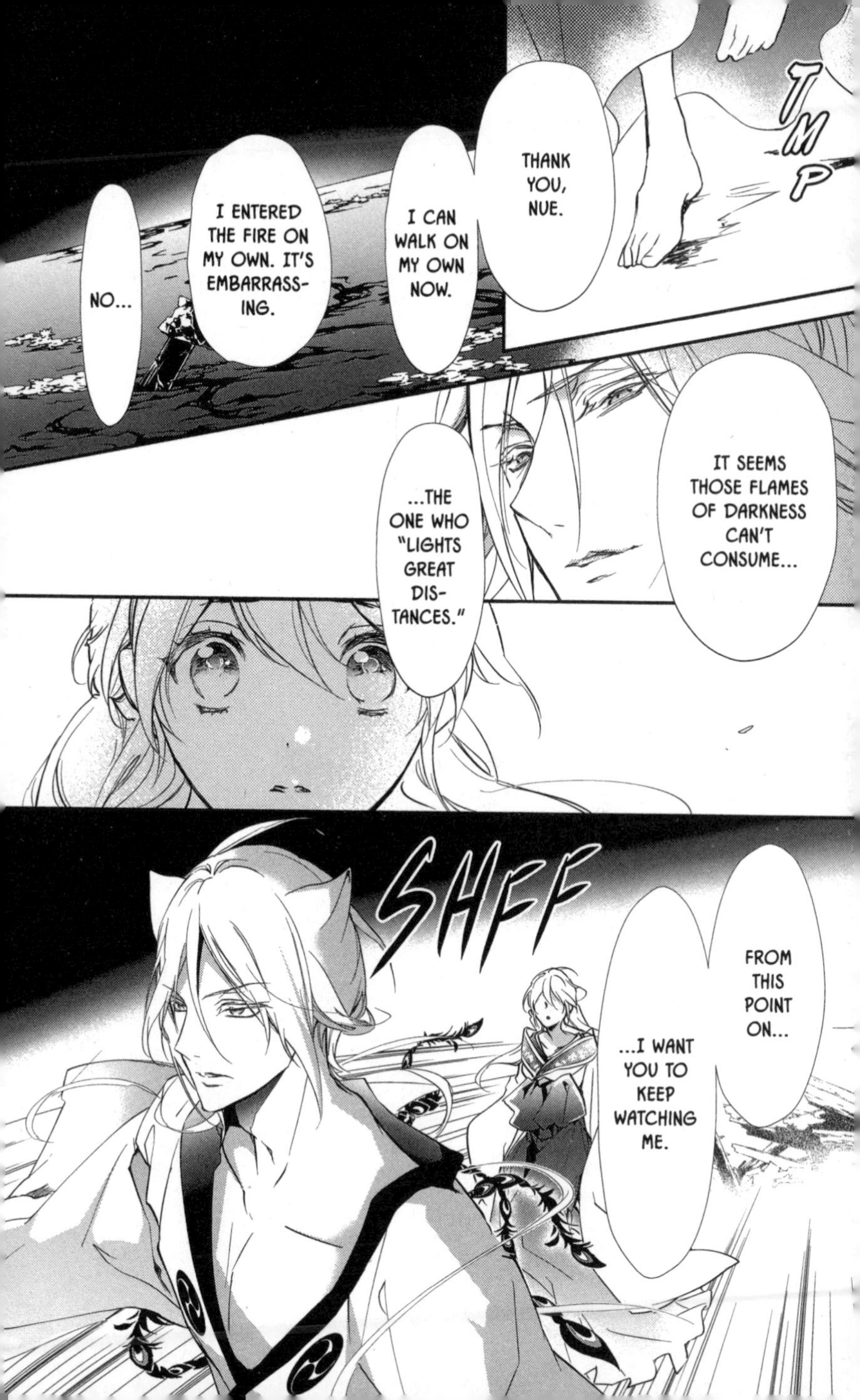
TMP
THANK YOU, NUE.
I CAN WALK ON MY OWN NOW.
I ENTERED THE FIRE ON MY OWN. IT'S EMBARRASSING.
NO...
IT SEEMS THOSE FLAMES OF DARKNESS CAN'T CONSUME...
...THE ONE WHO "LIGHTS GREAT DISTANCES."
SHFF
FROM THIS POINT ON...
...I WANT YOU TO KEEP WATCHING ME.

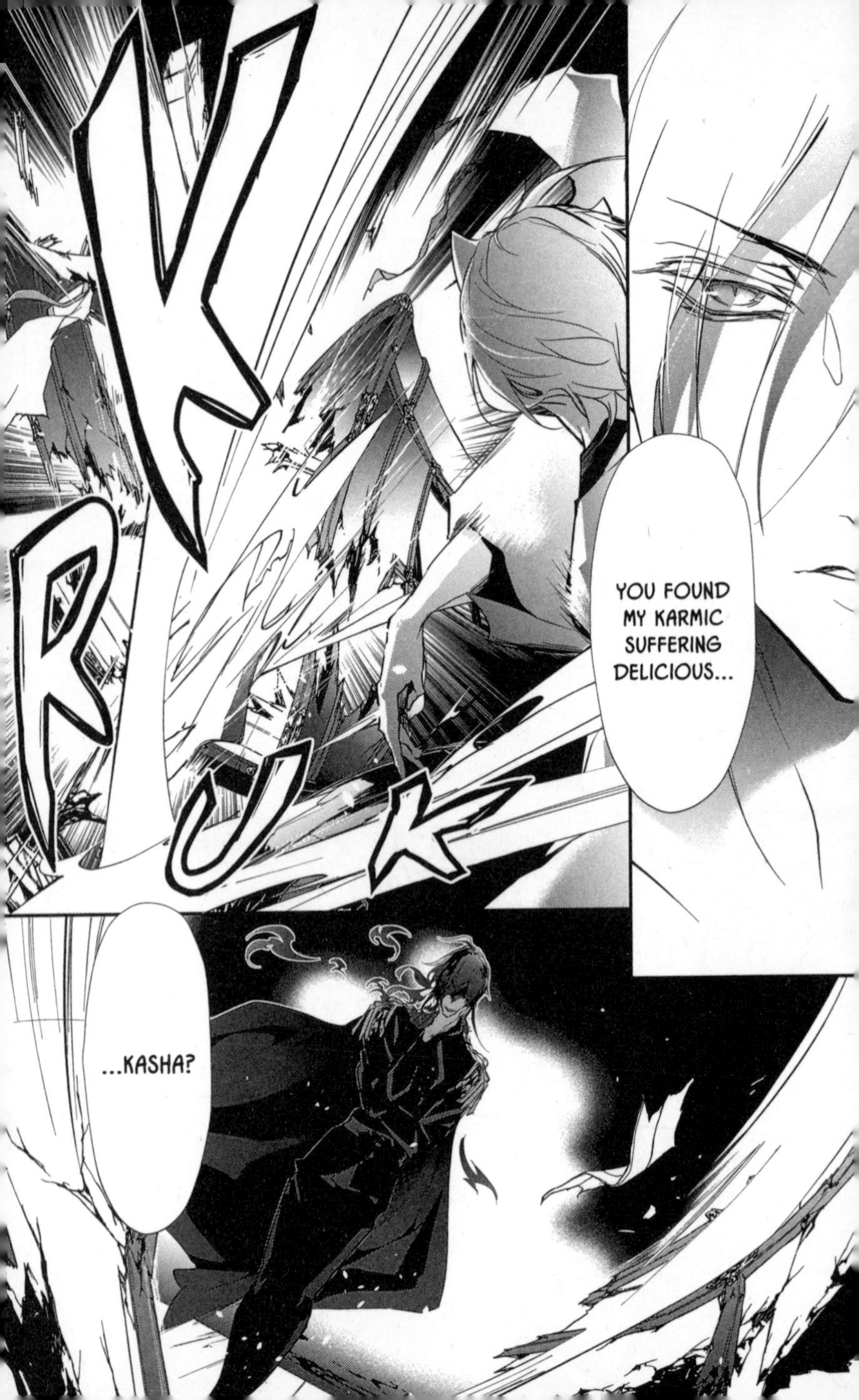
YOU FOUND MY KARMIC SUFFERING DELICIOUS...
KRUK
...KASHA?

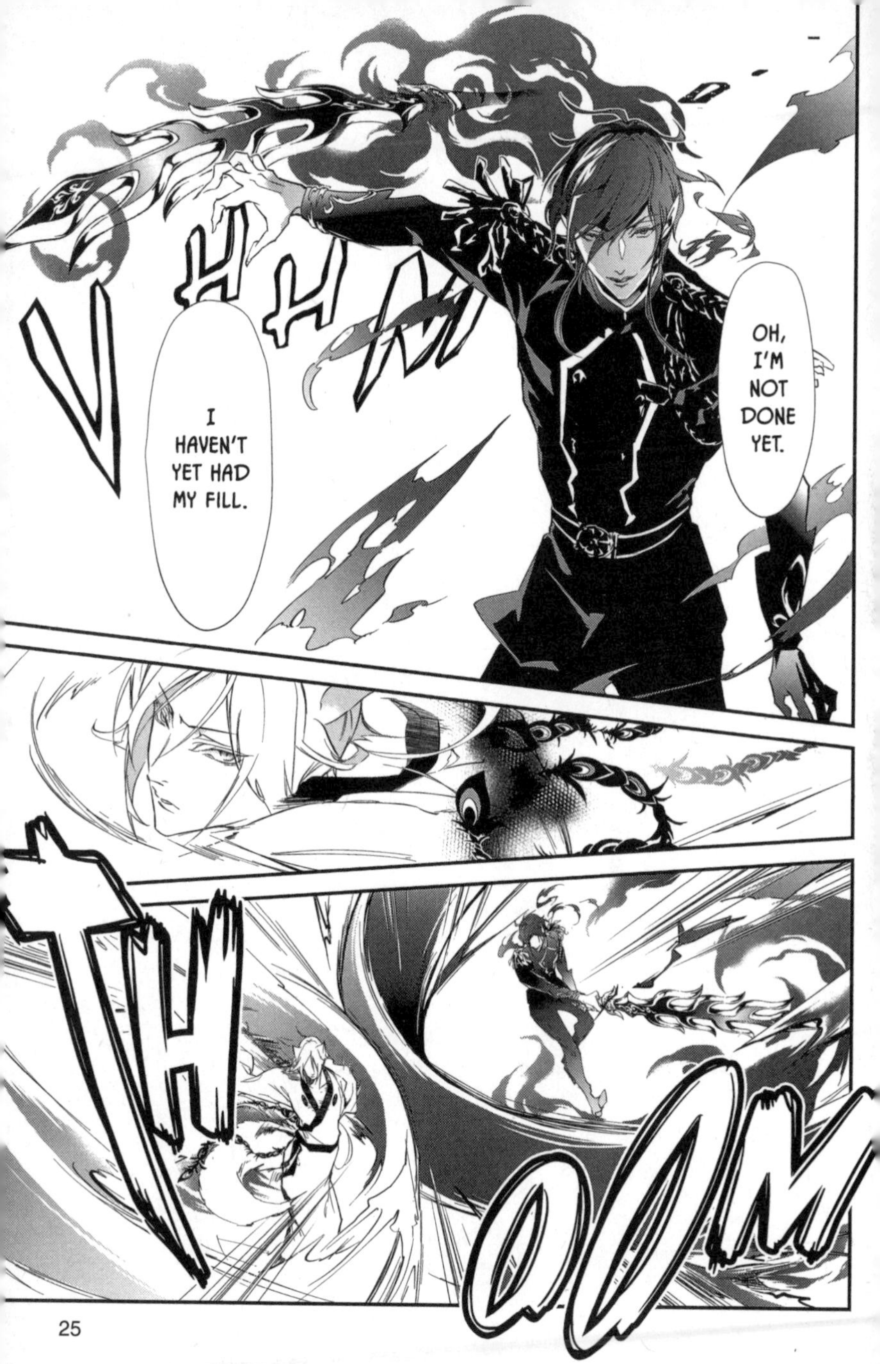
OH, I'M NOT DONE YET.
I HAVEN'T YET HAD MY FILL.
VHHM
THOOM

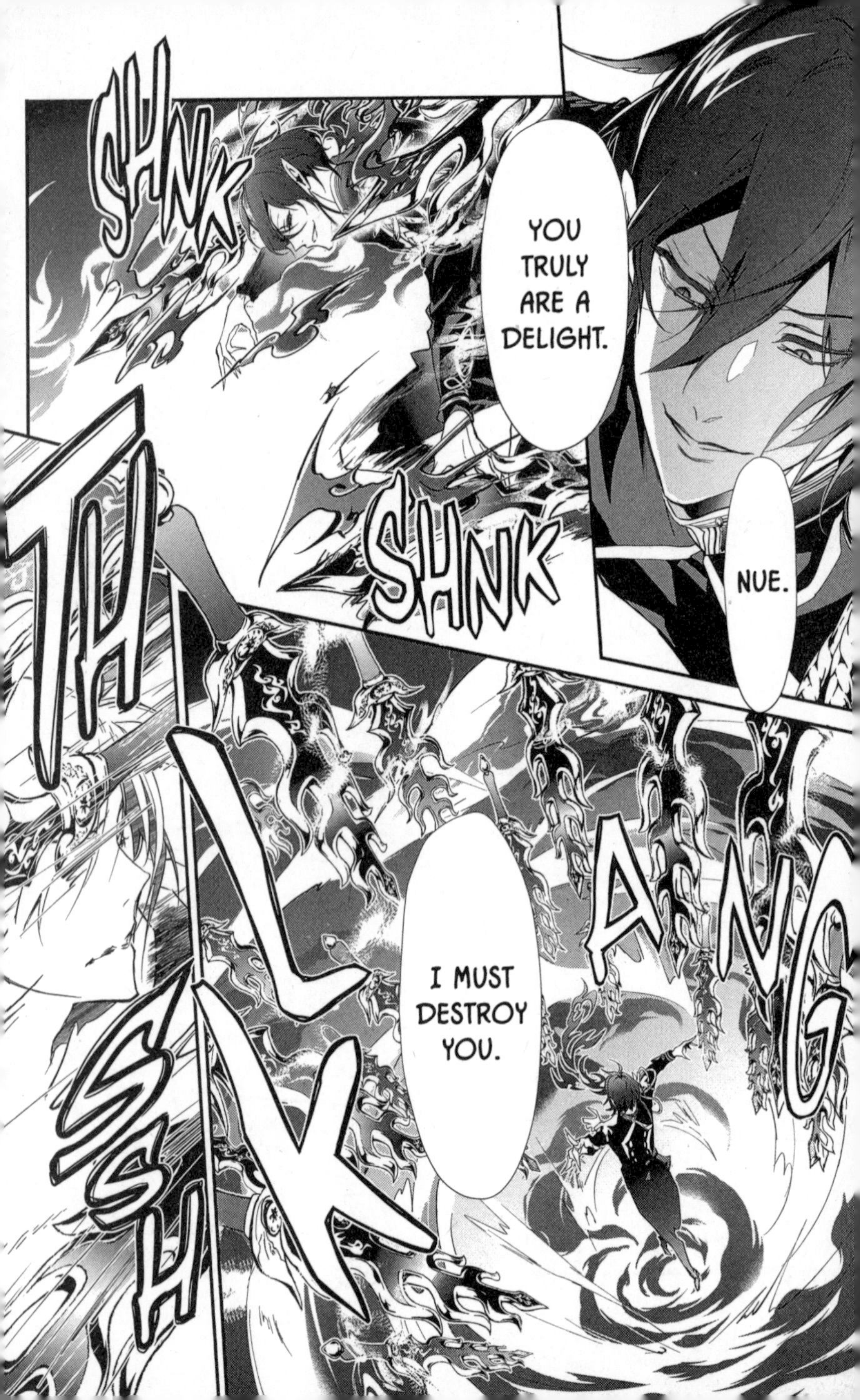
YOU TRULY ARE A DELIGHT.
NUE.
SHUNK
SHNK
I MUST DESTROY YOU.

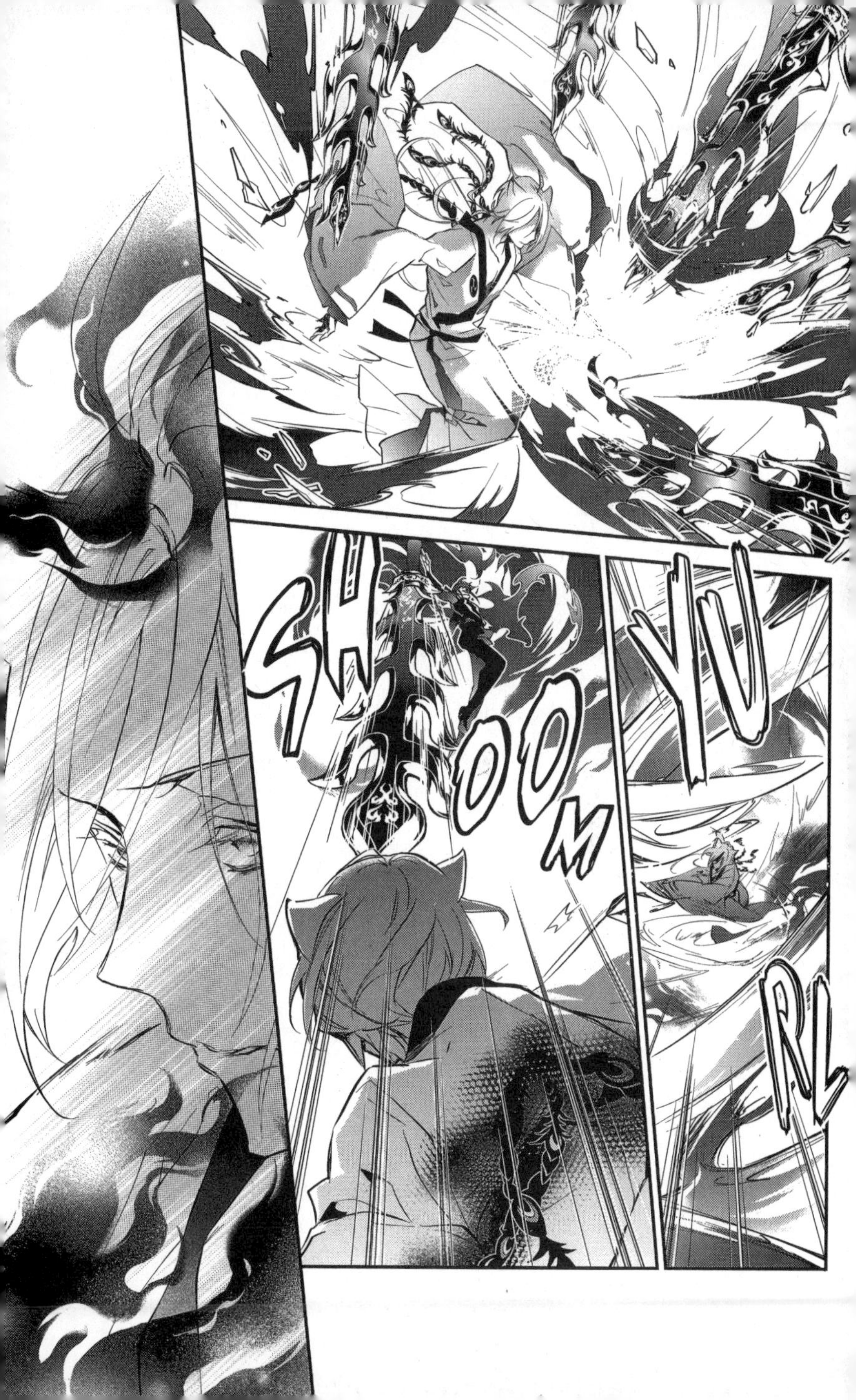
YURL
SHOOM

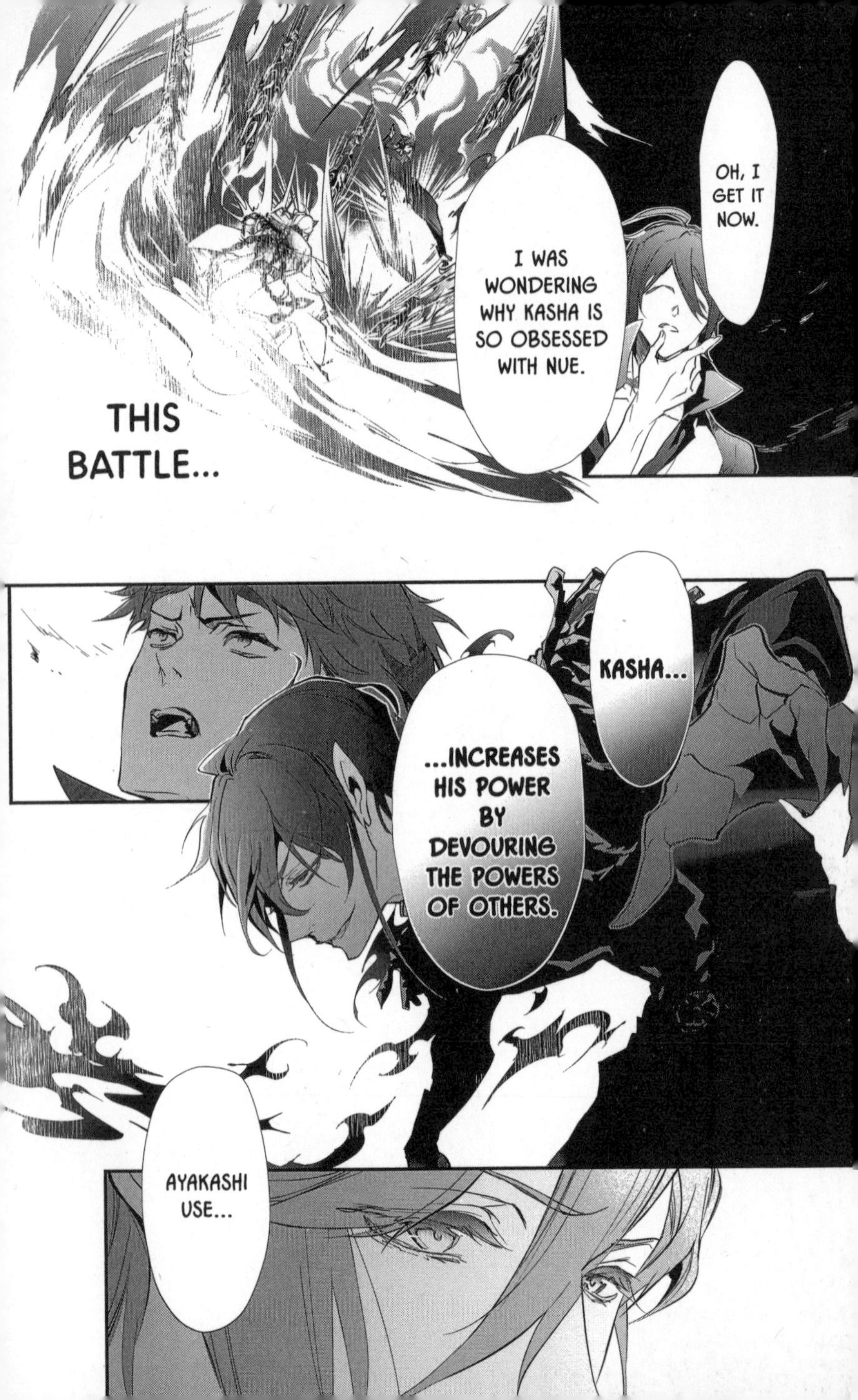
OH, I GET IT NOW.
I WAS WONDERING WHY KASHA IS SO OBSESSED WITH NUE.
THIS BATTLE...
KASHA...
...INCREASES HIS POWER BY DEVOURING THE POWERS OF OTHERS.
AYAKASHI USE...

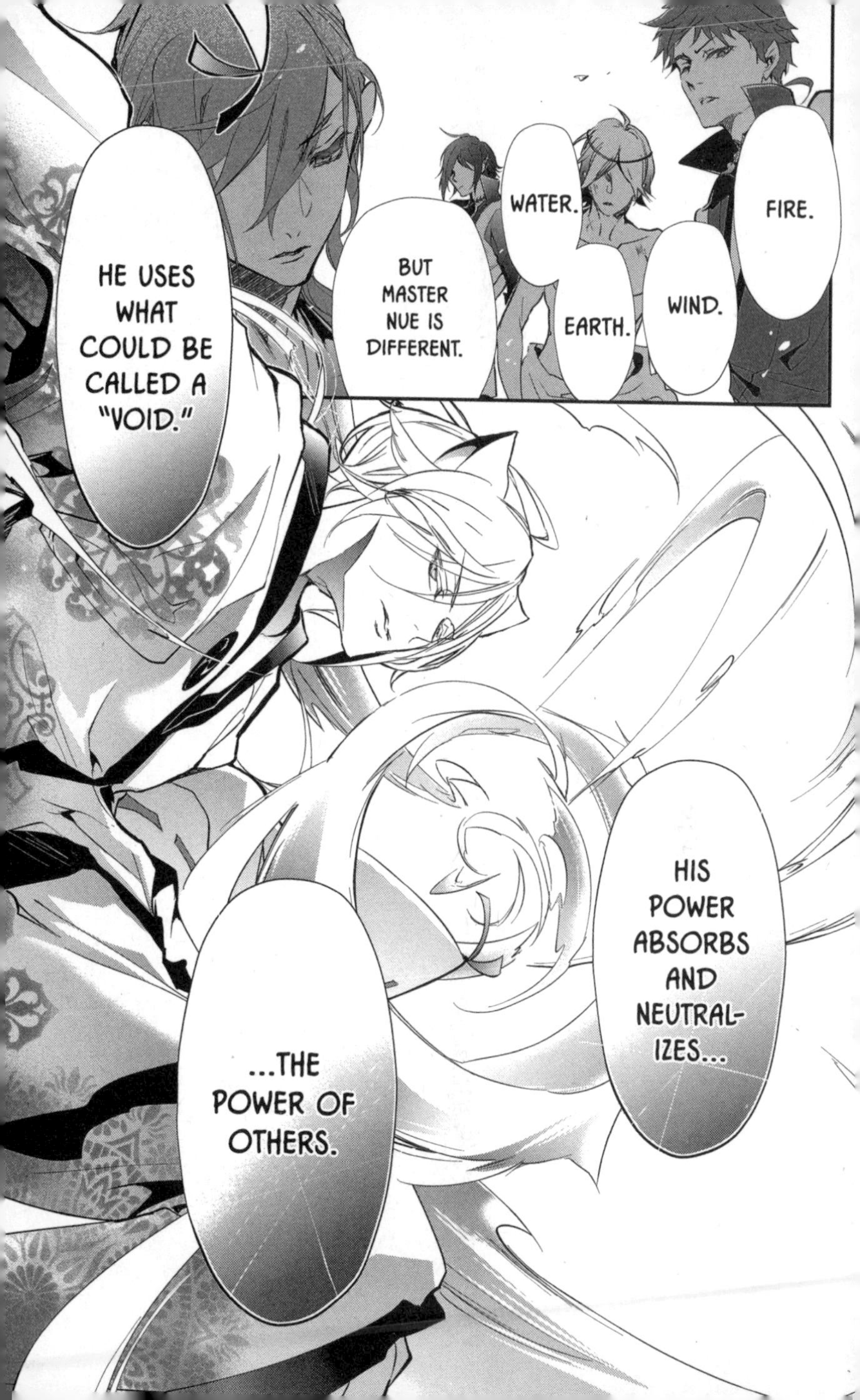
FIRE.
WIND.
EARTH.
WATER.
BUT MASTER NUE IS DIFFERENT.
HE USES WHAT COULD BE CALLED A "VOID."
HIS POWER ABSORBS AND NEUTRAL-IZES...
...THE POWER OF OTHERS.

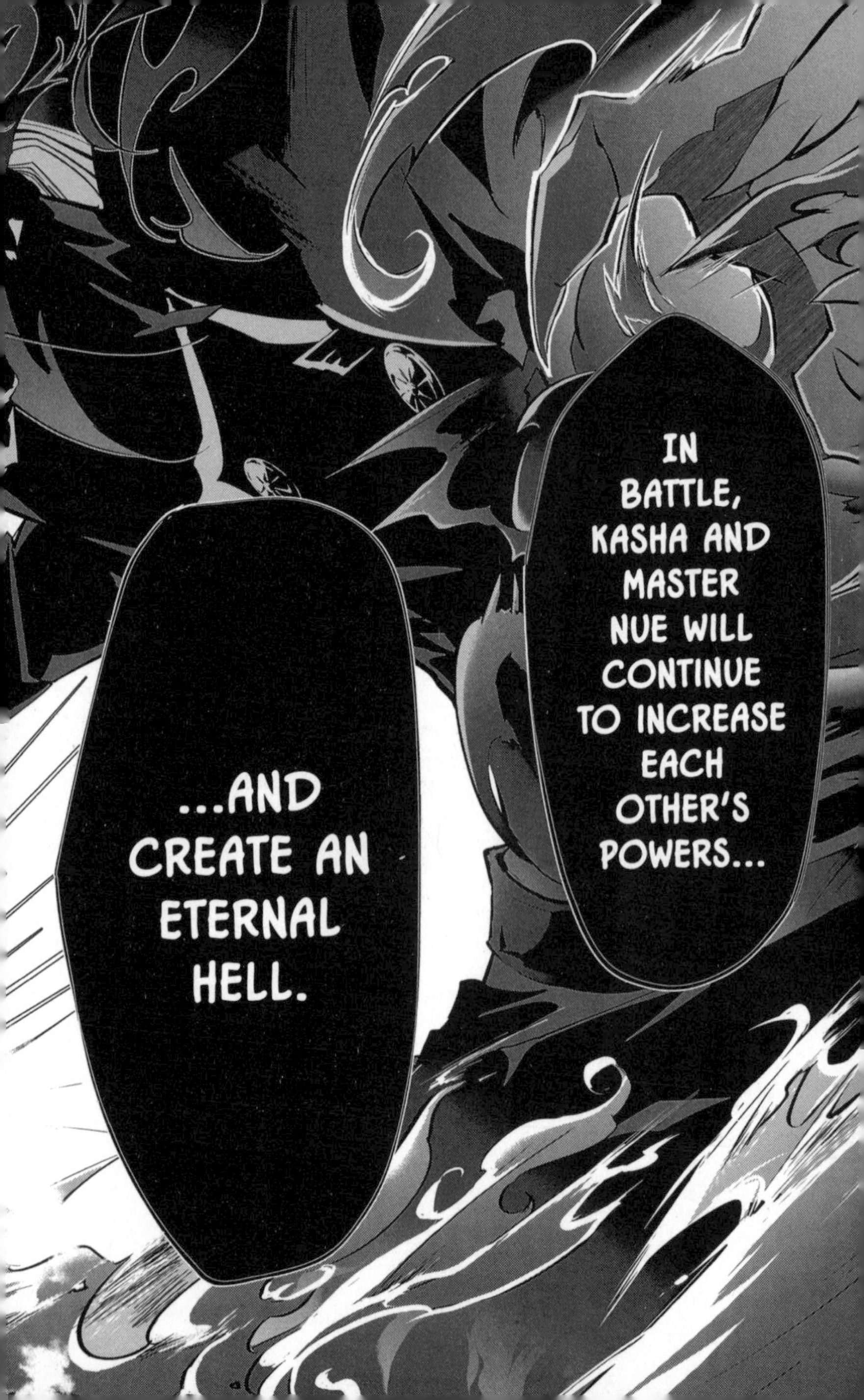
IN BATTLE, KASHA AND MASTER NUE WILL CONTINUE TO INCREASE EACH OTHER'S POWERS...
...AND CREATE AN ETERNAL HELL.

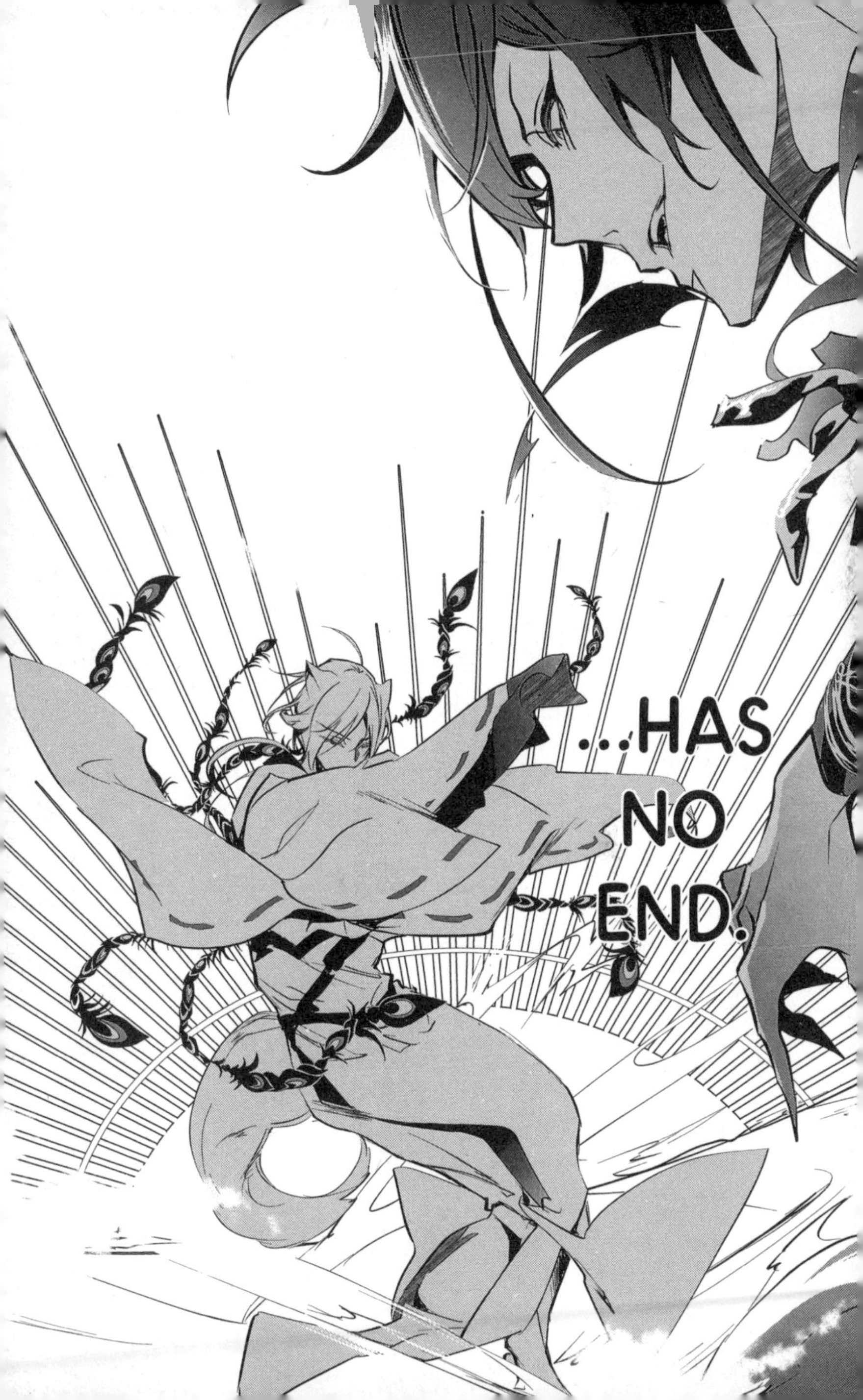
...HAS NO END.

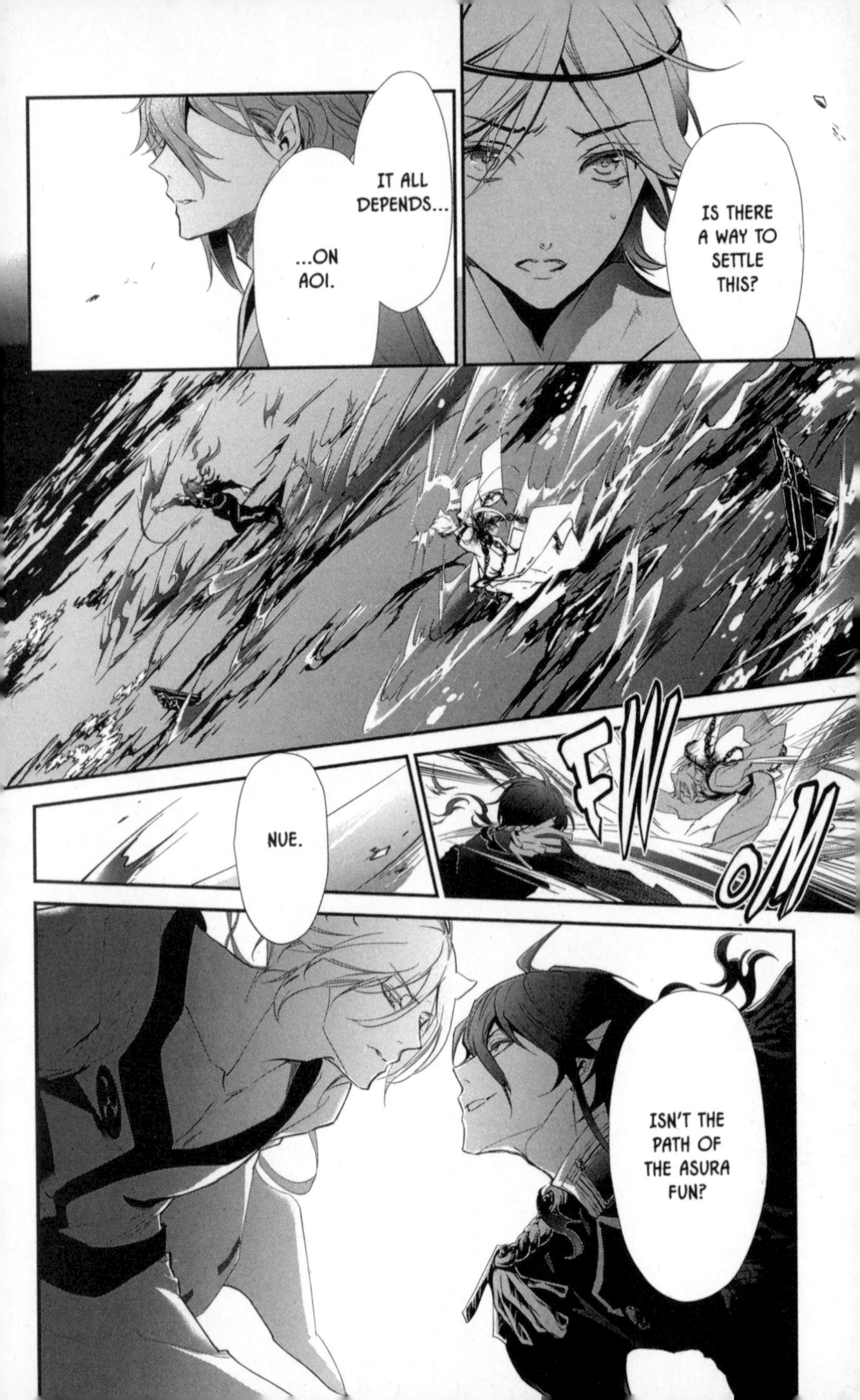
IS THERE A WAY TO SETTLE THIS?
IT ALL DEPENDS...
...ON AOI.
FWOM
NUE.
ISN'T THE PATH OF THE ASURA FUN?

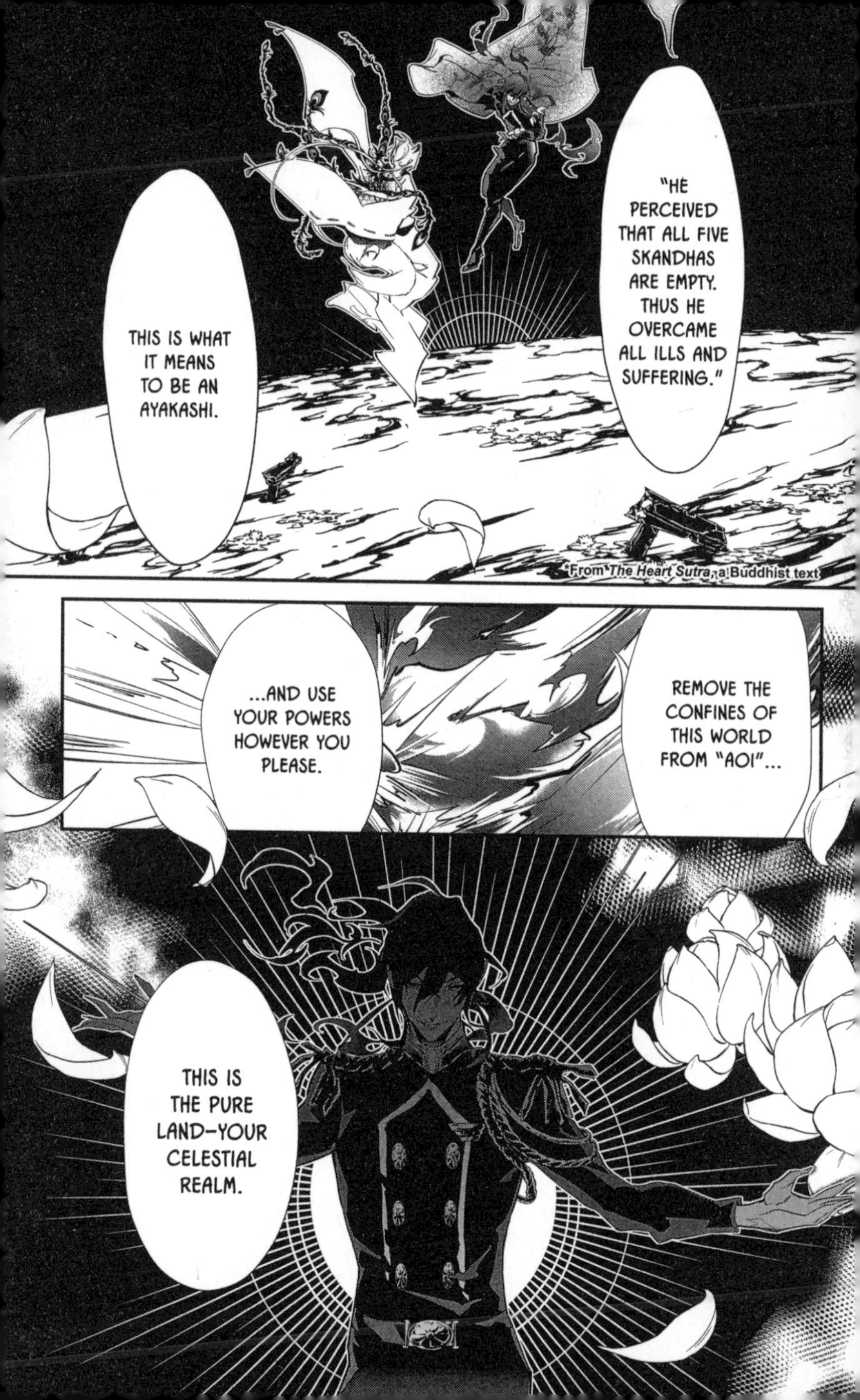
"HE PERCEIVED THAT ALL FIVE SKANDHAS ARE EMPTY. THUS HE OVERCAME ALL ILLS AND SUFFERING."
THIS IS WHAT IT MEANS TO BE AN AYAKASHI.
*From *The Heart Sutra*, a Buddhist text
REMOVE THE CONFINES OF THIS WORLD FROM "AOI"...
...AND USE YOUR POWERS HOWEVER YOU PLEASE.
THIS IS THE PURE LAND—YOUR CELESTIAL REALM.

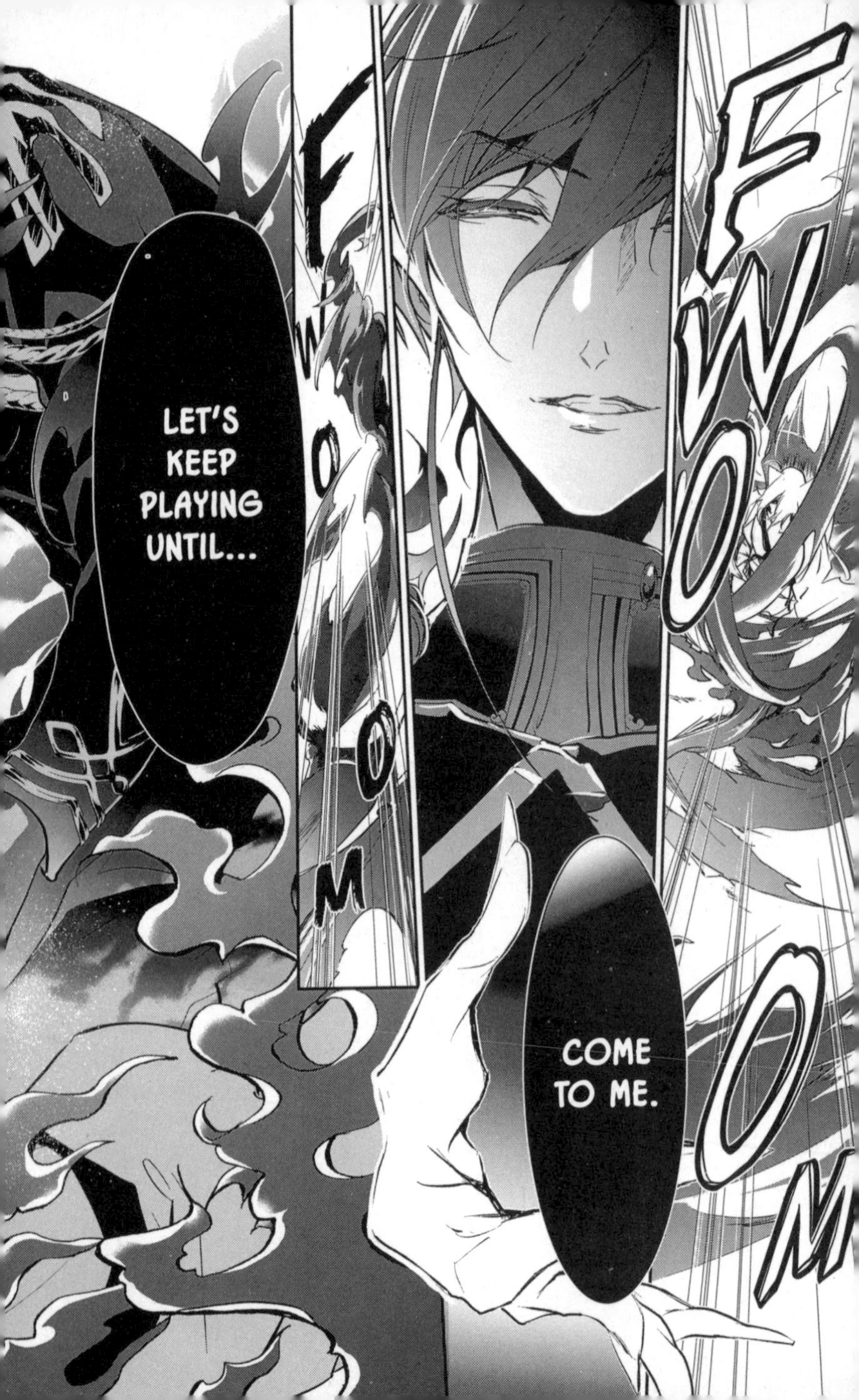
FWOOOOM
FWOOOM
LET'S KEEP PLAYING UNTIL...
COME TO ME.

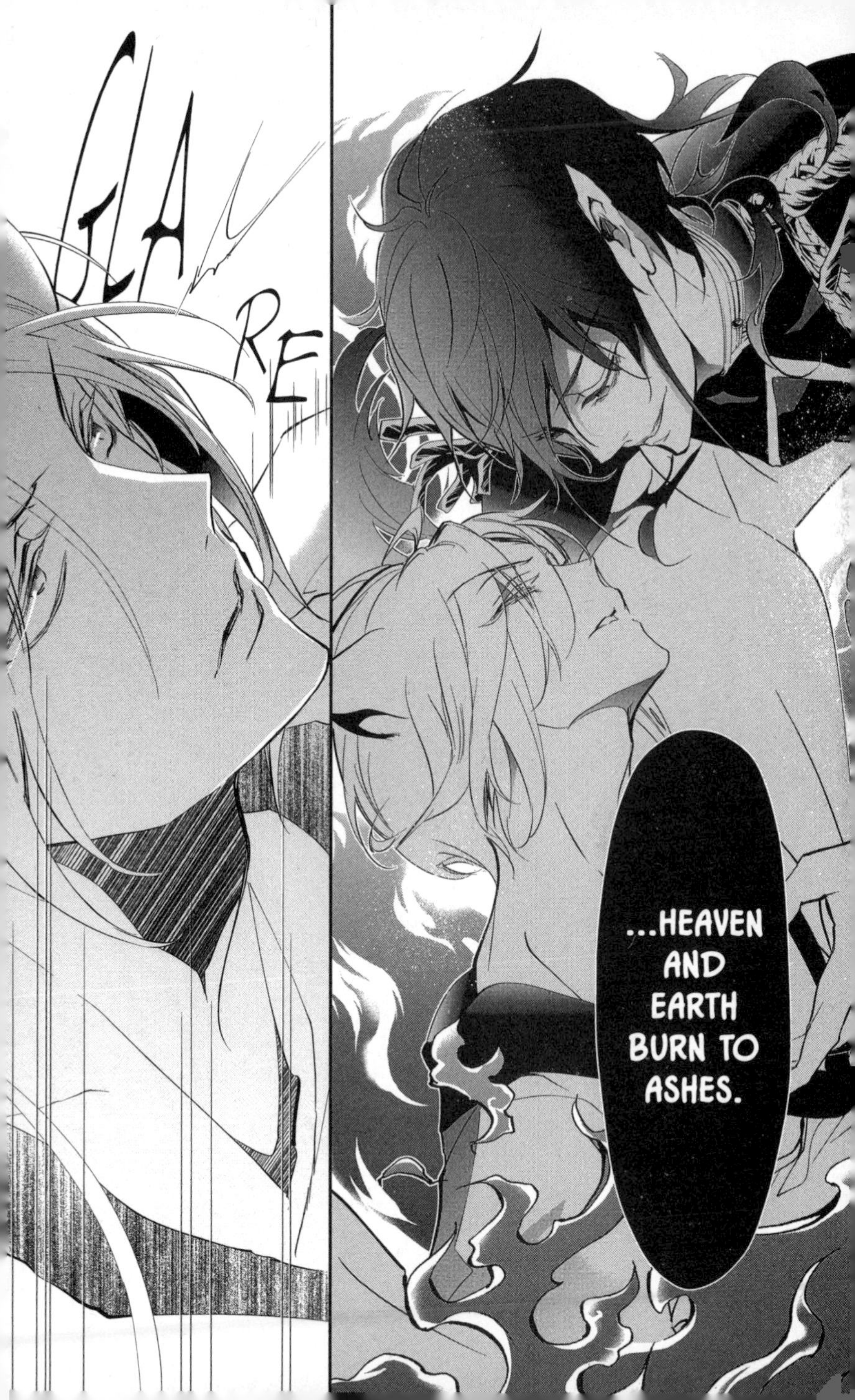
...HEAVEN AND EARTH BURN TO ASHES.
GLARE

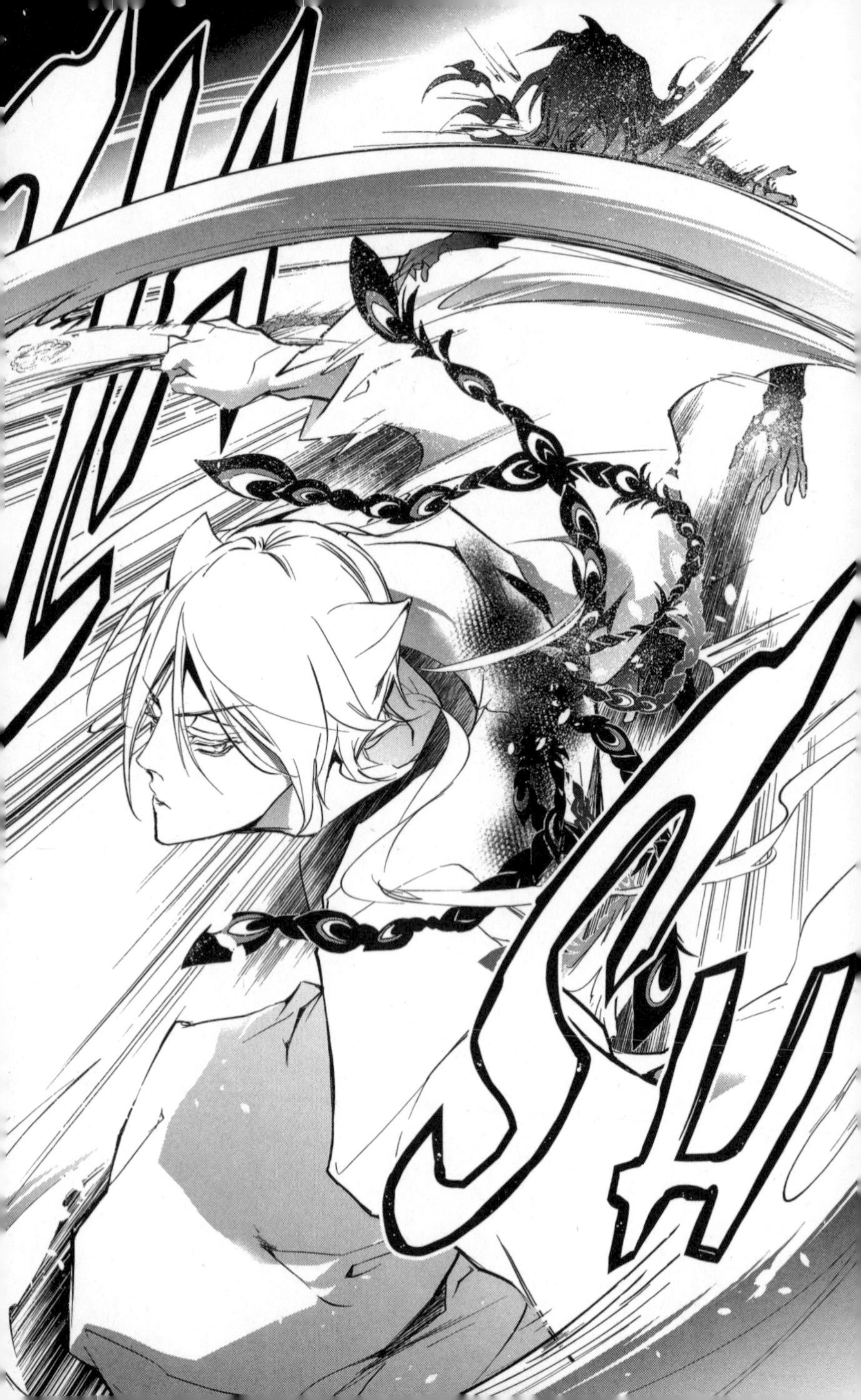

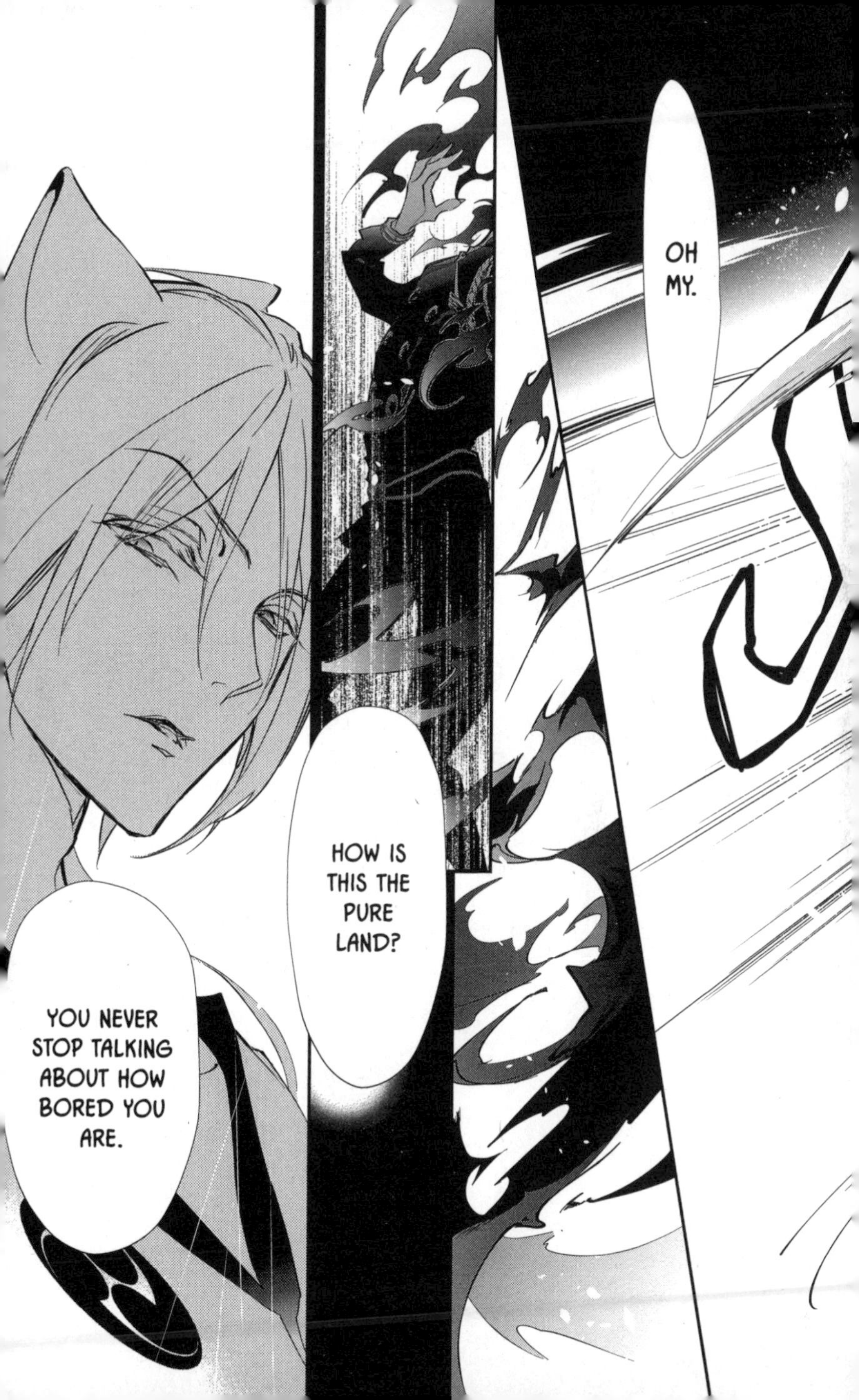
OH MY.
HOW IS THIS THE PURE LAND?
YOU NEVER STOP TALKING ABOUT HOW BORED YOU ARE.

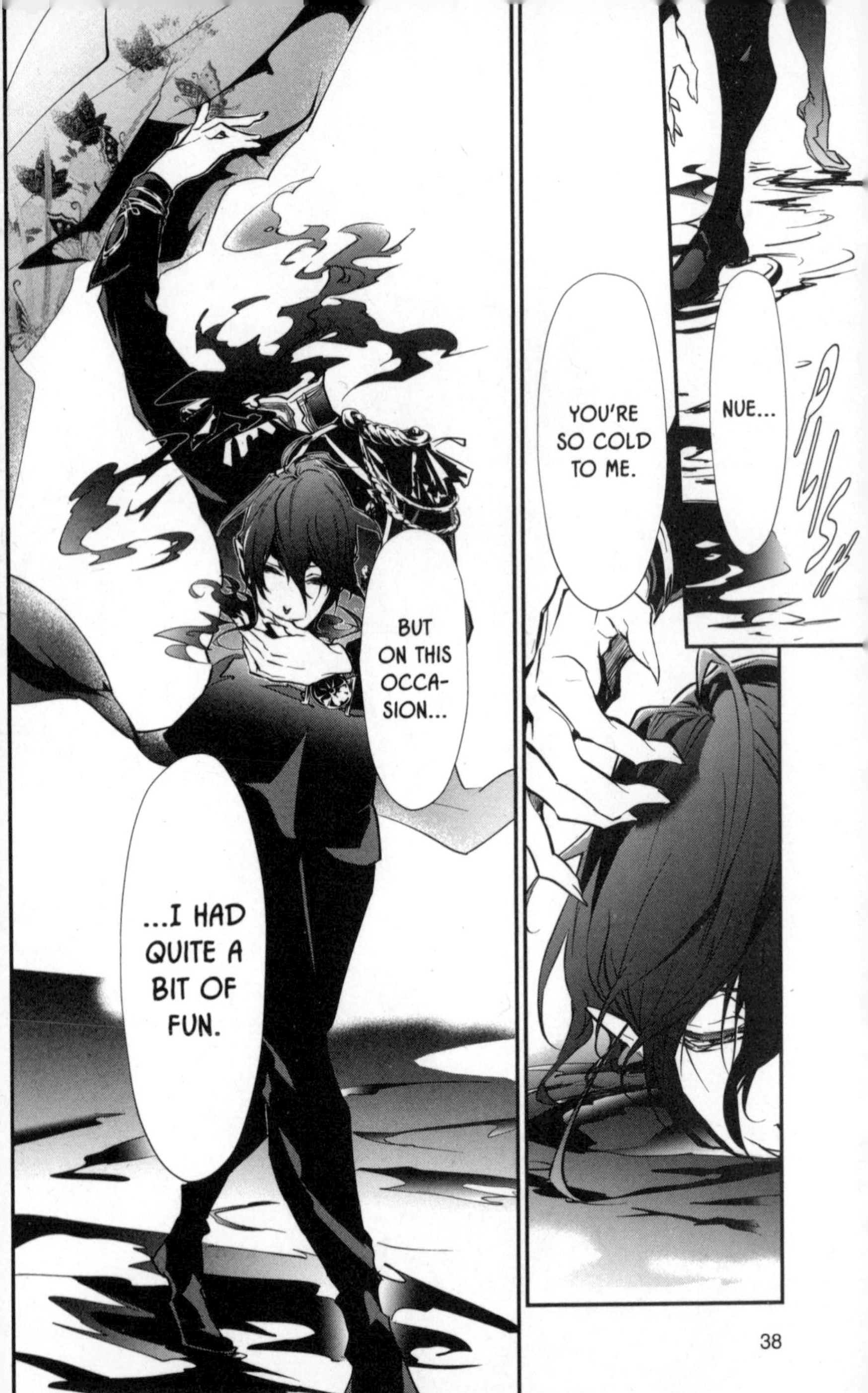
PLISH
NUE...
YOU'RE SO COLD TO ME.
BUT ON THIS OCCASION...
...I HAD QUITE A BIT OF FUN.

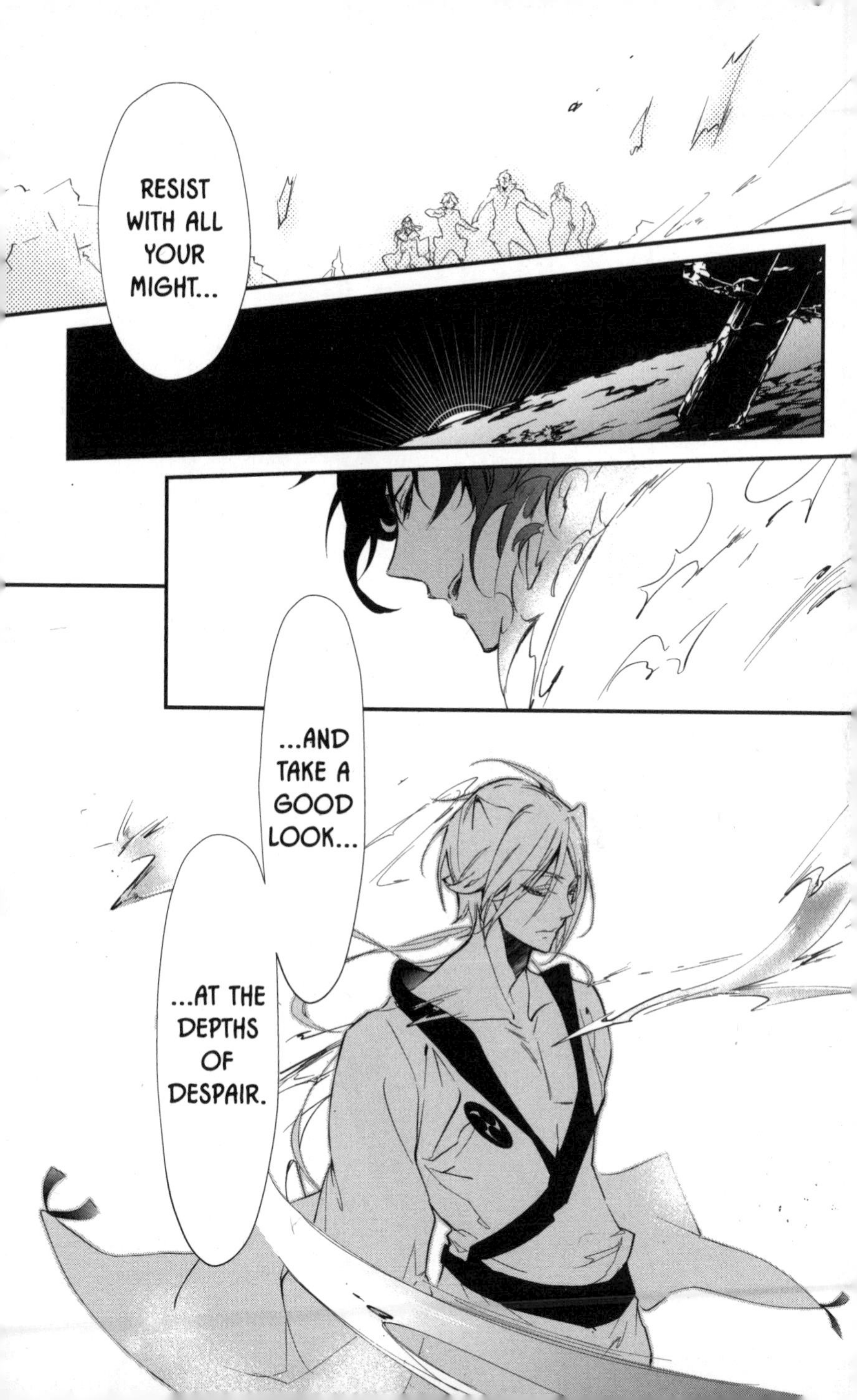
RESIST WITH ALL YOUR MIGHT...
...AND TAKE A GOOD LOOK...
...AT THE DEPTHS OF DESPAIR.

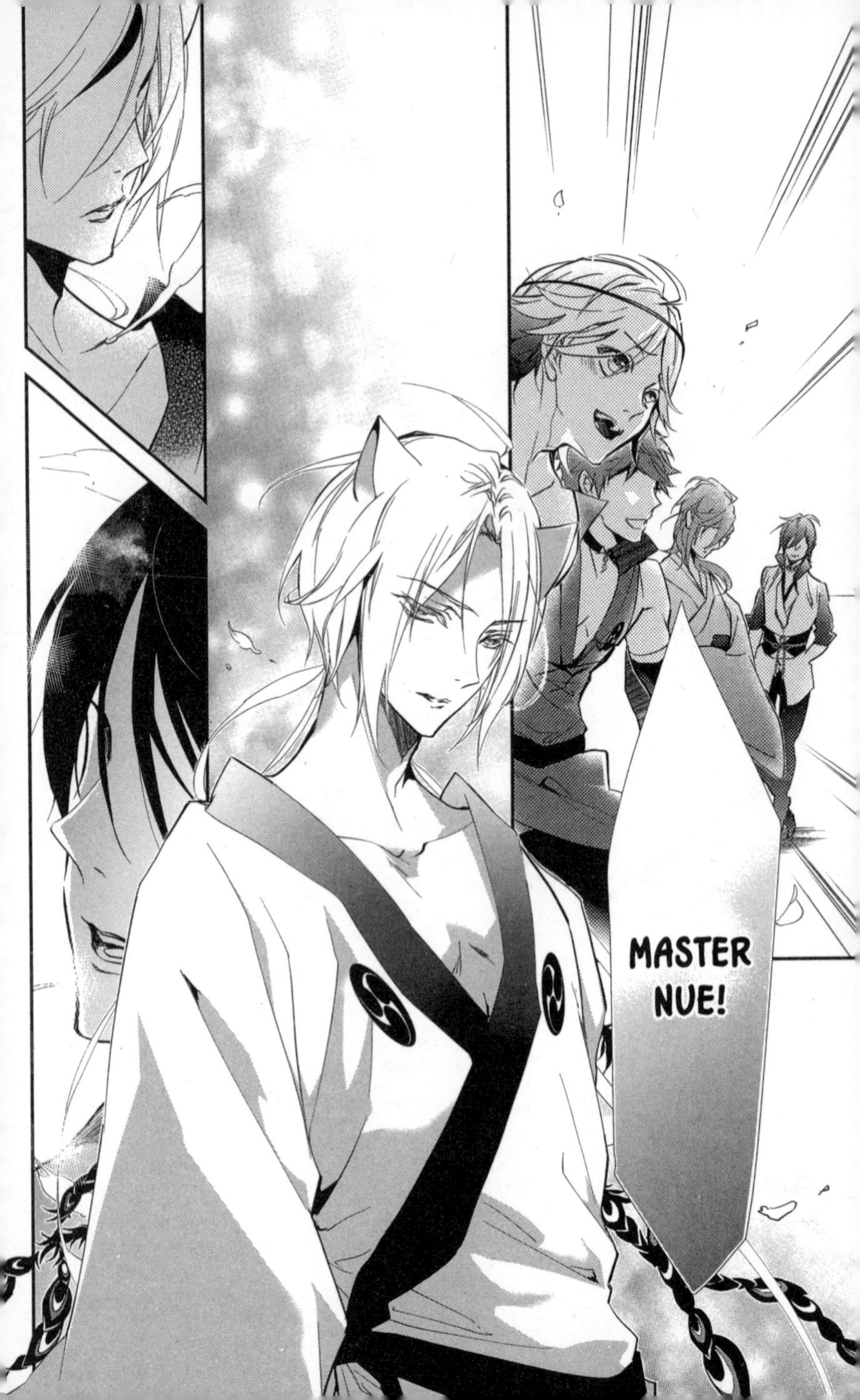
MASTER NUE!

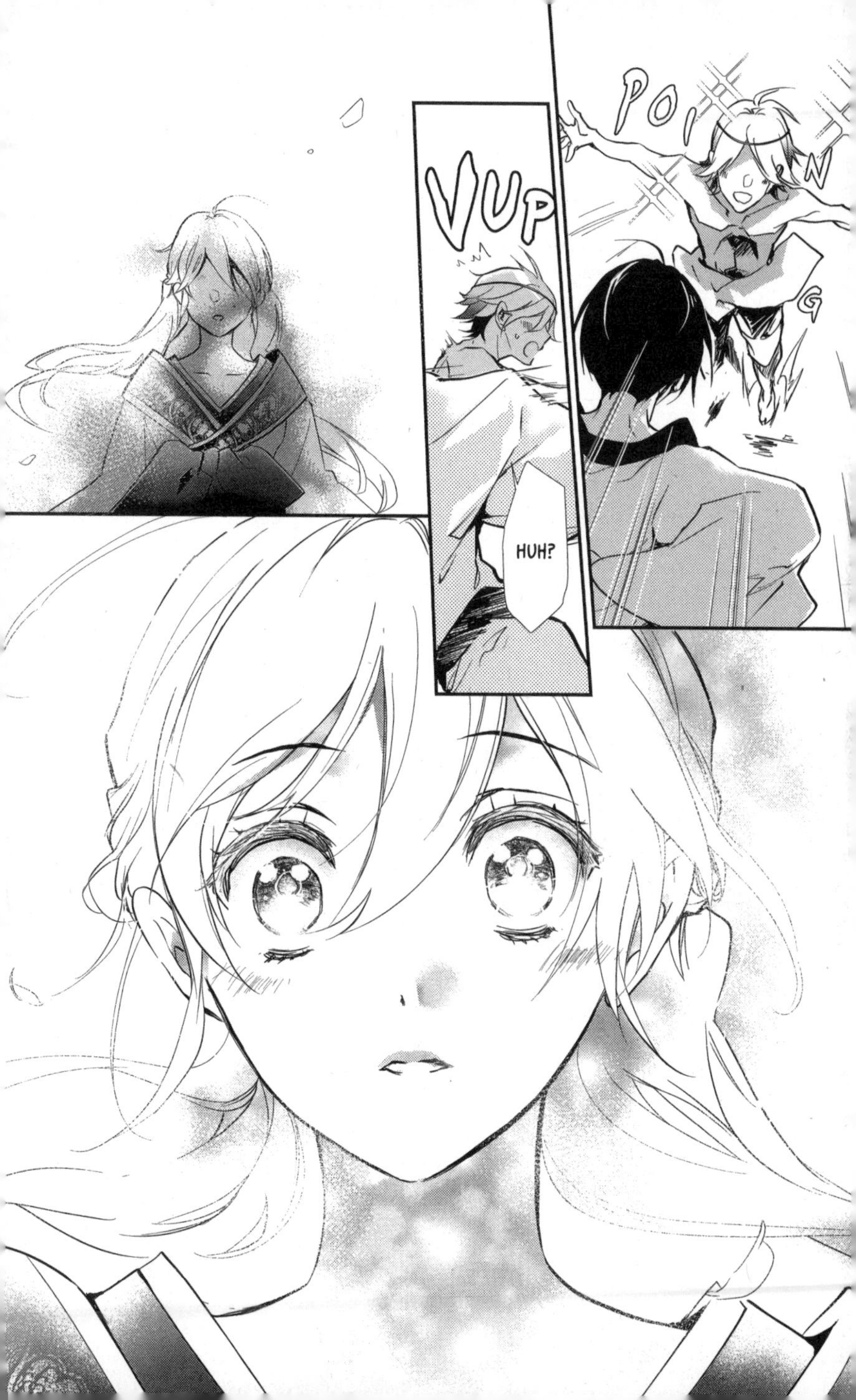
POING
VUP
HUH?

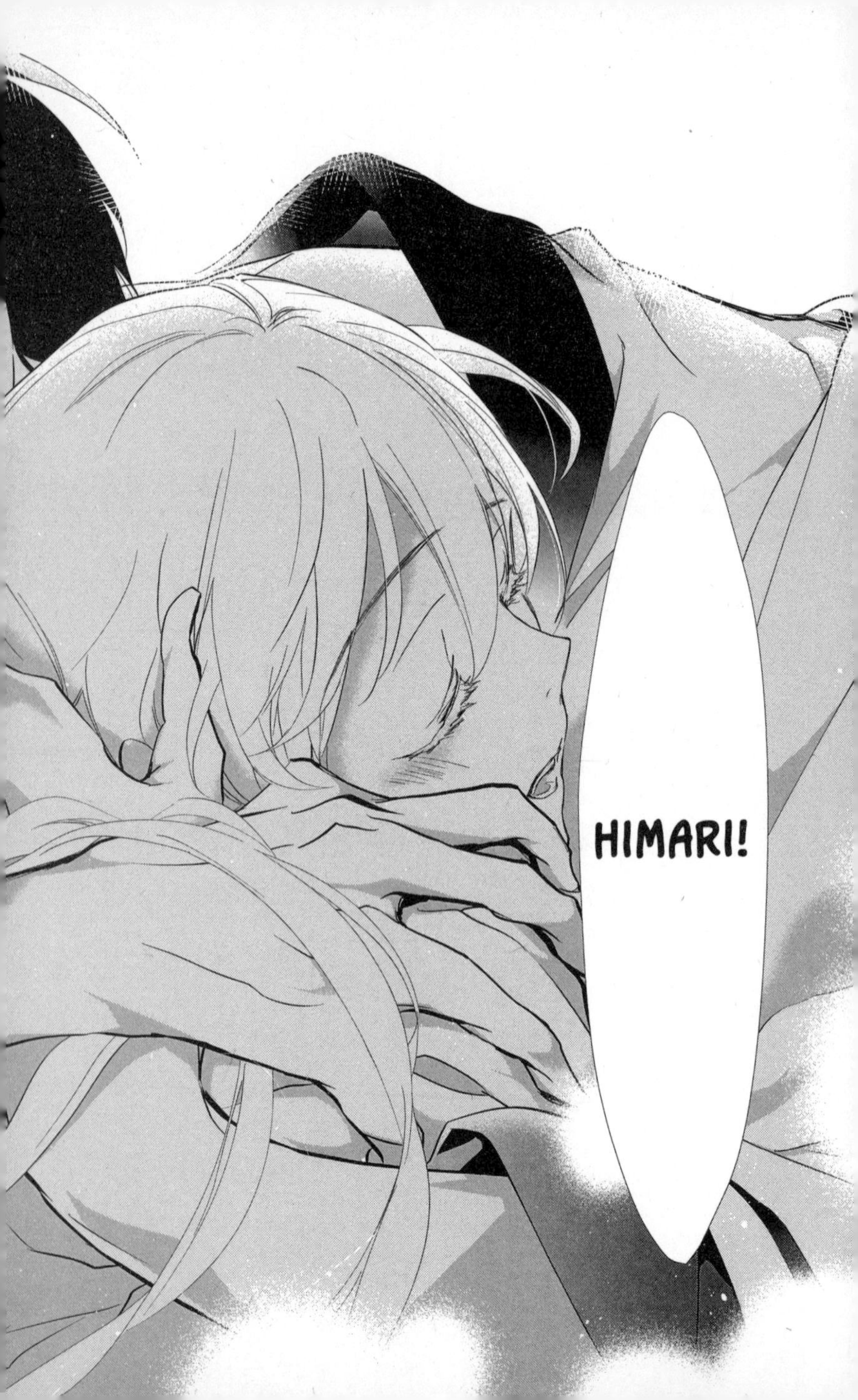
HIMARI!

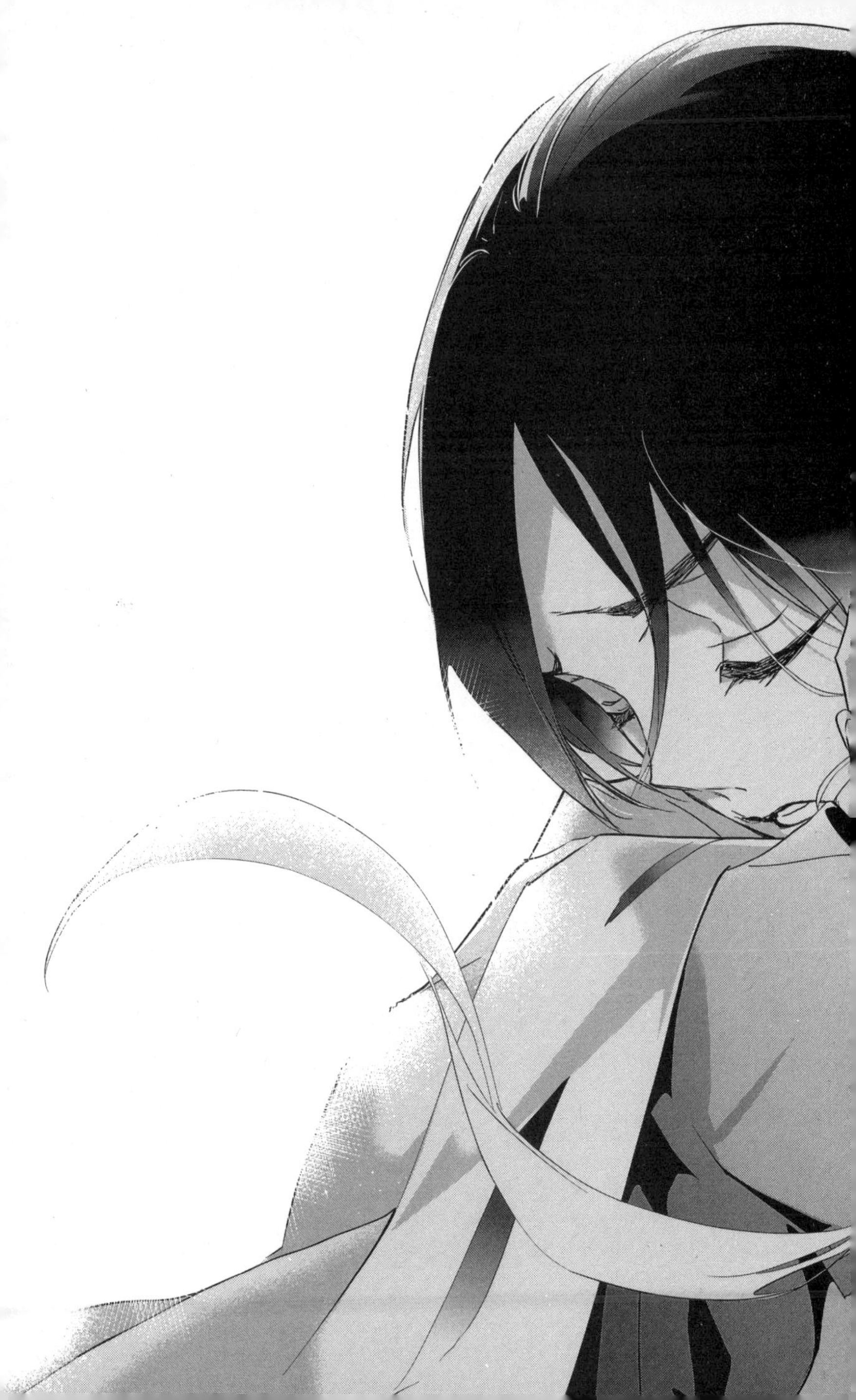

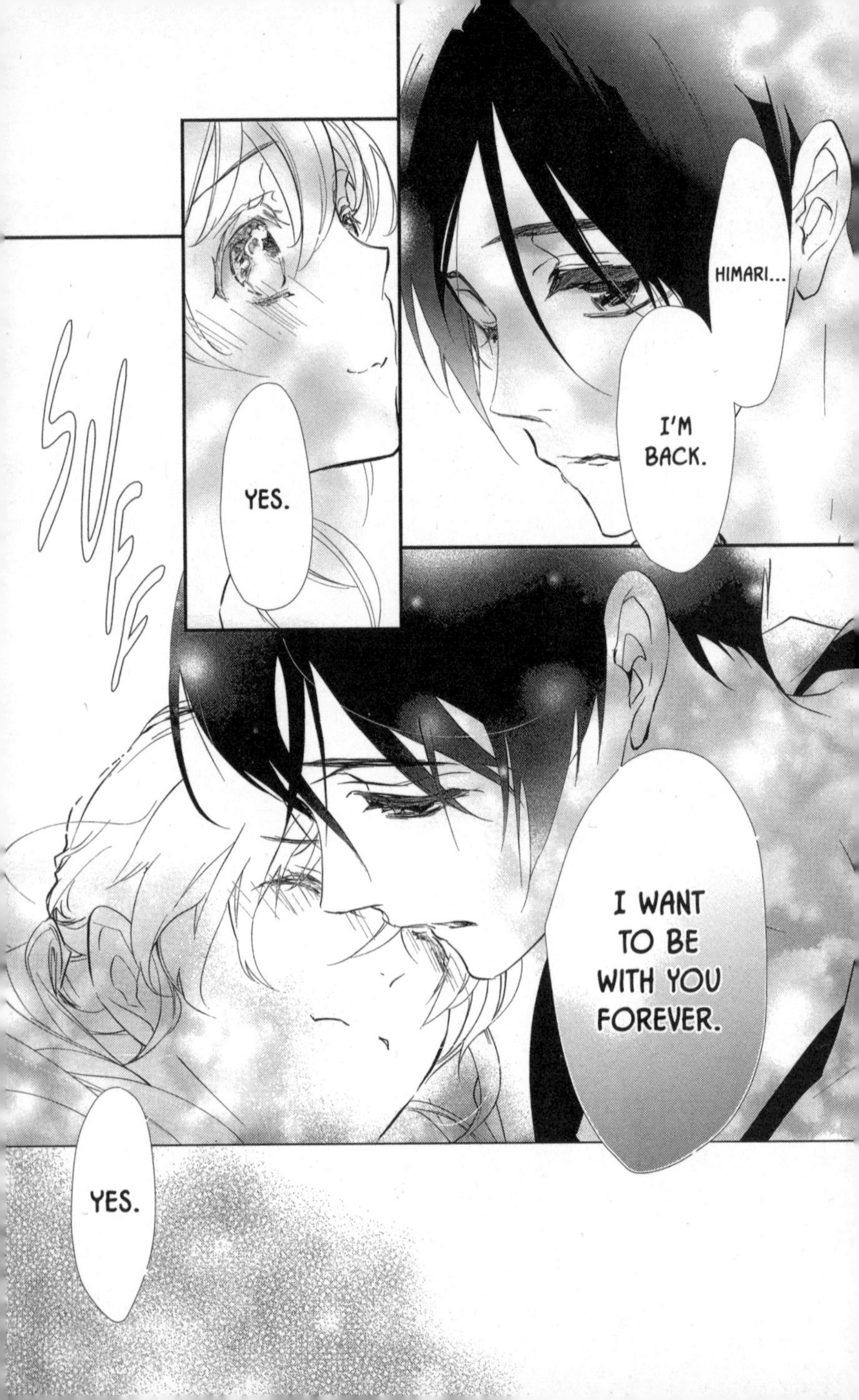
HIMARI...
I'M BACK.
YES.
I WANT TO BE WITH YOU FOREVER.
YES.

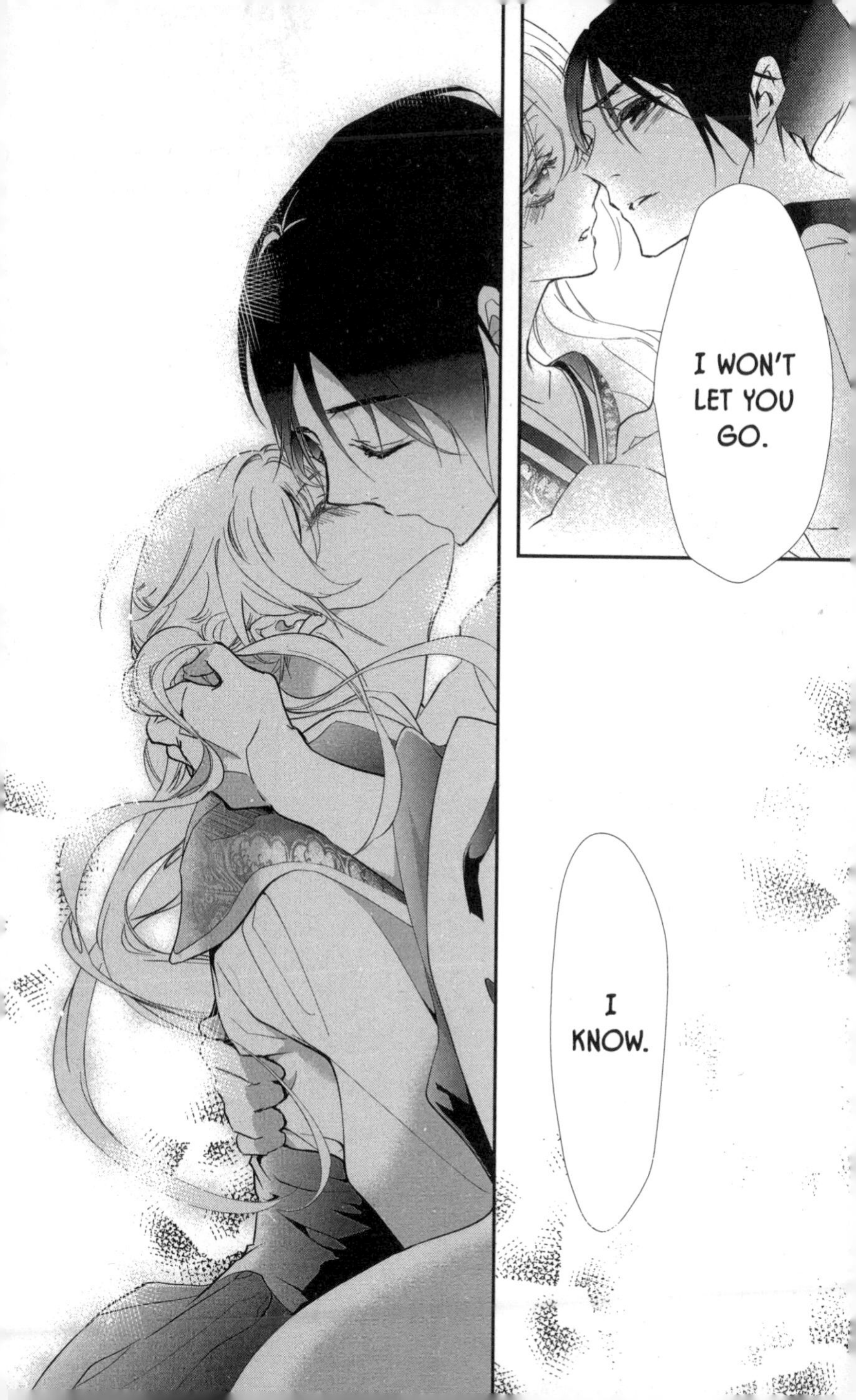
I WON'T LET YOU GO.
I KNOW.

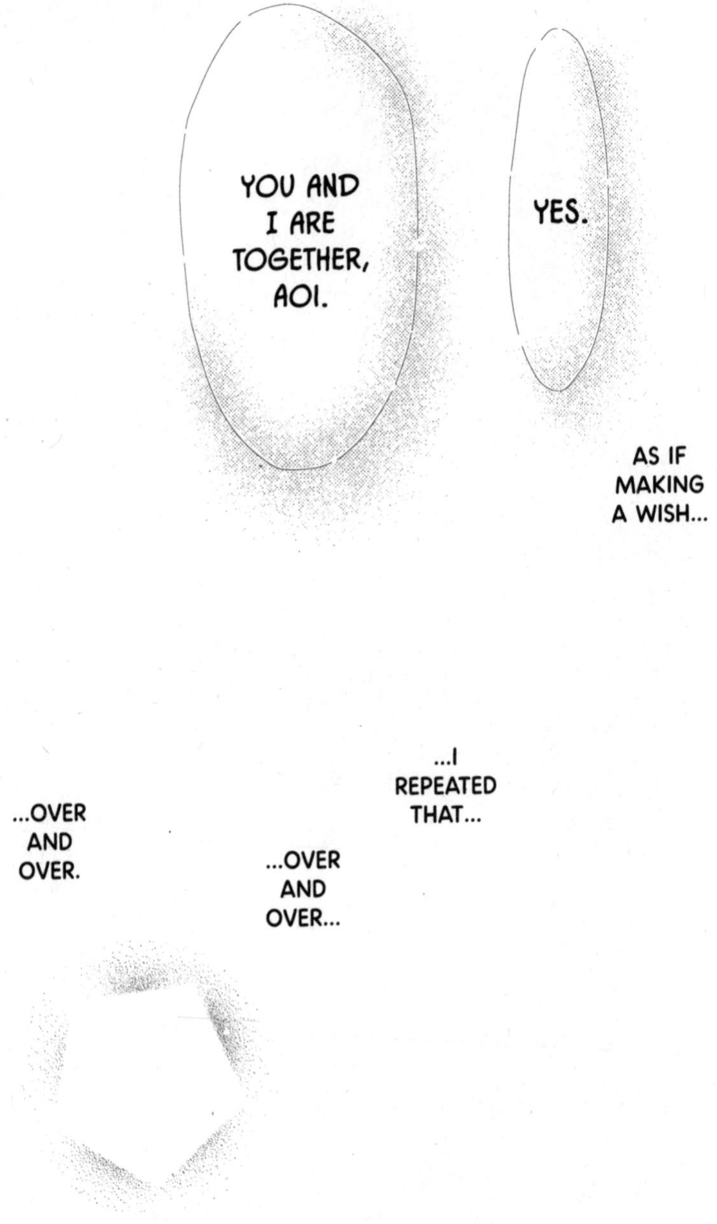
YES.
YOU AND I ARE TOGETHER, AOI.
AS IF MAKING A WISH...
...I REPEATED THAT...
...OVER AND OVER...
...OVER AND OVER.

Chapter 57/End

The DEMON PRINCE of MOMOCHI HOUSE

The DEMON PRINCE of MOMOCHI HOUSE

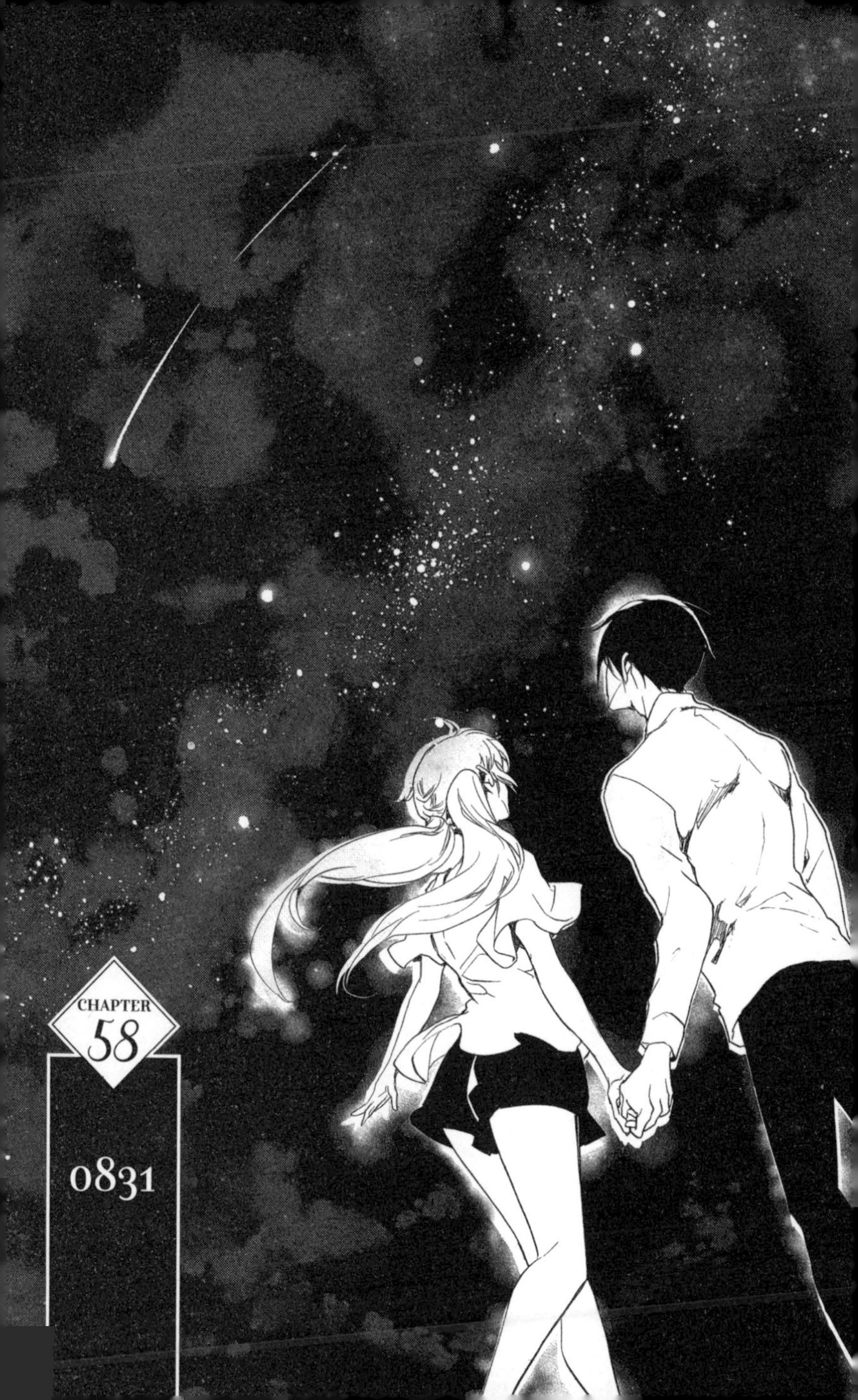
CHAPTER
58
0831

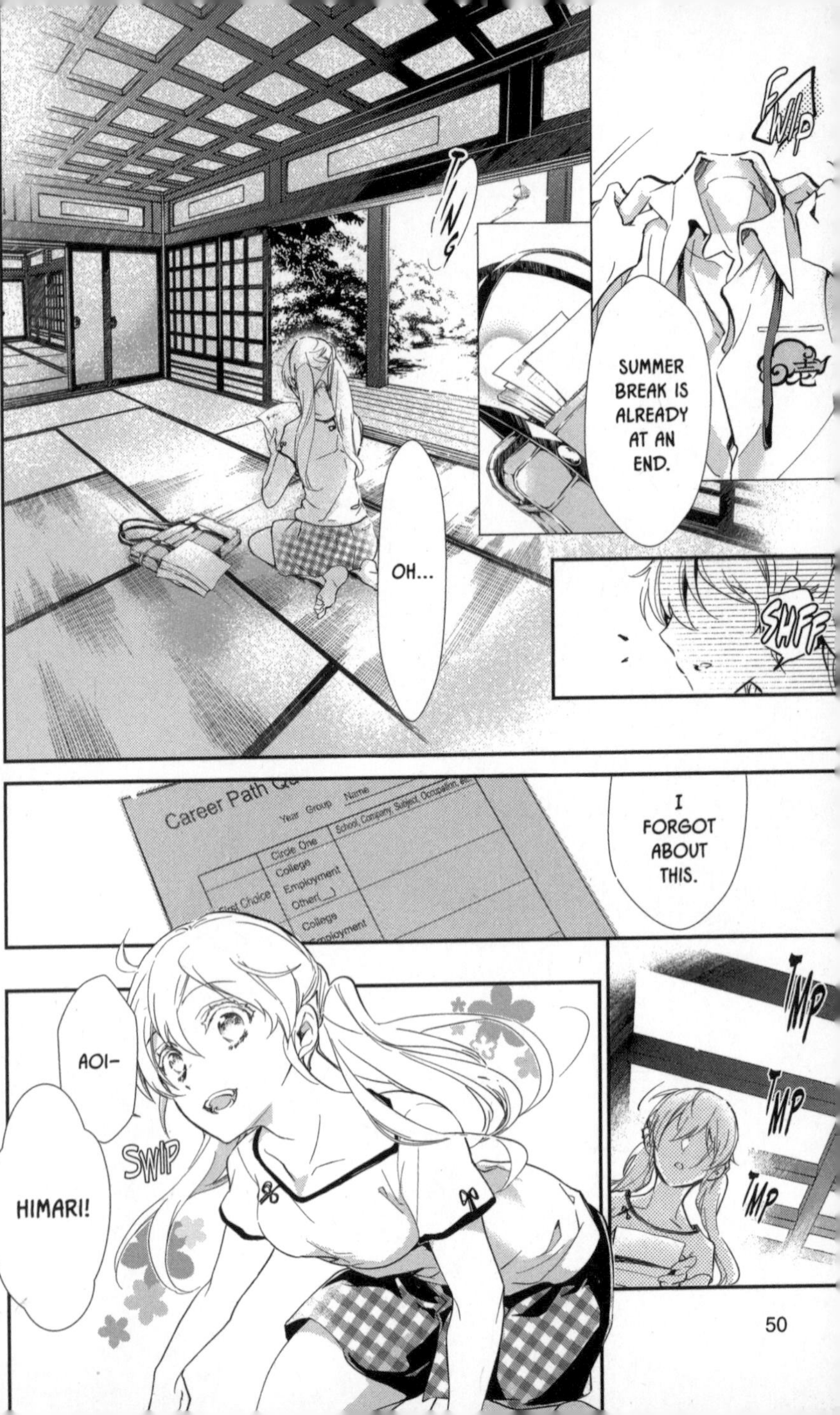
FWIP
SUMMER BREAK IS ALREADY AT AN END.
SHIFF
TING
OH...
I FORGOT ABOUT THIS.
Career Path
Year Group Name
School, Company, Subject, Occupation,
Circle One
College
Employment
Other( )
First Choice
College
TMP
TMP
TMP
AOI-
HIMARI!
SWIP

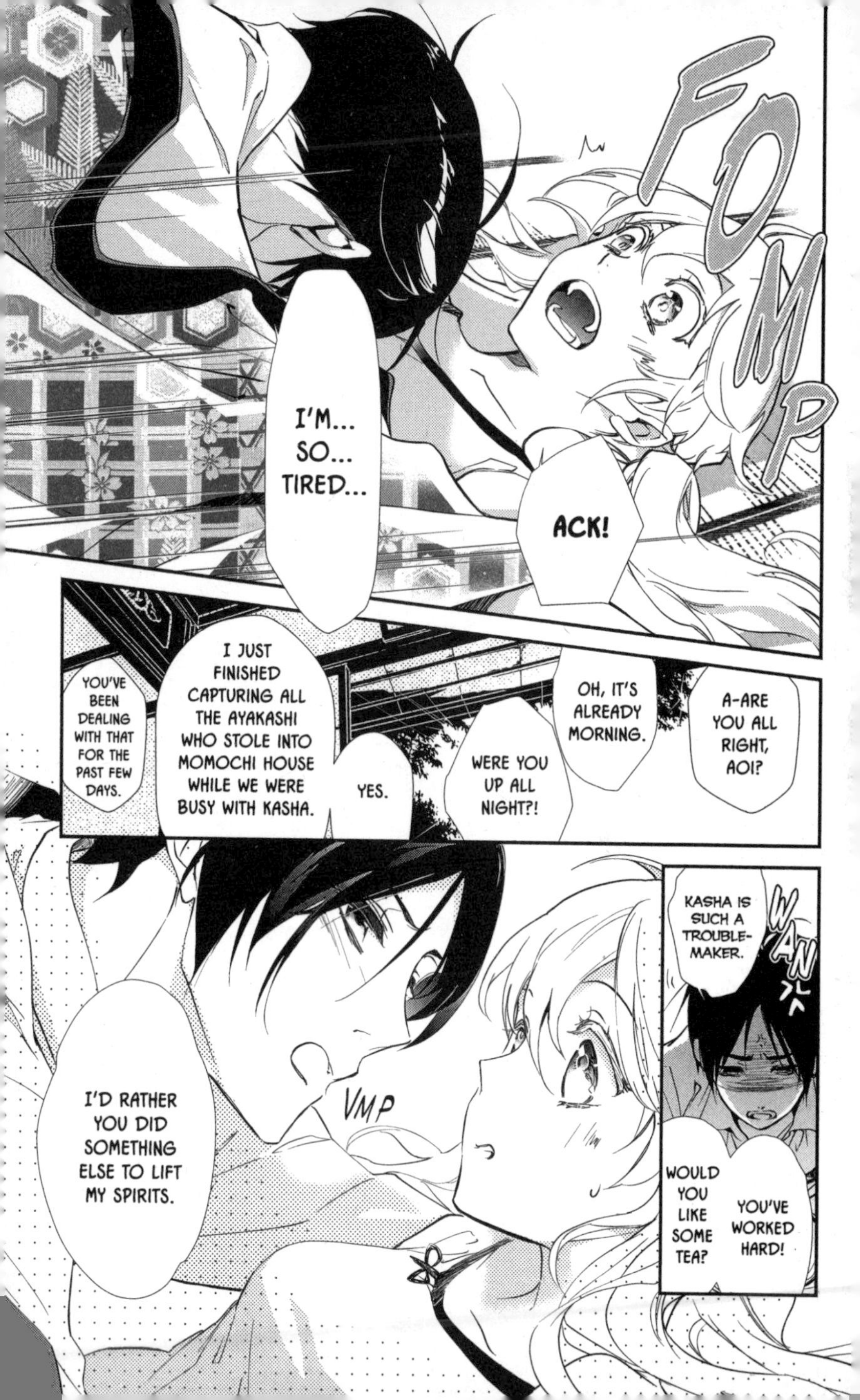
FOMP
ACK!
I'M... SO... TIRED...
A-ARE YOU ALL RIGHT, AOI?
OH, IT'S ALREADY MORNING.
WERE YOU UP ALL NIGHT?!
YES.
I JUST FINISHED CAPTURING ALL THE AYAKASHI WHO STOLE INTO MOMOCHI HOUSE WHILE WE WERE BUSY WITH KASHA.
YOU'VE BEEN DEALING WITH THAT FOR THE PAST FEW DAYS.
WAN
KASHA IS SUCH A TROUBLE-MAKER.
YOU'VE WORKED HARD!
WOULD YOU LIKE SOME TEA?
VMP
I'D RATHER YOU DID SOMETHING ELSE TO LIFT MY SPIRITS.

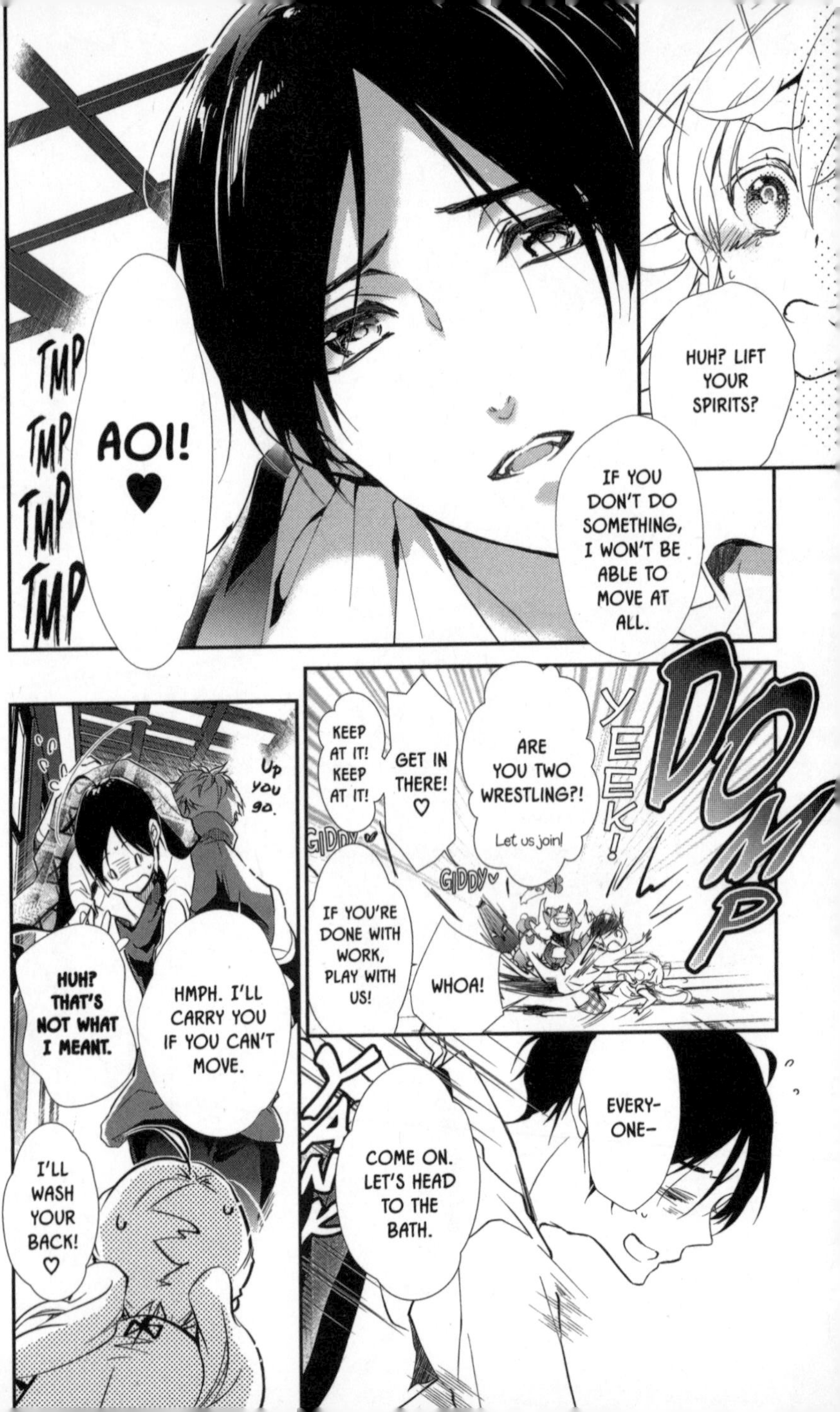
HUH? LIFT YOUR SPIRITS?
IF YOU DON'T DO SOMETHING, I WON'T BE ABLE TO MOVE AT ALL.
TMP TMP TMP TMP
AOI! ♥
DOMP
YEEK!
ARE YOU TWO WRESTLING?!
Let us join!
GET IN THERE! ♡
KEEP AT IT! KEEP AT IT!
GIDDY
GIDDY
WHOA!
IF YOU'RE DONE WITH WORK, PLAY WITH US!
Up you go.
HMPH. I'LL CARRY YOU IF YOU CAN'T MOVE.
HUH? THAT'S NOT WHAT I MEANT.
EVERY-ONE-
COME ON. LET'S HEAD TO THE BATH.
I'LL WASH YOUR BACK! ♡

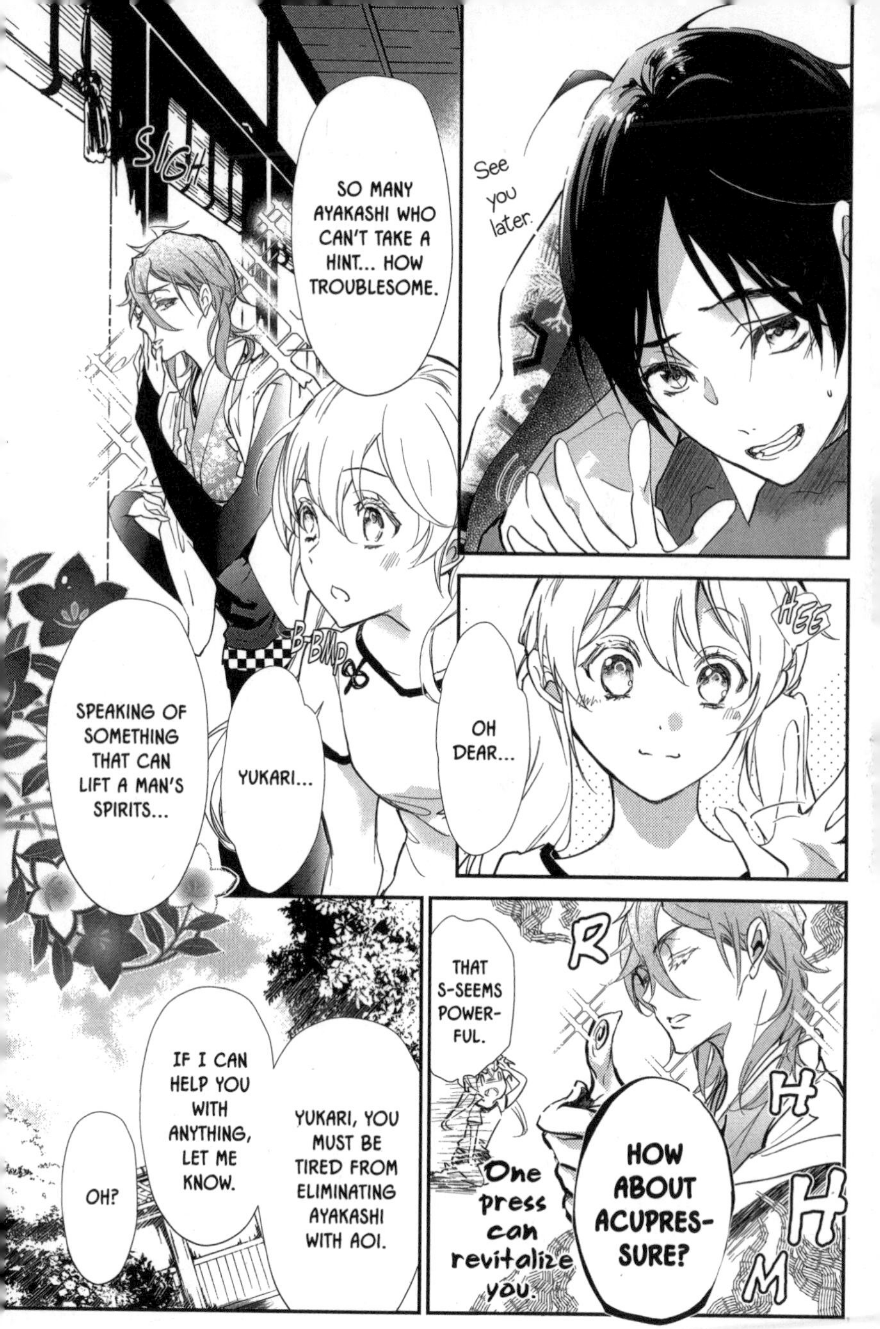
See you later.
HEE
OH DEAR...
SIGH
SO MANY AYAKASHI WHO CAN'T TAKE A HINT... HOW TROUBLESOME.
B-BMP
YUKARI...
SPEAKING OF SOMETHING THAT CAN LIFT A MAN'S SPIRITS...
R
H
HOW ABOUT ACUPRESSURE?
One press can revitalize you.
H
M
THAT S-SEEMS POWERFUL.
YUKARI, YOU MUST BE TIRED FROM ELIMINATING AYAKASHI WITH AOI.
IF I CAN HELP YOU WITH ANYTHING, LET ME KNOW.
OH?

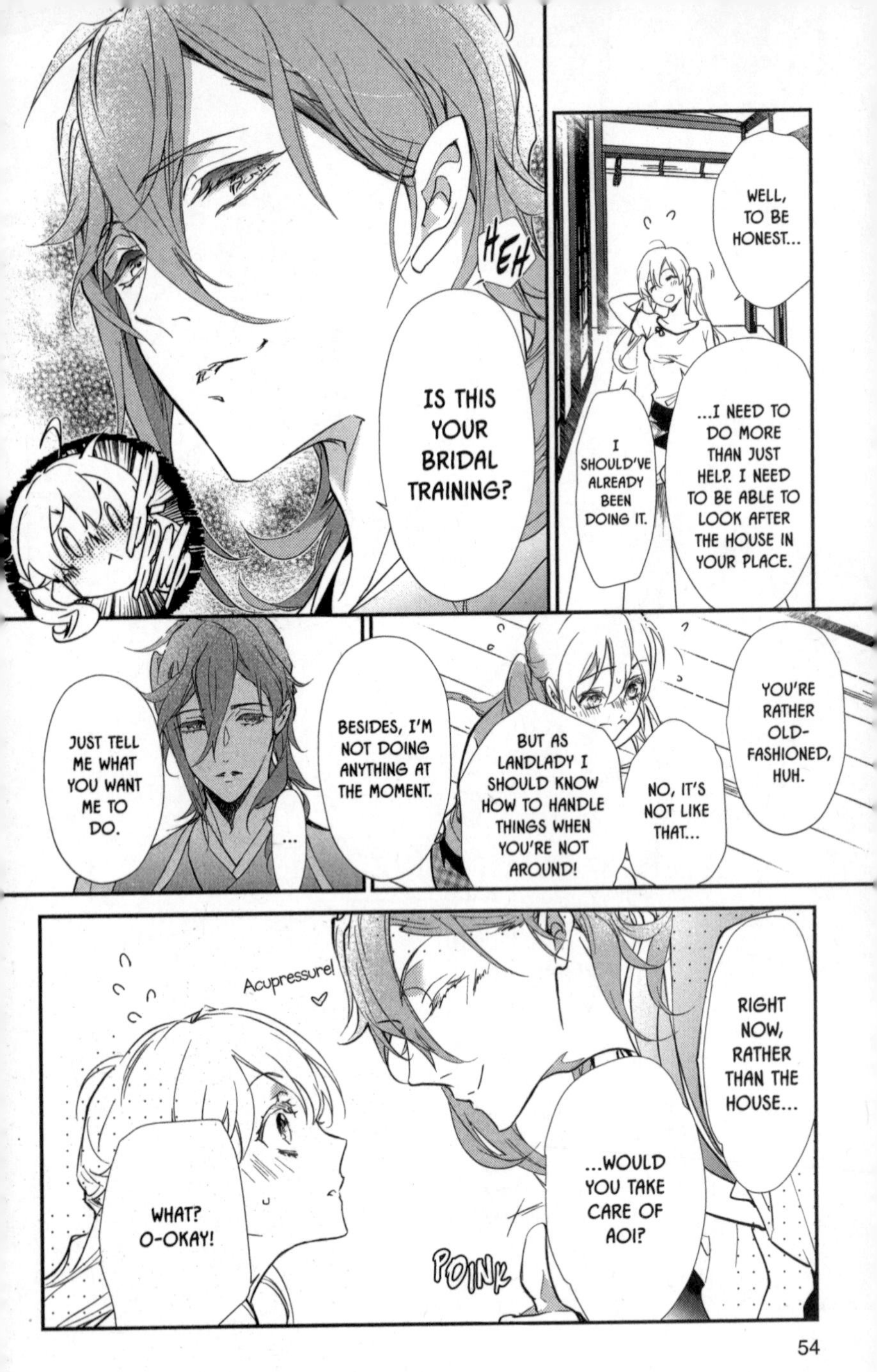
WELL, TO BE HONEST...
...I NEED TO DO MORE THAN JUST HELP. I NEED TO BE ABLE TO LOOK AFTER THE HOUSE IN YOUR PLACE.
I SHOULD'VE ALREADY BEEN DOING IT.
HEH
IS THIS YOUR BRIDAL TRAINING?
YOU'RE RATHER OLD-FASHIONED, HUH.
NO, IT'S NOT LIKE THAT...
BUT AS LANDLADY I SHOULD KNOW HOW TO HANDLE THINGS WHEN YOU'RE NOT AROUND!
BESIDES, I'M NOT DOING ANYTHING AT THE MOMENT.
...
JUST TELL ME WHAT YOU WANT ME TO DO.
RIGHT NOW, RATHER THAN THE HOUSE...
...WOULD YOU TAKE CARE OF AOI?
Acupressure!
POINK
WHAT? O-OKAY!

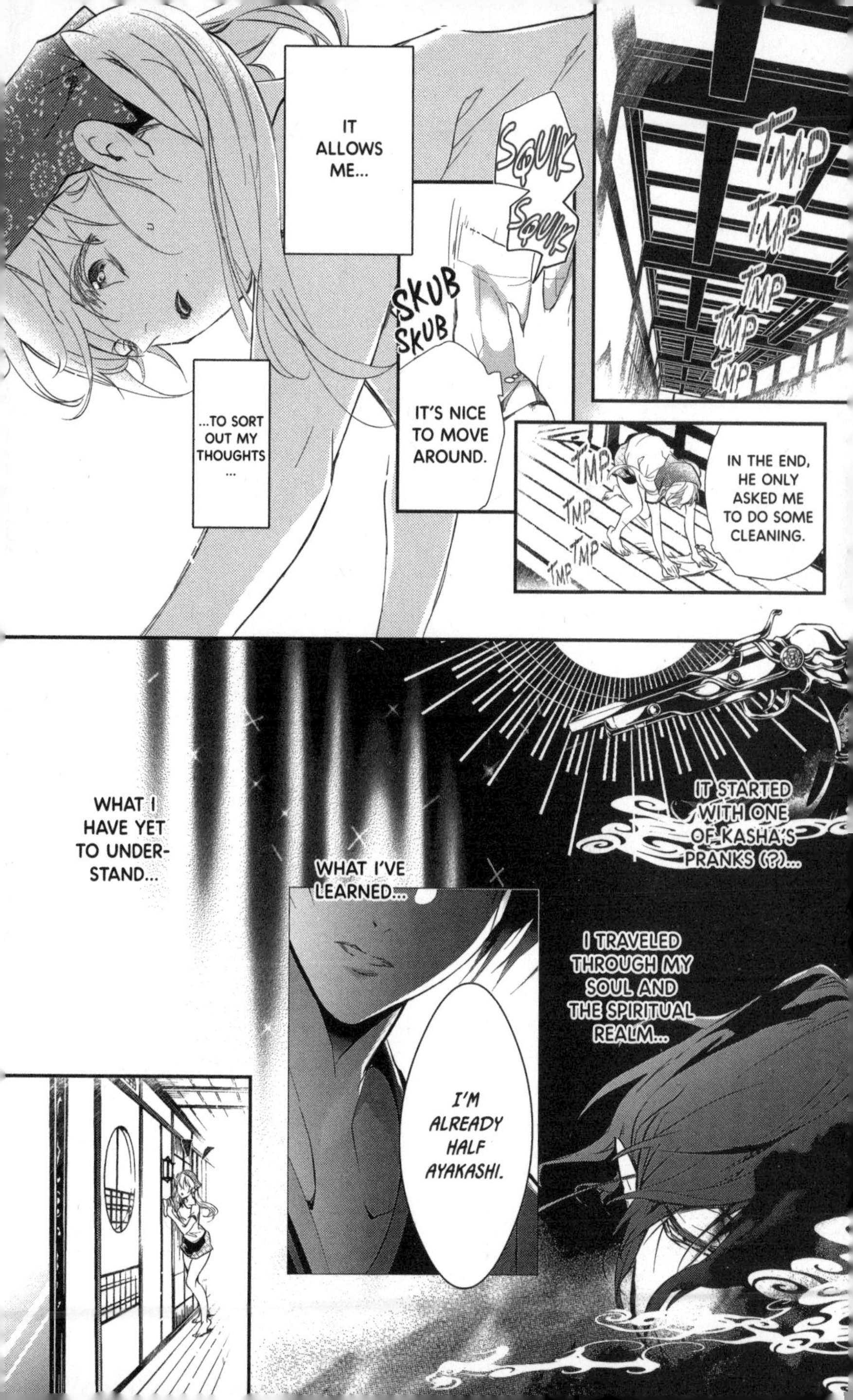

TMP TMP TMP TMP TMP
IN THE END, HE ONLY ASKED ME TO DO SOME CLEANING.
TMP TMP TMP TMP
SQUIK SQUIK
SKUB SKUB
IT'S NICE TO MOVE AROUND.
IT ALLOWS ME...
...TO SORT OUT MY THOUGHTS...
IT STARTED WITH ONE OF KASHA'S PRANKS (?)...
I TRAVELED THROUGH MY SOUL AND THE SPIRITUAL REALM...
WHAT I'VE LEARNED...
I'M ALREADY HALF AYAKASHI.
WHAT I HAVE YET TO UNDER-STAND...

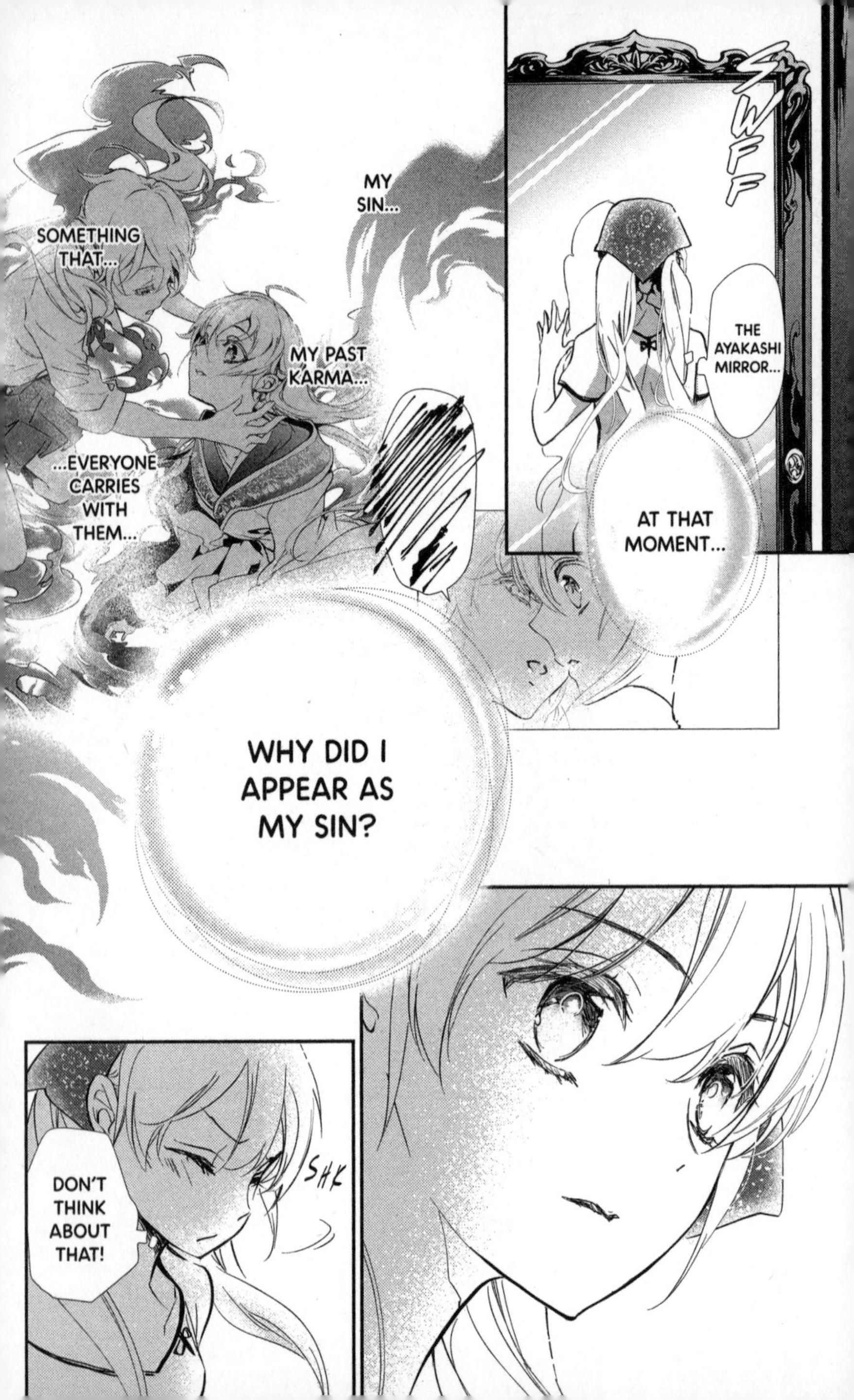
SWFF
THE AYAKASHI MIRROR...
AT THAT MOMENT...
MY SIN...
MY PAST KARMA...
SOMETHING THAT...
...EVERYONE CARRIES WITH THEM...
WHY DID I APPEAR AS MY SIN?
SHK
DON'T THINK ABOUT THAT!

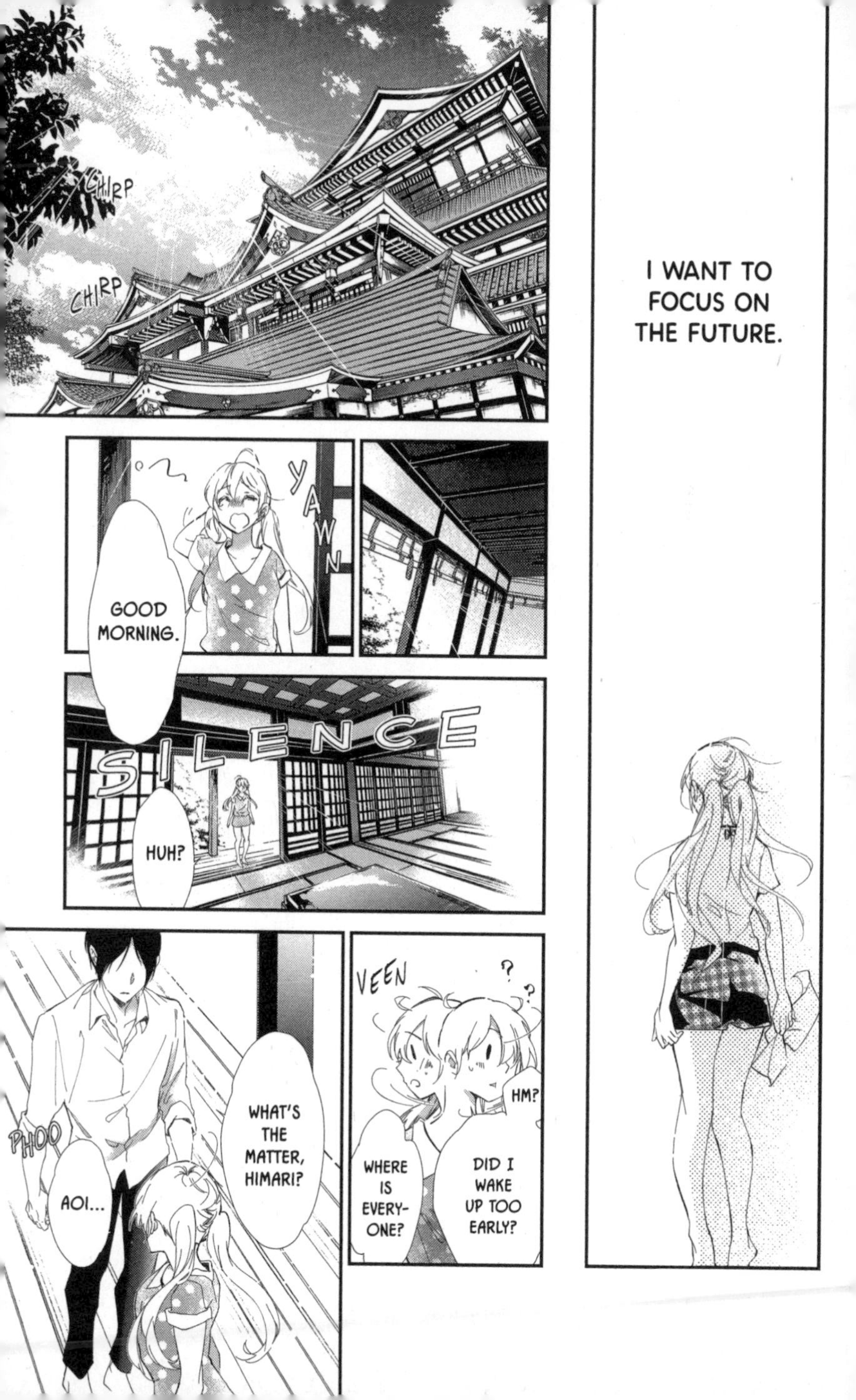
I WANT TO FOCUS ON THE FUTURE.
CHIRP
CHIRP
YAWN
GOOD MORNING.
SILENCE
HUH?
VEEN
HM?
DID I WAKE UP TOO EARLY?
WHERE IS EVERYONE?
WHAT'S THE MATTER, HIMARI?
PHOO
AOI...

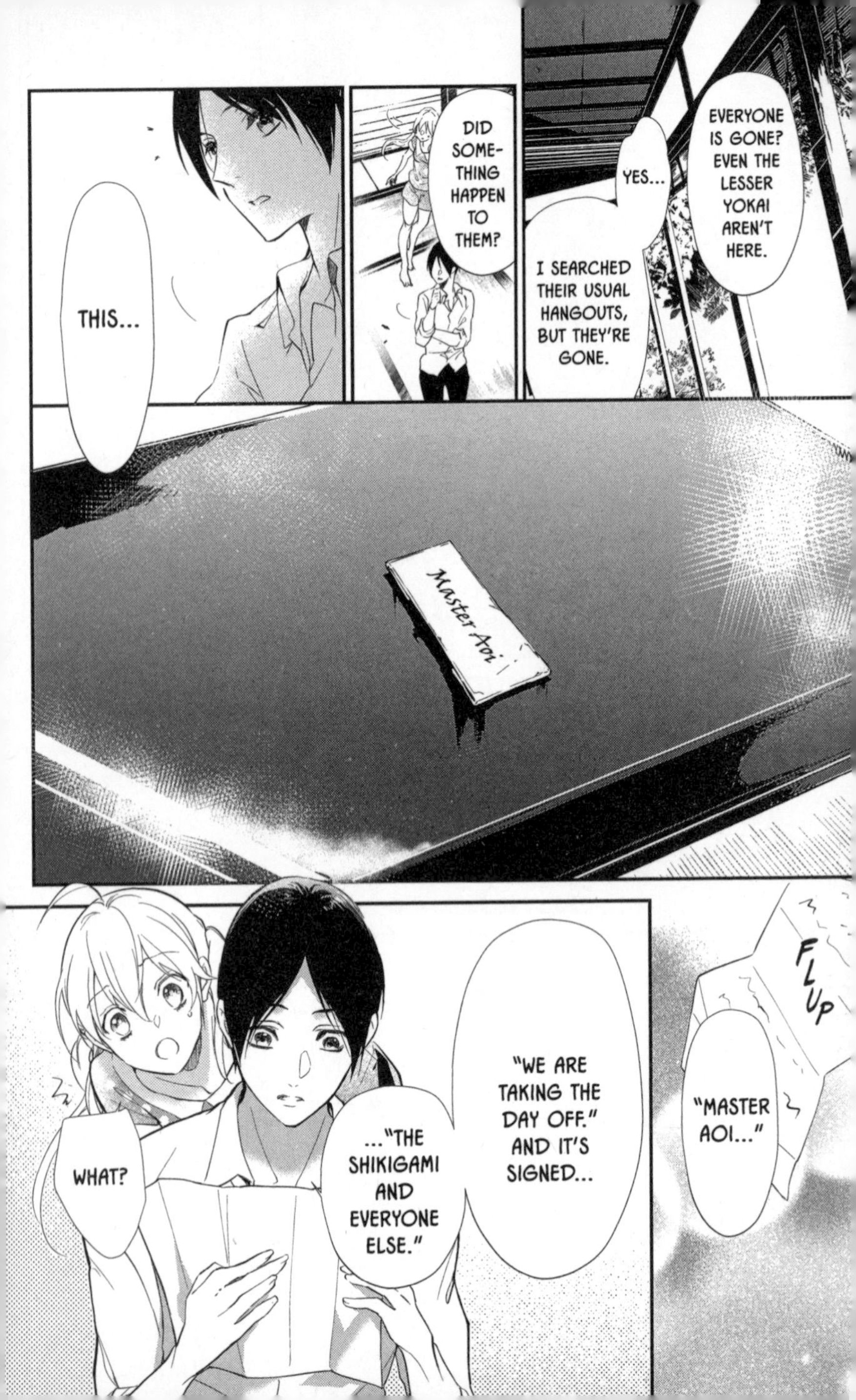
EVERYONE IS GONE? EVEN THE LESSER YOKAI AREN'T HERE.
YES...
I SEARCHED THEIR USUAL HANGOUTS, BUT THEY'RE GONE.
DID SOME-THING HAPPEN TO THEM?
THIS...
Master Aoi
FLUP
"MASTER AOI..."
"WE ARE TAKING THE DAY OFF." AND IT'S SIGNED...
..."THE SHIKIGAMI AND EVERYONE ELSE."
WHAT?

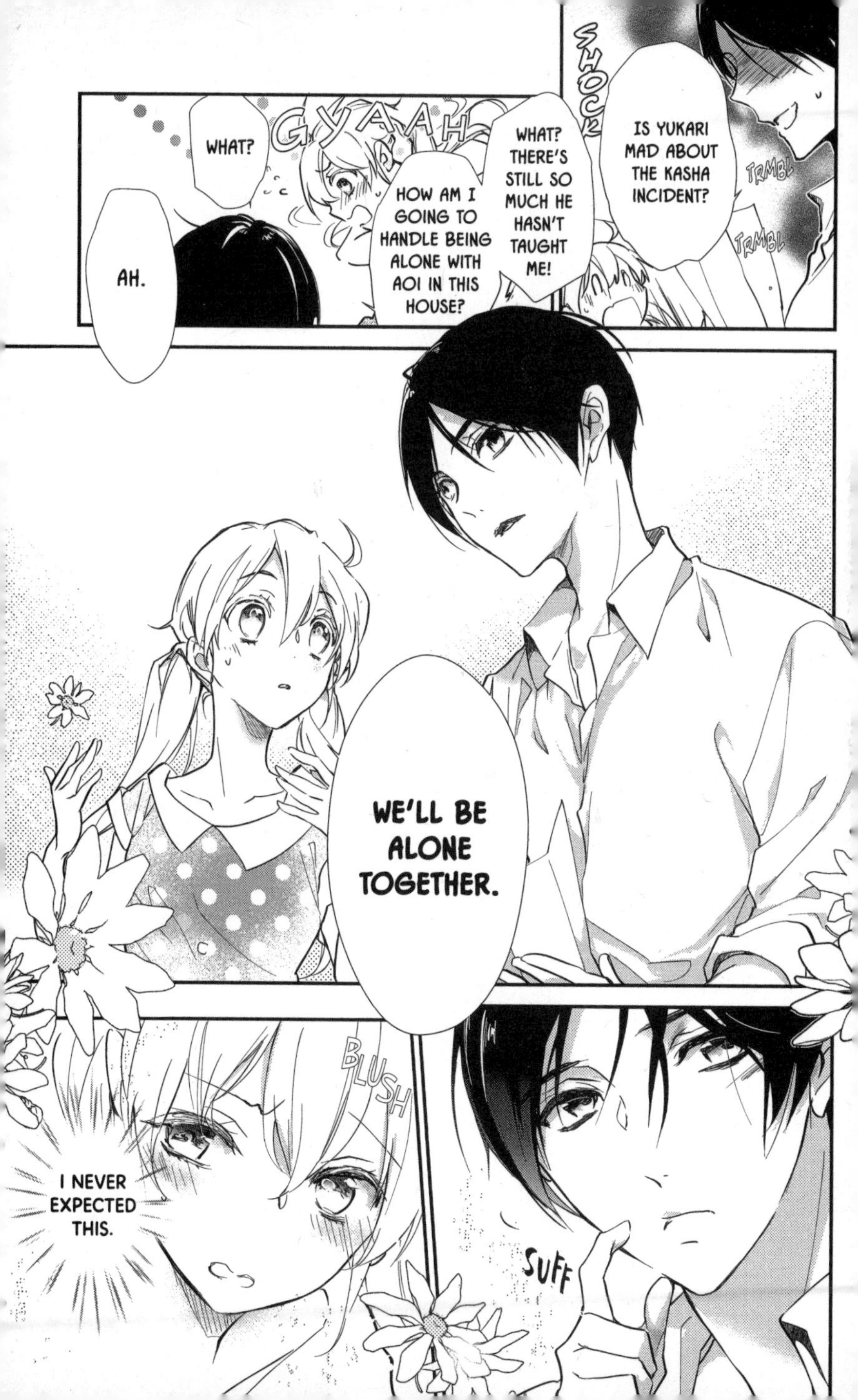
SHOCK
IS YUKARI MAD ABOUT THE KASHA INCIDENT?
TRMBL
TRMBL
WHAT? THERE'S STILL SO MUCH HE HASN'T TAUGHT ME!
GYAAH
HOW AM I GOING TO HANDLE BEING ALONE WITH AOI IN THIS HOUSE?
WHAT?
AH.
WE'LL BE ALONE TOGETHER.
SUFF
BLUSH
I NEVER EXPECTED THIS.

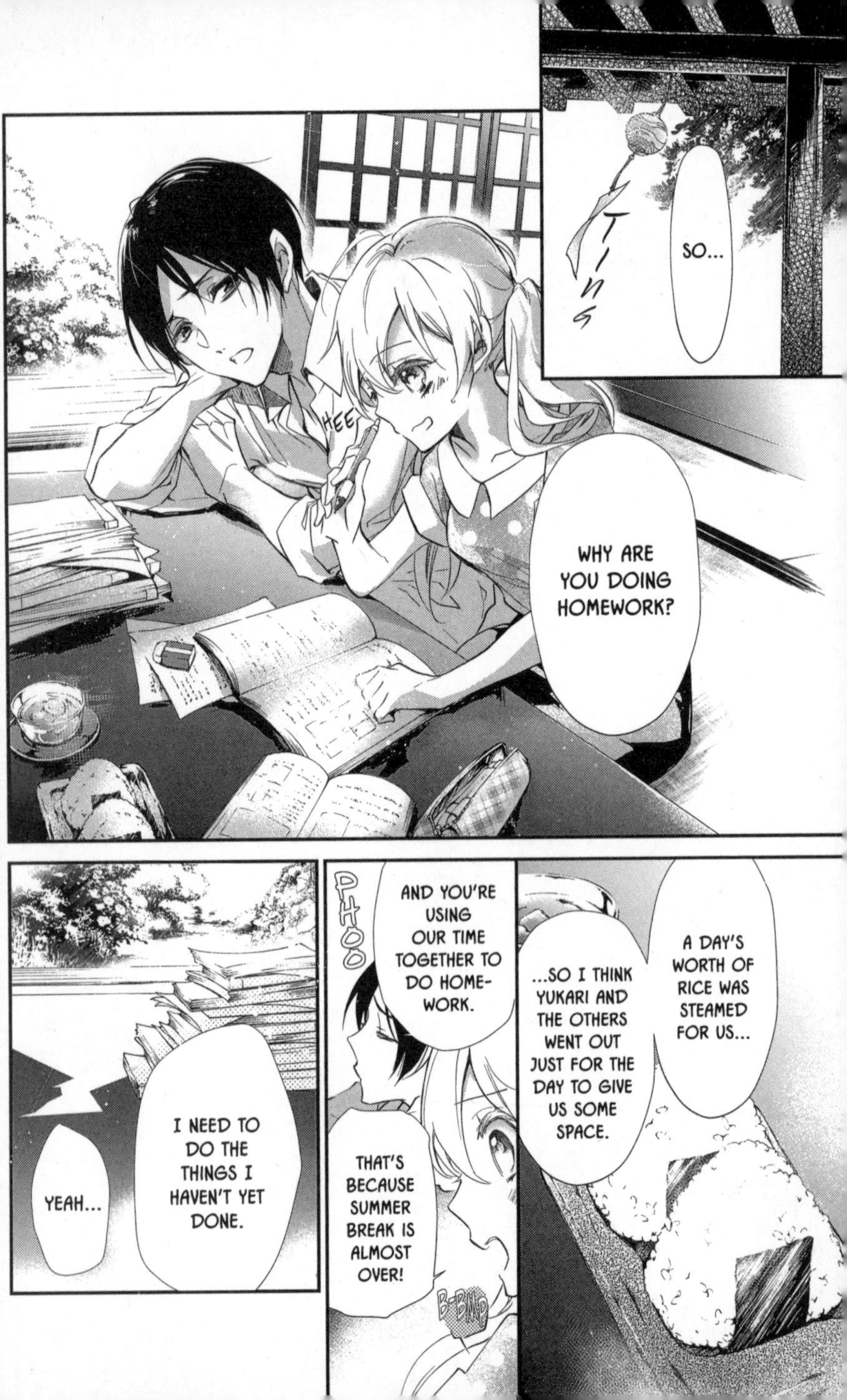
SO...
HEE
WHY ARE YOU DOING HOMEWORK?
A DAY'S WORTH OF RICE WAS STEAMED FOR US...
...SO I THINK YUKARI AND THE OTHERS WENT OUT JUST FOR THE DAY TO GIVE US SOME SPACE.
AND YOU'RE USING OUR TIME TOGETHER TO DO HOME-WORK.
PHOO
THAT'S BECAUSE SUMMER BREAK IS ALMOST OVER!
B-BMP
I NEED TO DO THE THINGS I HAVEN'T YET DONE.
YEAH...

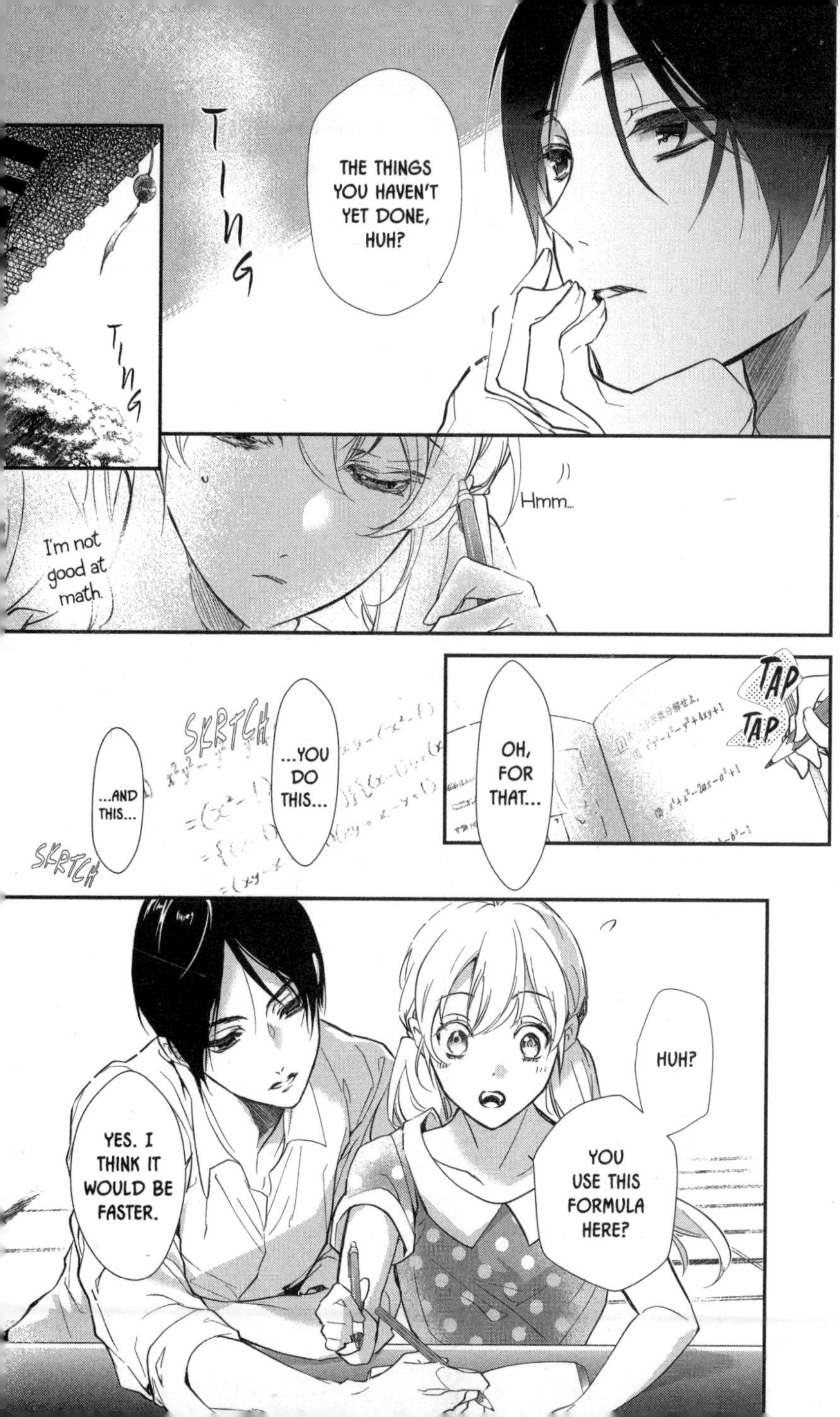
THE THINGS YOU HAVEN'T YET DONE, HUH?
TING
TING
Hmm...
I'm not good at math.
TAP TAP
OH, FOR THAT...
...YOU DO THIS...
SKRTCH
...AND THIS...
SKRTCH
HUH?
YOU USE THIS FORMULA HERE?
YES. I THINK IT WOULD BE FASTER.

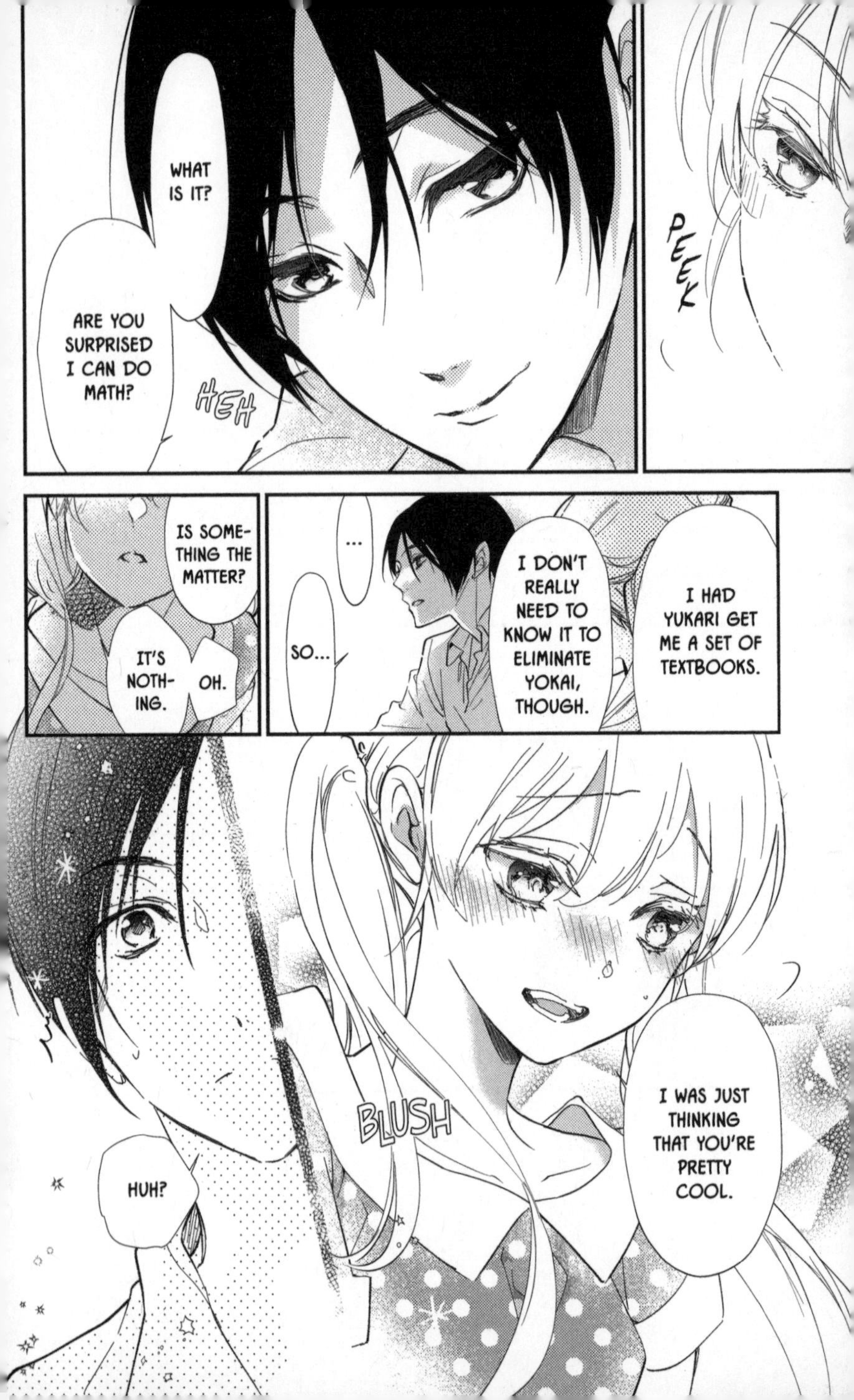
PEEK
WHAT IS IT?
ARE YOU SURPRISED I CAN DO MATH?
HEH
I HAD YUKARI GET ME A SET OF TEXTBOOKS.
I DON'T REALLY NEED TO KNOW IT TO ELIMINATE YOKAI, THOUGH.
...
SO...
IS SOMETHING THE MATTER?
OH.
IT'S NOTHING.
I WAS JUST THINKING THAT YOU'RE PRETTY COOL.
BLUSH
HUH?

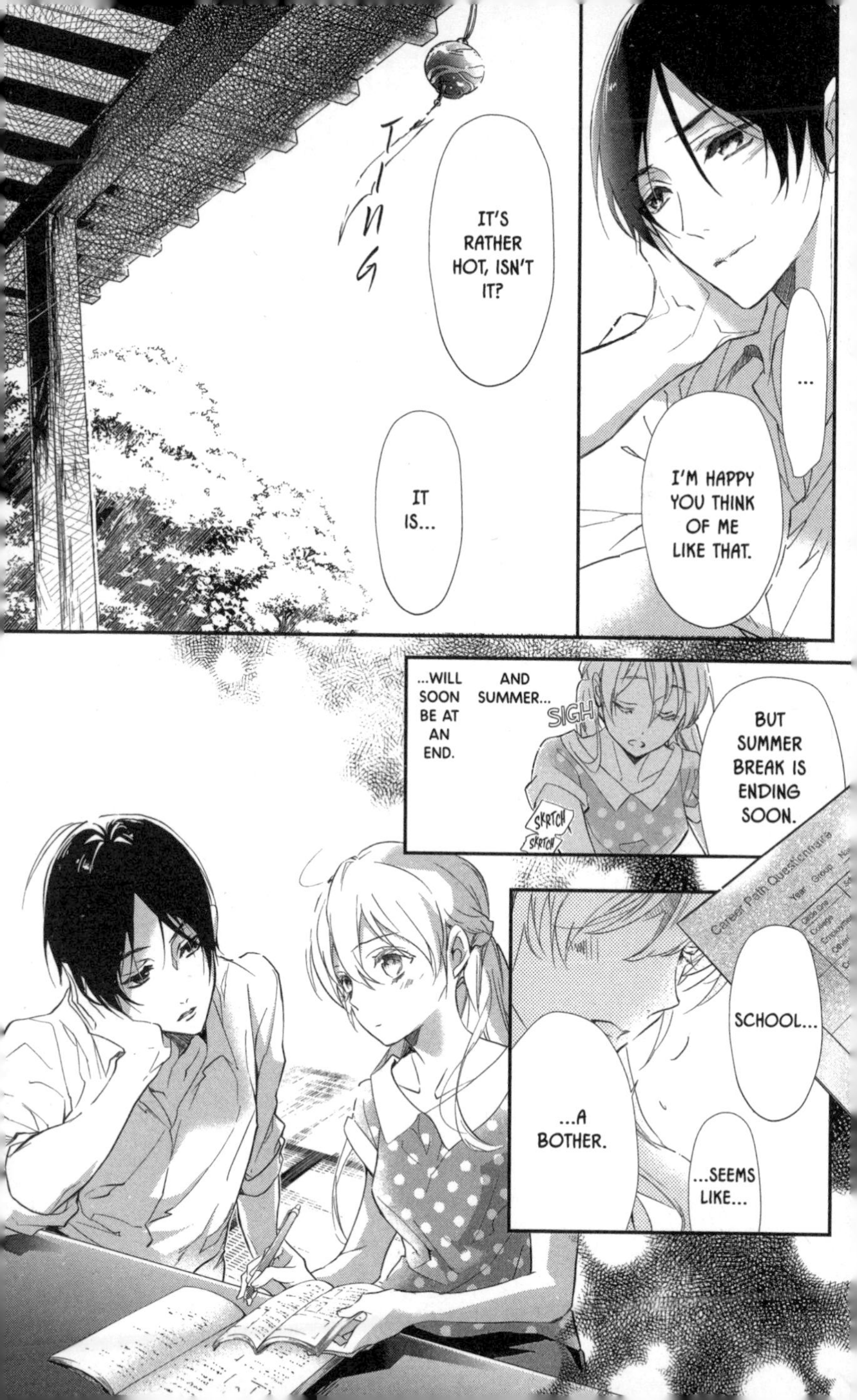
...
I'M HAPPY YOU THINK OF ME LIKE THAT.
TING
IT'S RATHER HOT, ISN'T IT?
IT IS...
BUT SUMMER BREAK IS ENDING SOON.
SIGH
SKRTCH
SKRTCH
AND SUMMER...
...WILL SOON BE AT AN END.
Career Path Questionnaire
Year Group
SCHOOL...
...SEEMS LIKE...
...A BOTHER.

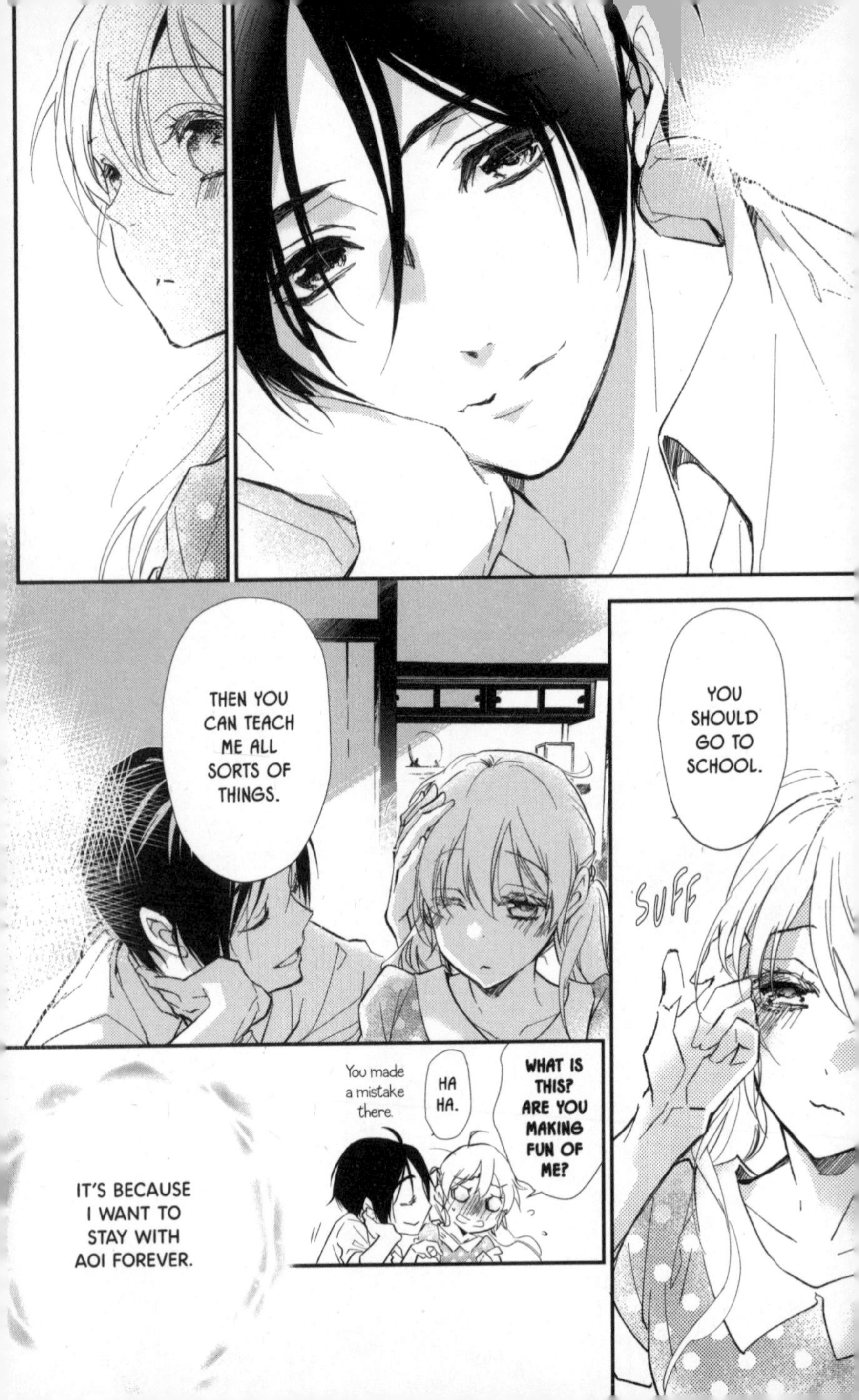
YOU SHOULD GO TO SCHOOL.
SUFF
THEN YOU CAN TEACH ME ALL SORTS OF THINGS.
WHAT IS THIS? ARE YOU MAKING FUN OF ME?
HA HA.
You made a mistake there.
IT'S BECAUSE I WANT TO STAY WITH AOI FOREVER.

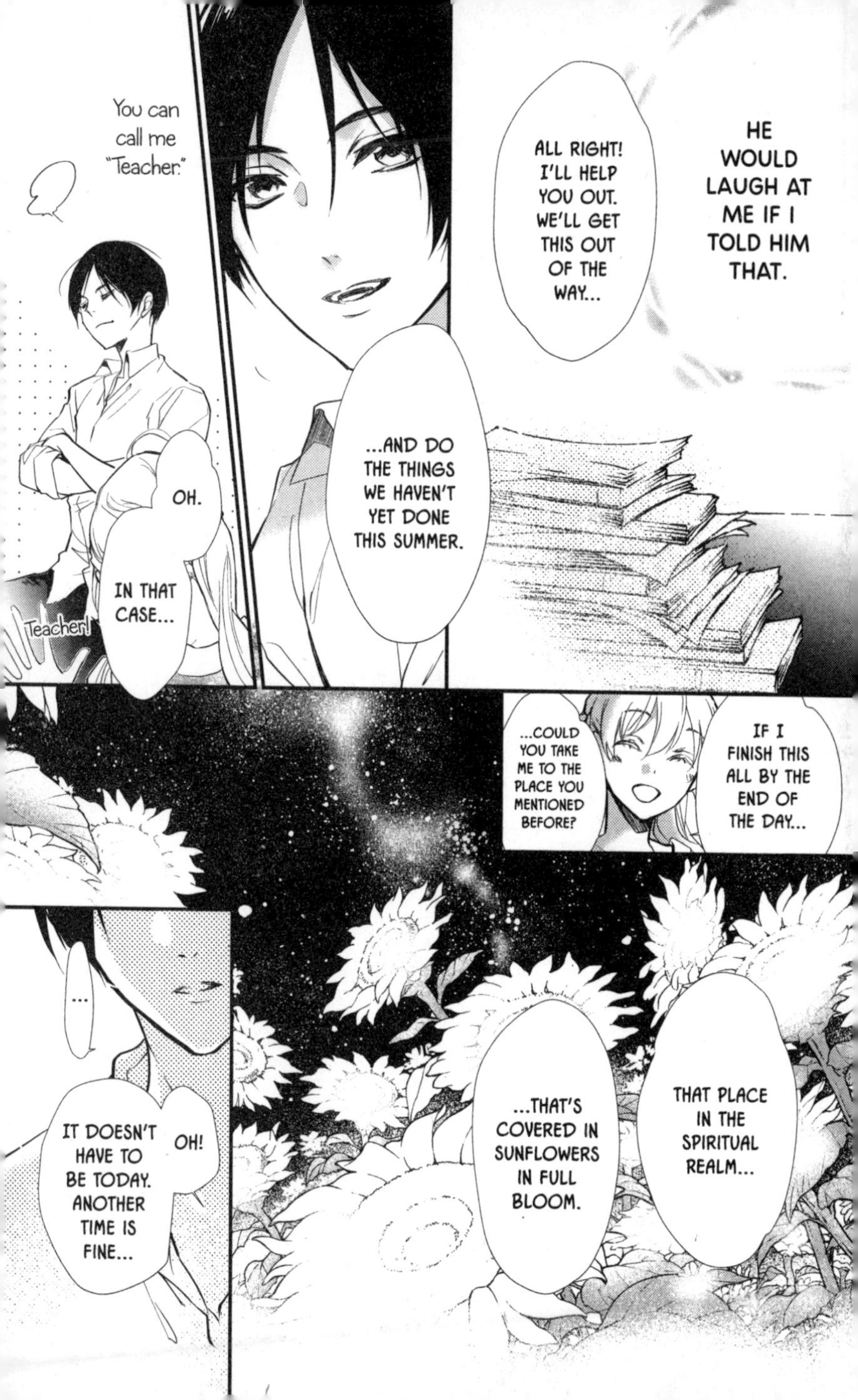
HE WOULD LAUGH AT ME IF I TOLD HIM THAT.
ALL RIGHT! I'LL HELP YOU OUT. WE'LL GET THIS OUT OF THE WAY...
...AND DO THE THINGS WE HAVEN'T YET DONE THIS SUMMER.
You can call me "Teacher."
OH.
IN THAT CASE...
Teacher!
IF I FINISH THIS ALL BY THE END OF THE DAY...
...COULD YOU TAKE ME TO THE PLACE YOU MENTIONED BEFORE?
THAT PLACE IN THE SPIRITUAL REALM...
...THAT'S COVERED IN SUNFLOWERS IN FULL BLOOM.
...
OH!
IT DOESN'T HAVE TO BE TODAY. ANOTHER TIME IS FINE...

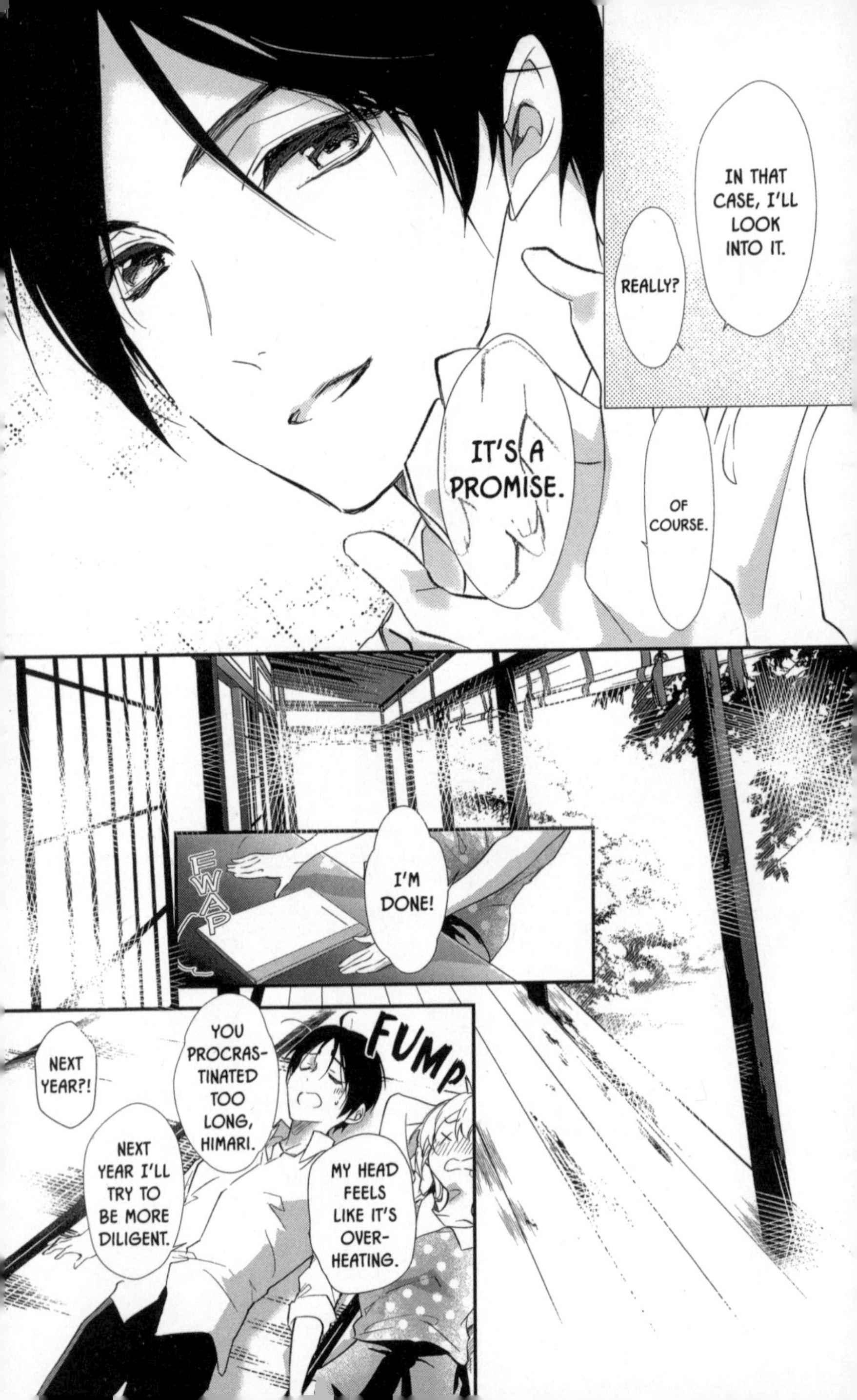
IN THAT CASE, I'LL LOOK INTO IT.
REALLY?
IT'S A PROMISE.
OF COURSE.
I'M DONE!
FWAP
FUMP
YOU PROCRAS-TINATED TOO LONG, HIMARI.
MY HEAD FEELS LIKE IT'S OVER-HEATING.
NEXT YEAR I'LL TRY TO BE MORE DILIGENT.
NEXT YEAR?!

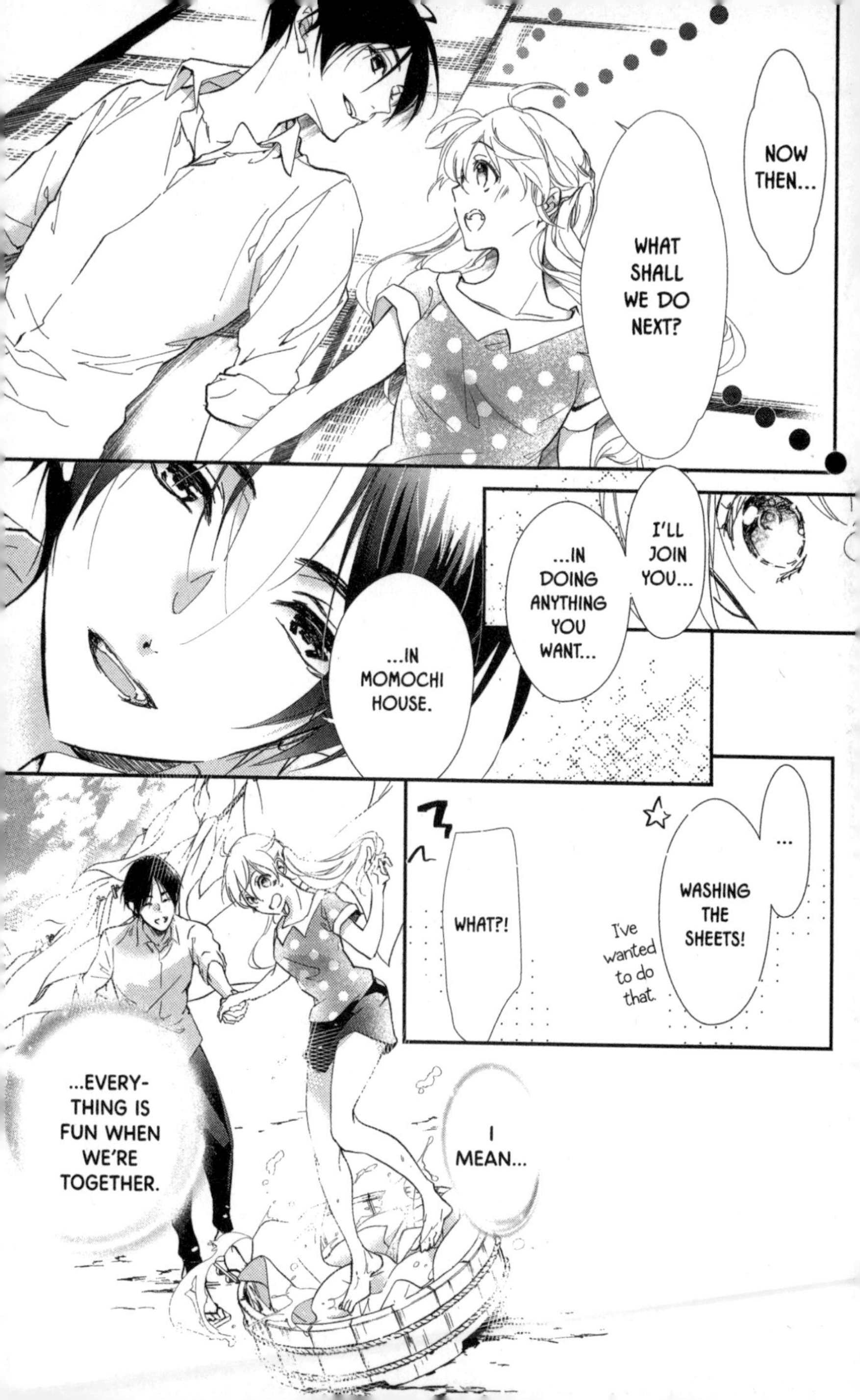
NOW THEN...
WHAT SHALL WE DO NEXT?
I'LL JOIN YOU...
...IN DOING ANYTHING YOU WANT...
...IN MOMOCHI HOUSE.
...
WASHING THE SHEETS!
I've wanted to do that.
WHAT?!
I MEAN...
...EVERY-THING IS FUN WHEN WE'RE TOGETHER.

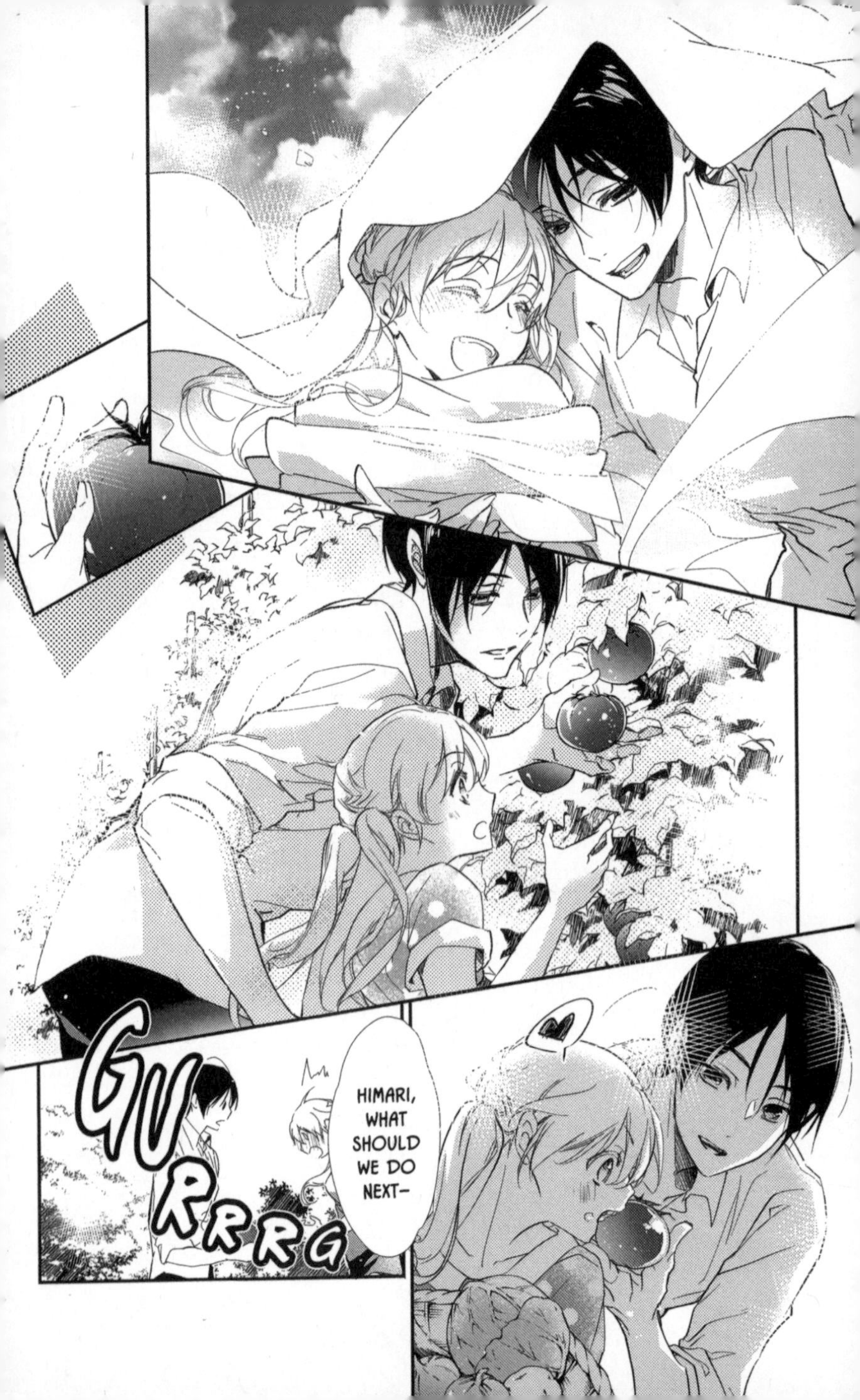
HIMARI, WHAT SHOULD WE DO NEXT–
GURRRRG

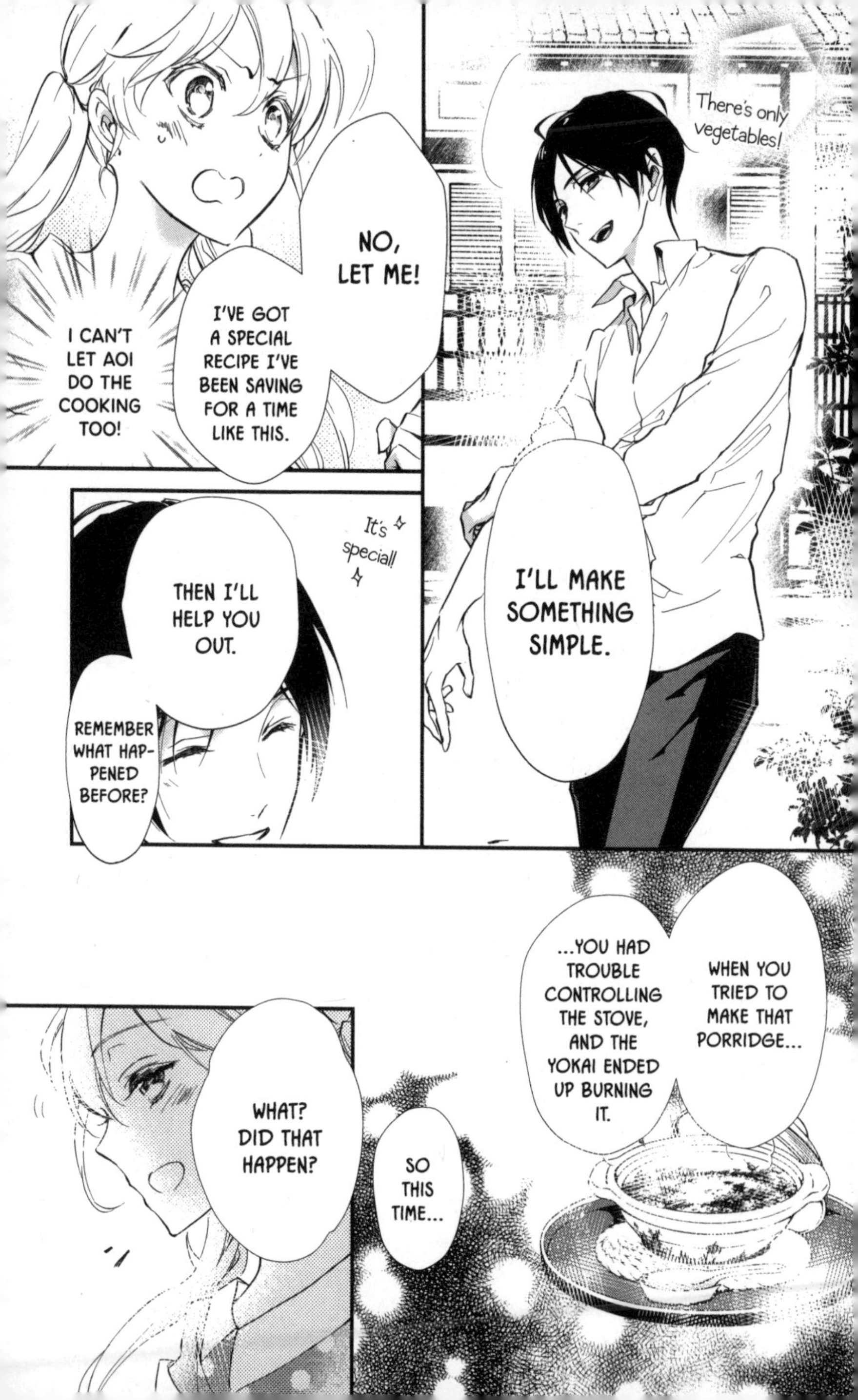
There's only vegetables!
I'LL MAKE SOMETHING SIMPLE.
NO, LET ME!
I'VE GOT A SPECIAL RECIPE I'VE BEEN SAVING FOR A TIME LIKE THIS.
I CAN'T LET AOI DO THE COOKING TOO!
It's special!
THEN I'LL HELP YOU OUT.
REMEMBER WHAT HAP-PENED BEFORE?
WHEN YOU TRIED TO MAKE THAT PORRIDGE...
...YOU HAD TROUBLE CONTROLLING THE STOVE, AND THE YOKAI ENDED UP BURNING IT.
SO THIS TIME...
WHAT? DID THAT HAPPEN?

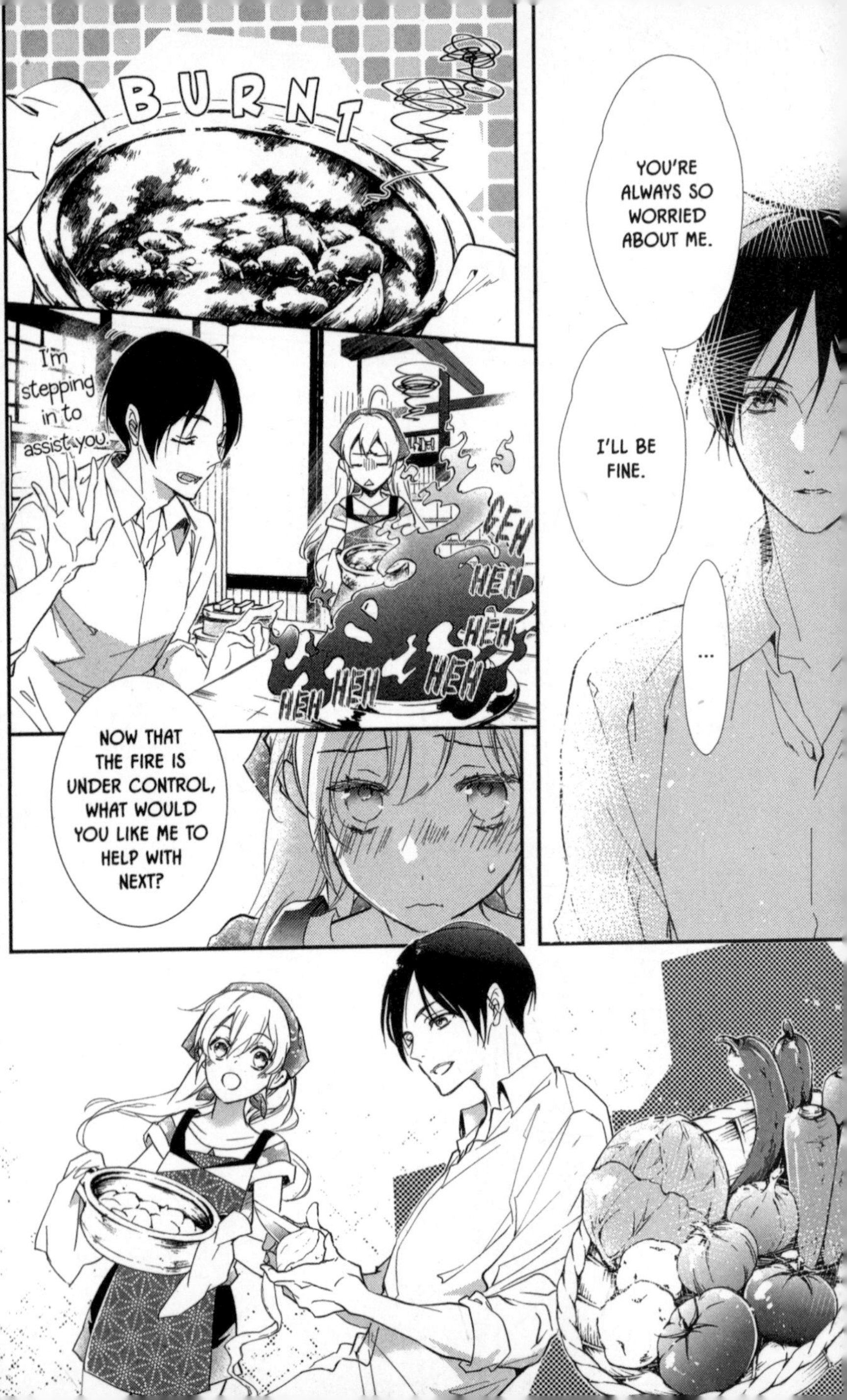
YOU'RE ALWAYS SO WORRIED ABOUT ME.
I'LL BE FINE.
...
BURNT
GEH HEH HEH HEH HEH HEH
I'm stepping in to assist you.
NOW THAT THE FIRE IS UNDER CONTROL, WHAT WOULD YOU LIKE ME TO HELP WITH NEXT?

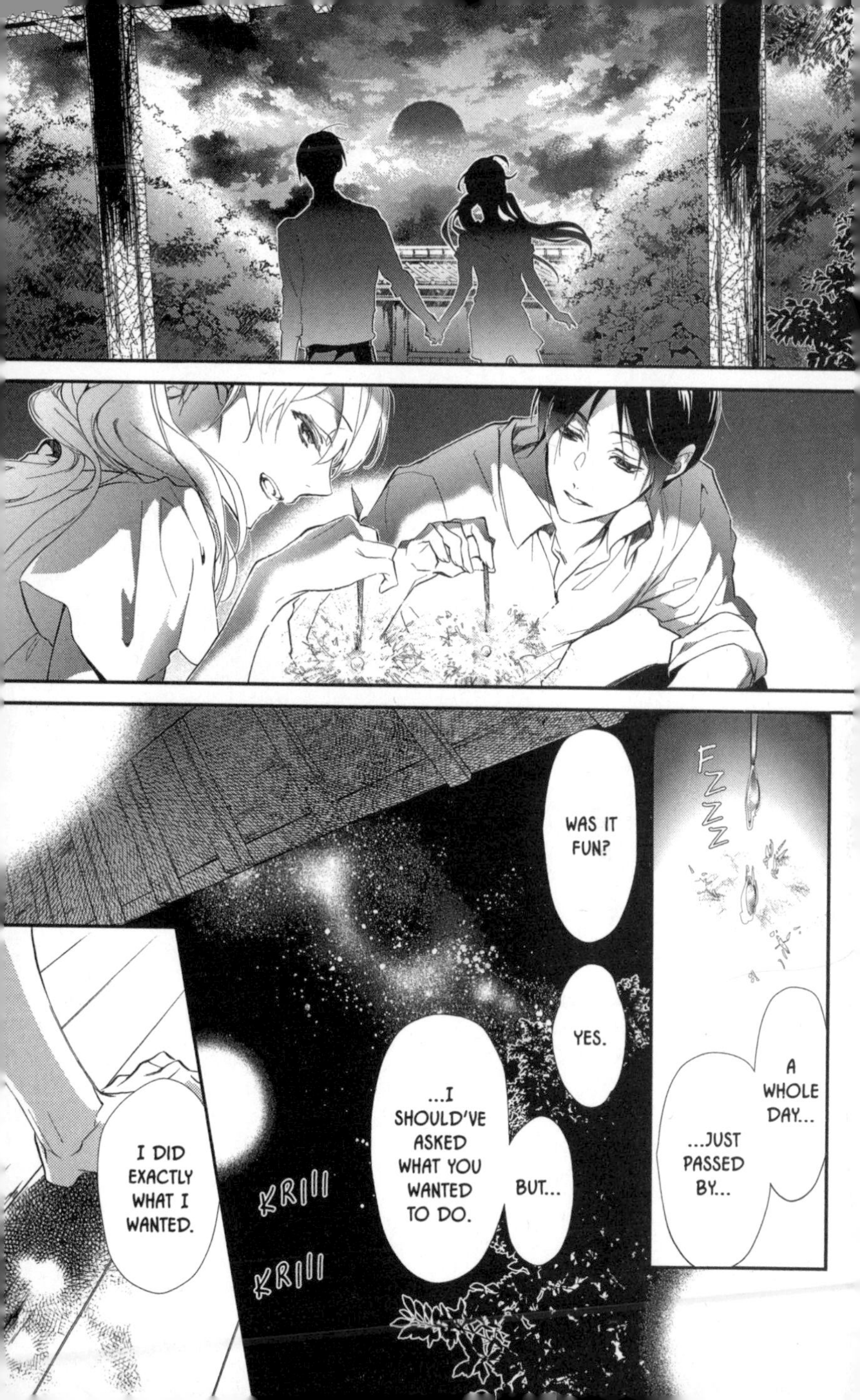
FZZZ
A WHOLE DAY...
...JUST PASSED BY...
WAS IT FUN?
YES.
BUT...
...I SHOULD'VE ASKED WHAT YOU WANTED TO DO.
KRIII
KRIII
I DID EXACTLY WHAT I WANTED.

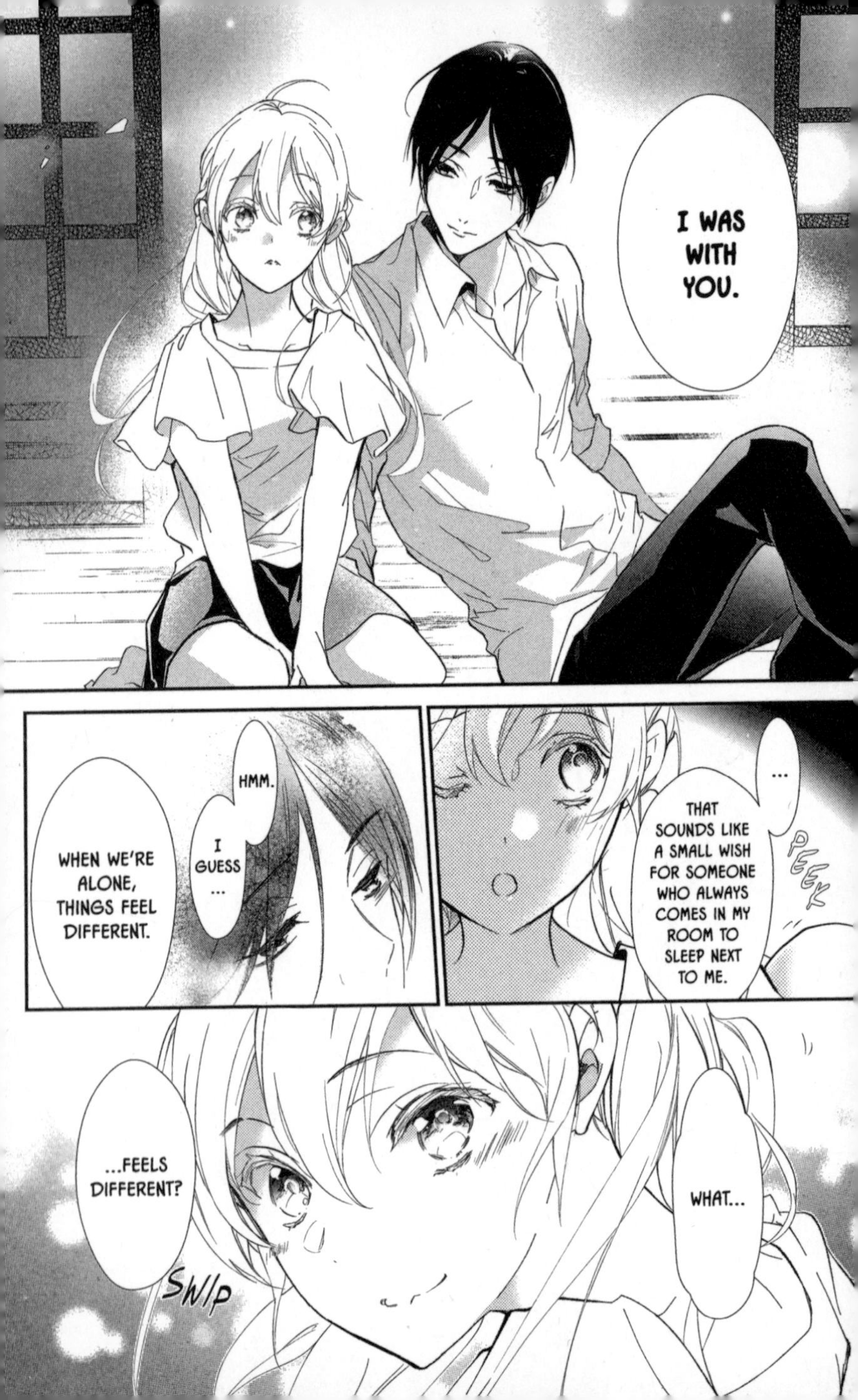
I WAS WITH YOU.
...
THAT SOUNDS LIKE A SMALL WISH FOR SOMEONE WHO ALWAYS COMES IN MY ROOM TO SLEEP NEXT TO ME.
PEEK
HMM.
I GUESS ...
WHEN WE'RE ALONE, THINGS FEEL DIFFERENT.
WHAT...
...FEELS DIFFERENT?
SWIP

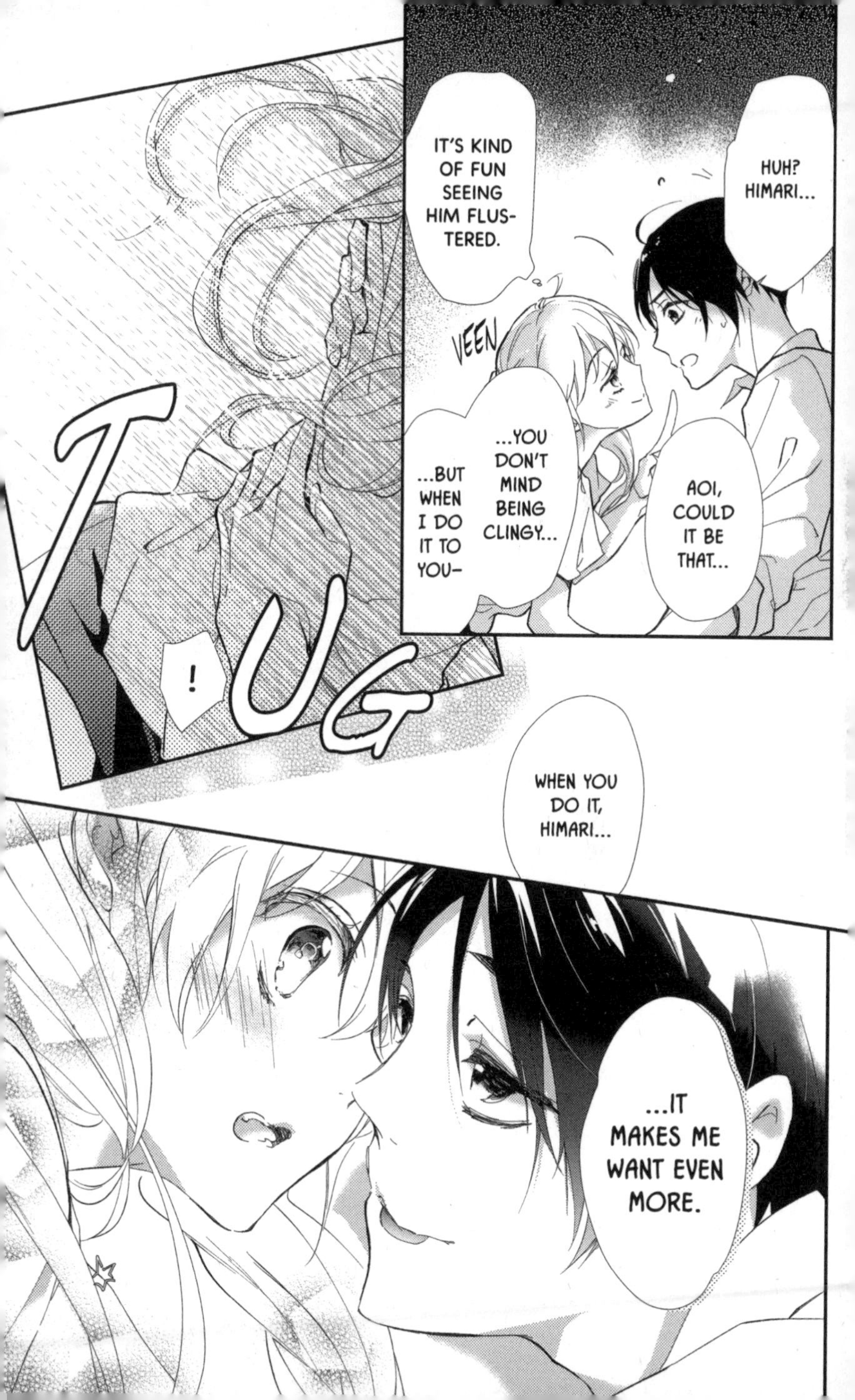
HUH? HIMARI...
IT'S KIND OF FUN SEEING HIM FLUS-TERED.
VEEN
AOI, COULD IT BE THAT...
...YOU DON'T MIND BEING CLINGY...
...BUT WHEN I DO IT TO YOU–
TUG
!
WHEN YOU DO IT, HIMARI...
...IT MAKES ME WANT EVEN MORE.

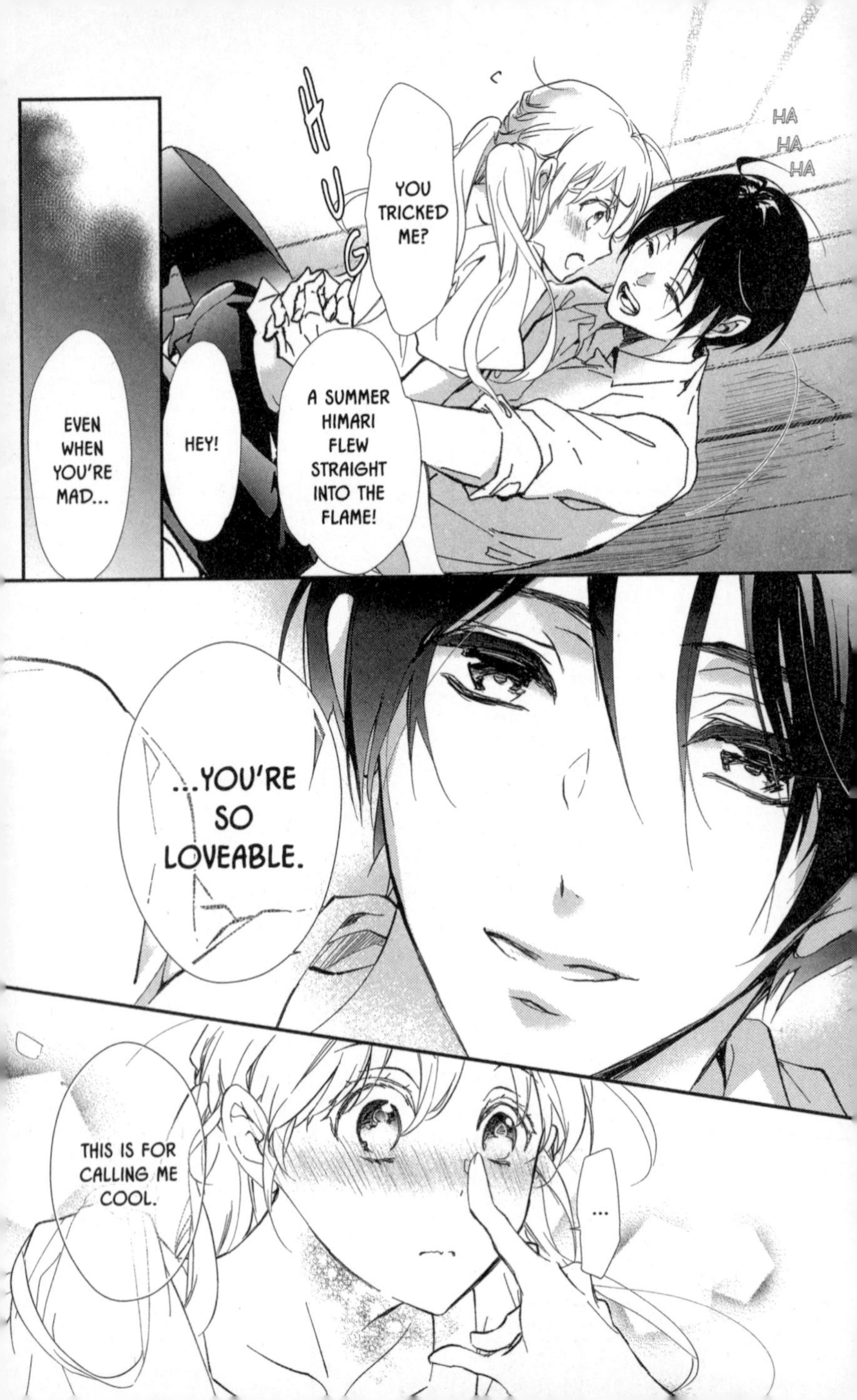
HA HA HA
HUG
YOU TRICKED ME?
A SUMMER HIMARI FLEW STRAIGHT INTO THE FLAME!
HEY!
EVEN WHEN YOU'RE MAD...
...YOU'RE SO LOVEABLE.
...
THIS IS FOR CALLING ME COOL.

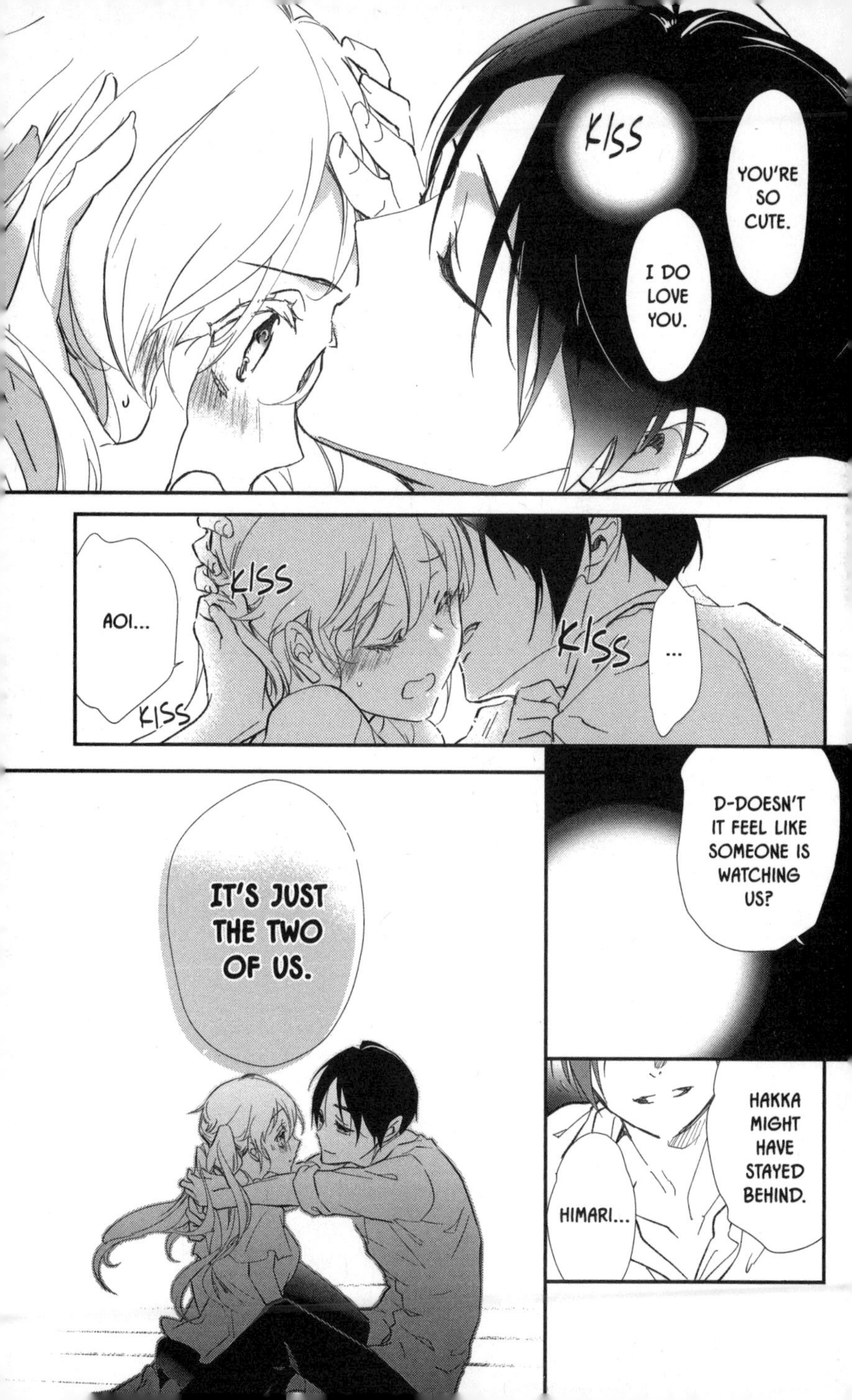
KISS
YOU'RE SO CUTE.
I DO LOVE YOU.
...
KISS
KISS
AOI...
KISS
D-DOESN'T IT FEEL LIKE SOMEONE IS WATCHING US?
HAKKA MIGHT HAVE STAYED BEHIND.
HIMARI...
IT'S JUST THE TWO OF US.

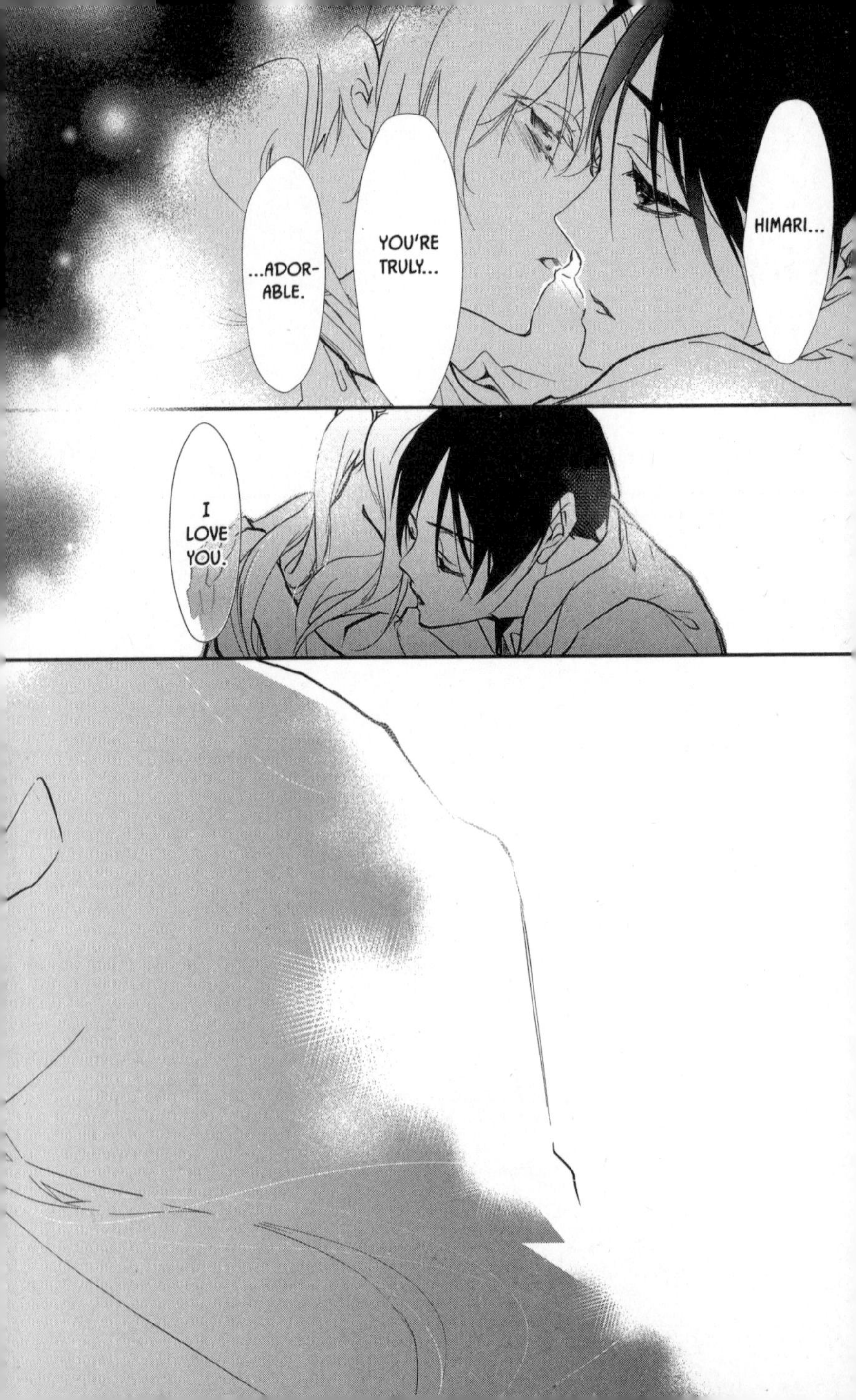
HIMARI...
YOU'RE TRULY...
...ADORABLE.
I LOVE YOU.

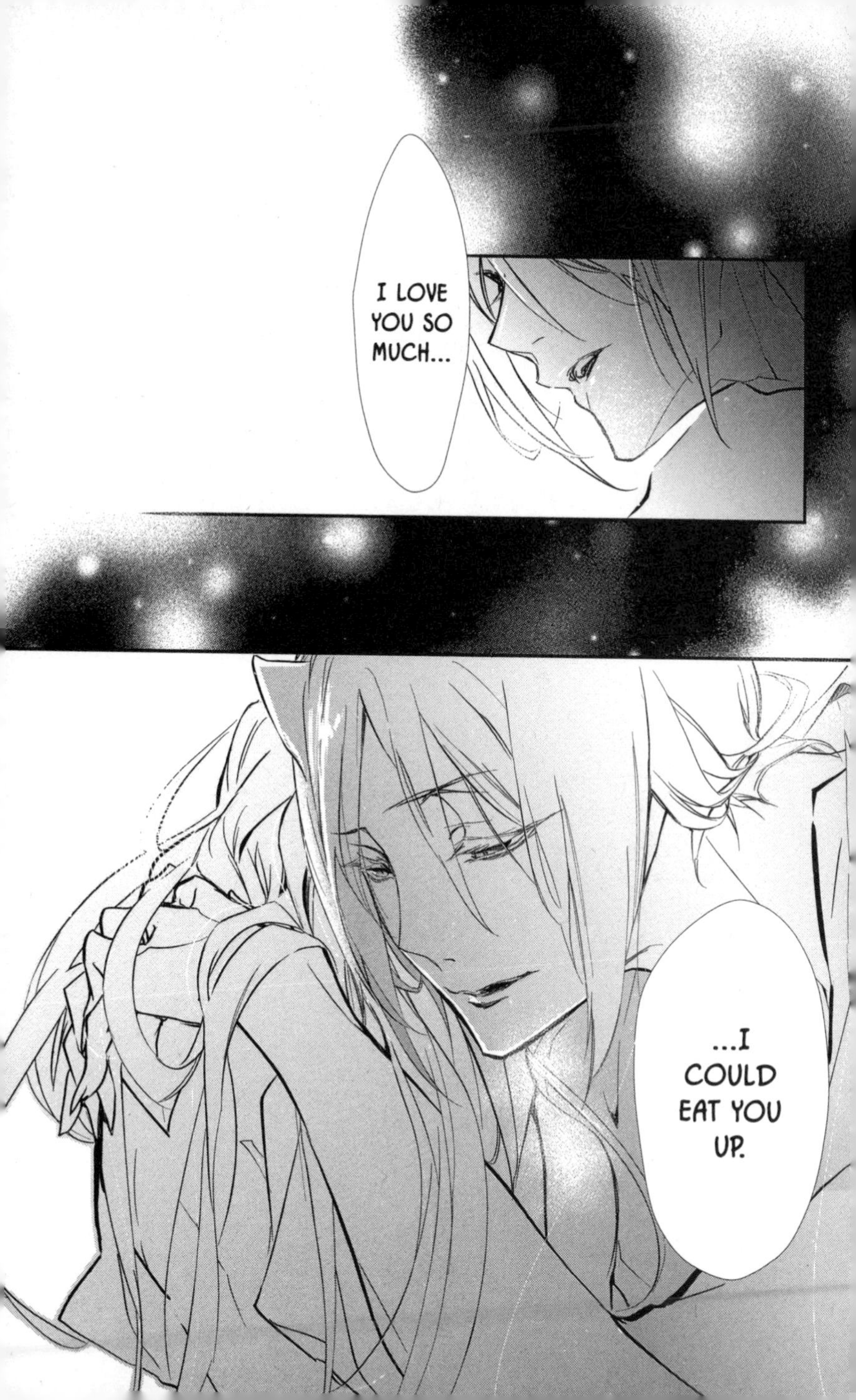
I LOVE YOU SO MUCH...
...I COULD EAT YOU UP.

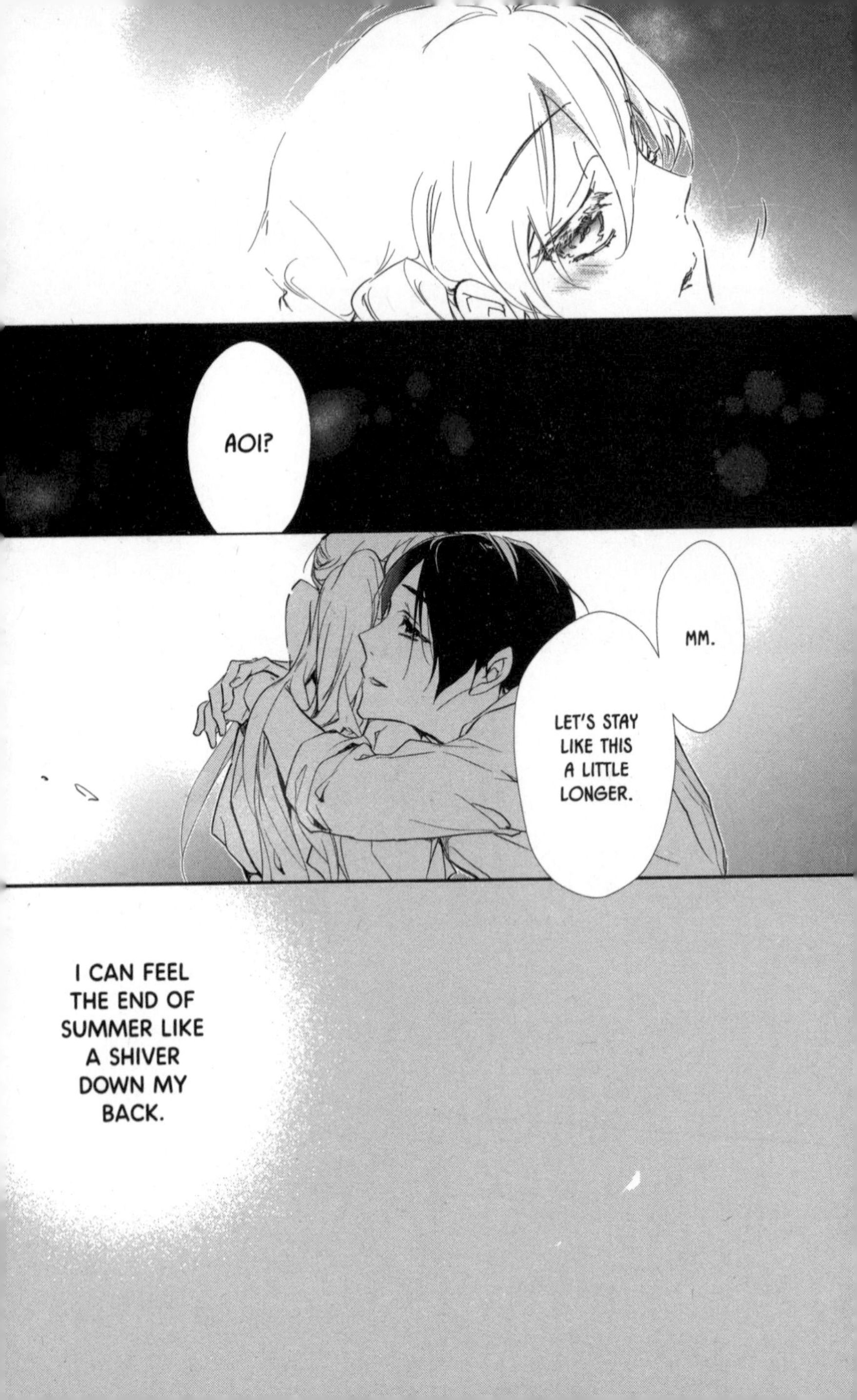
AOI?
MM.
LET'S STAY LIKE THIS A LITTLE LONGER.
I CAN FEEL THE END OF SUMMER LIKE A SHIVER DOWN MY BACK.

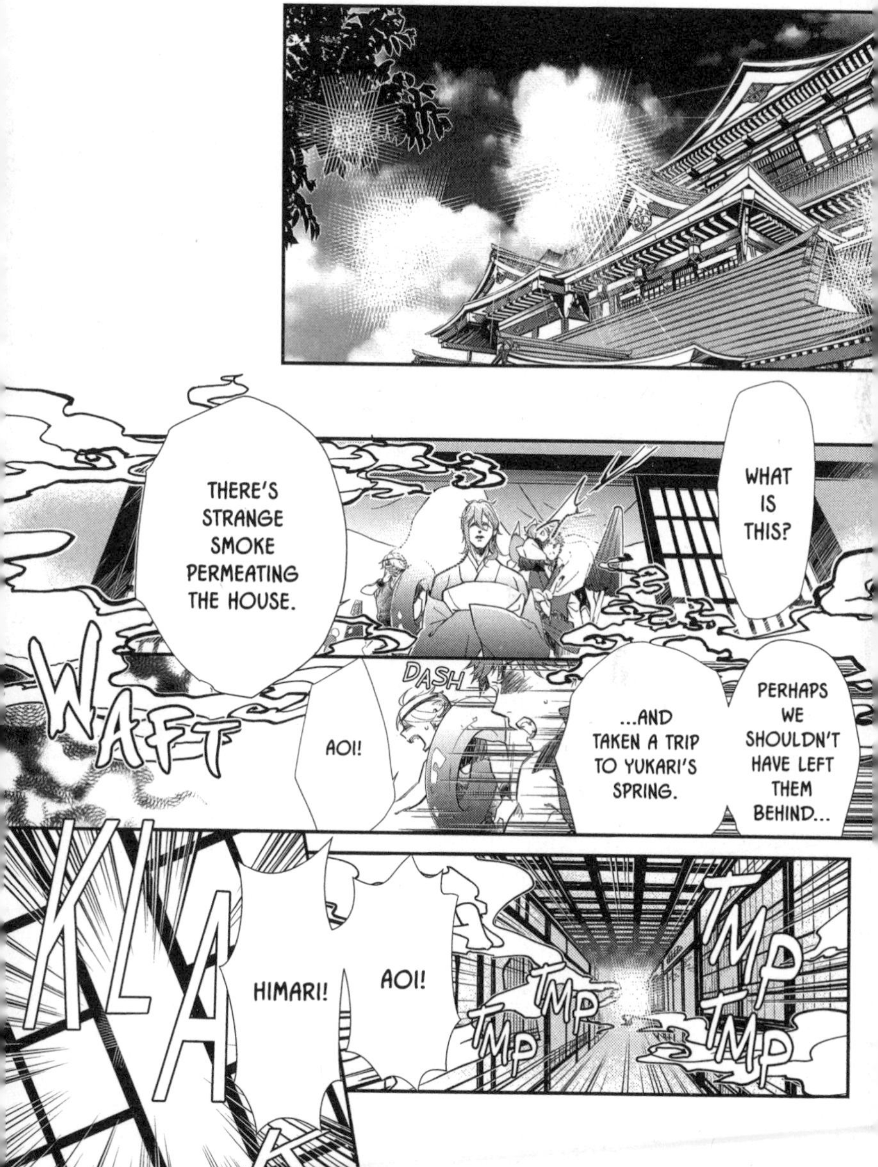
WHAT IS THIS?
THERE'S STRANGE SMOKE PERMEATING THE HOUSE.
WAFT
PERHAPS WE SHOULDN'T HAVE LEFT THEM BEHIND...
...AND TAKEN A TRIP TO YUKARI'S SPRING.
DASH
AOI!
TMP TMP
TMP TMP
AOI!
HIMARI!
KLAAK

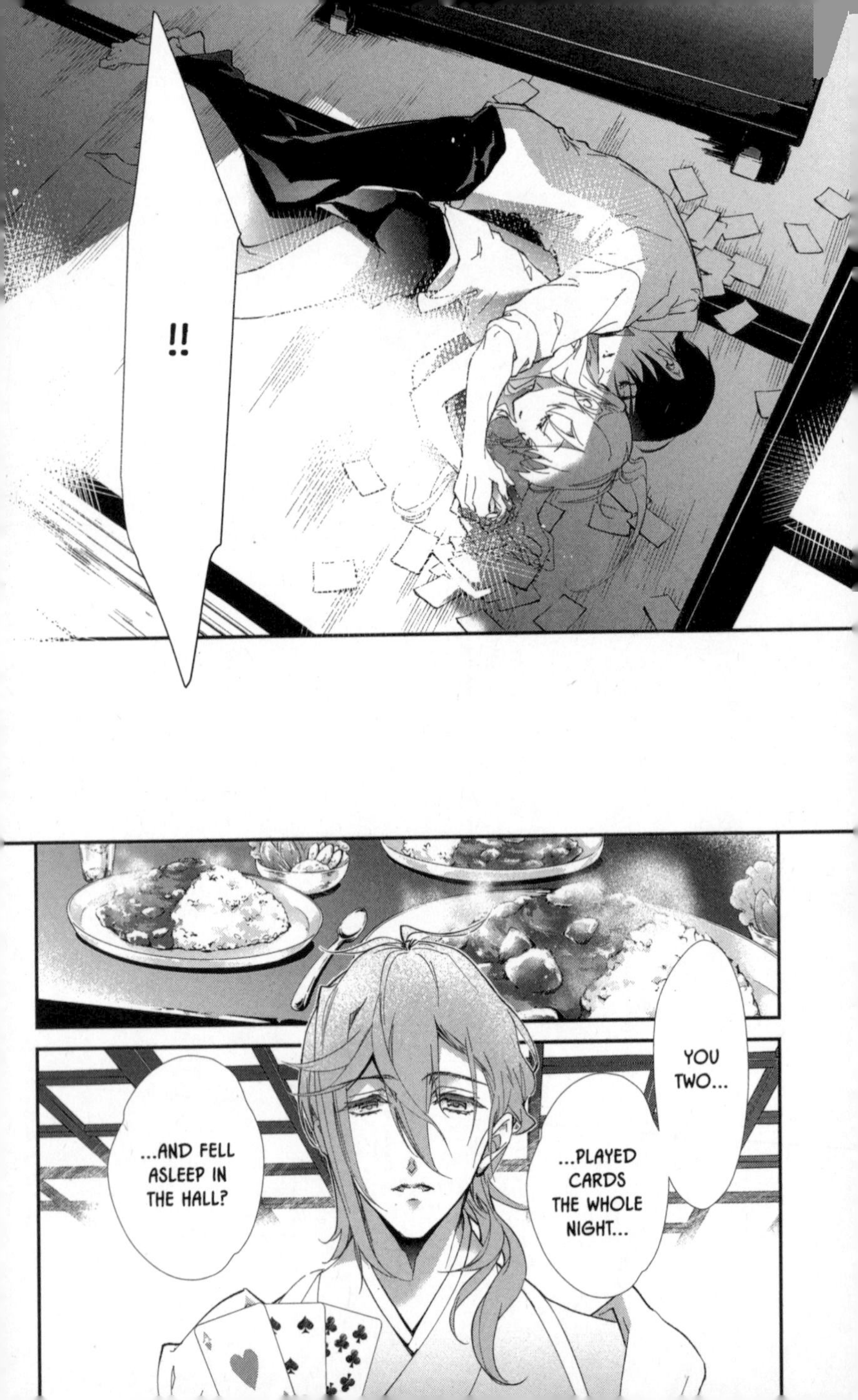
!!
YOU TWO...
...PLAYED CARDS THE WHOLE NIGHT...
...AND FELL ASLEEP IN THE HALL?

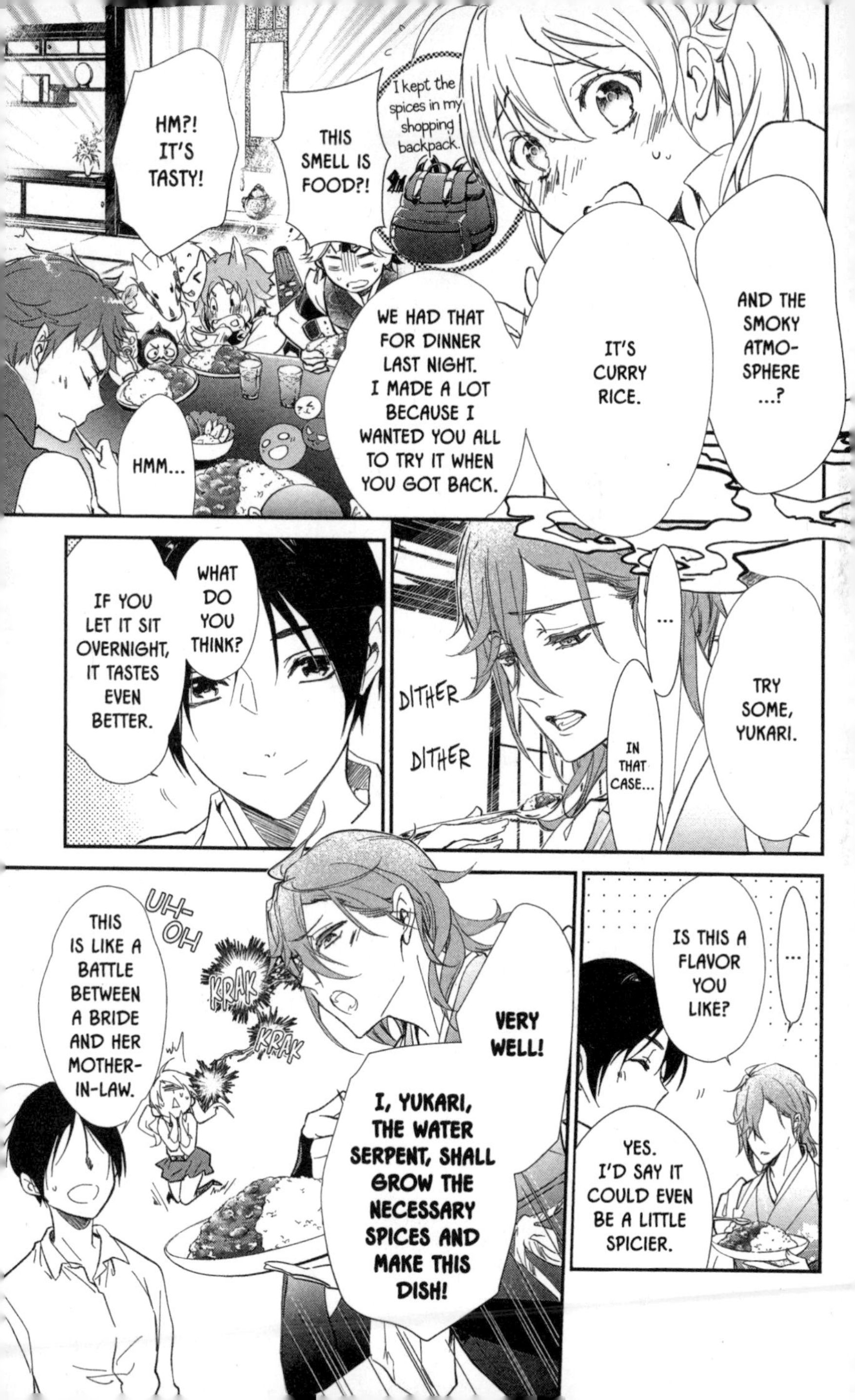
AND THE SMOKY ATMOSPHERE ...?
IT'S CURRY RICE.
I kept the spices in my shopping backpack.
WE HAD THAT FOR DINNER LAST NIGHT. I MADE A LOT BECAUSE I WANTED YOU ALL TO TRY IT WHEN YOU GOT BACK.
THIS SMELL IS FOOD?!
HM?! IT'S TASTY!
HMM...
...
TRY SOME, YUKARI.
IN THAT CASE...
DITHER
DITHER
WHAT DO YOU THINK?
IF YOU LET IT SIT OVERNIGHT, IT TASTES EVEN BETTER.
...
IS THIS A FLAVOR YOU LIKE?
YES. I'D SAY IT COULD EVEN BE A LITTLE SPICIER.
VERY WELL!
I, YUKARI, THE WATER SERPENT, SHALL GROW THE NECESSARY SPICES AND MAKE THIS DISH!
KRAK
KRAK
UH-OH
THIS IS LIKE A BATTLE BETWEEN A BRIDE AND HER MOTHER-IN-LAW.

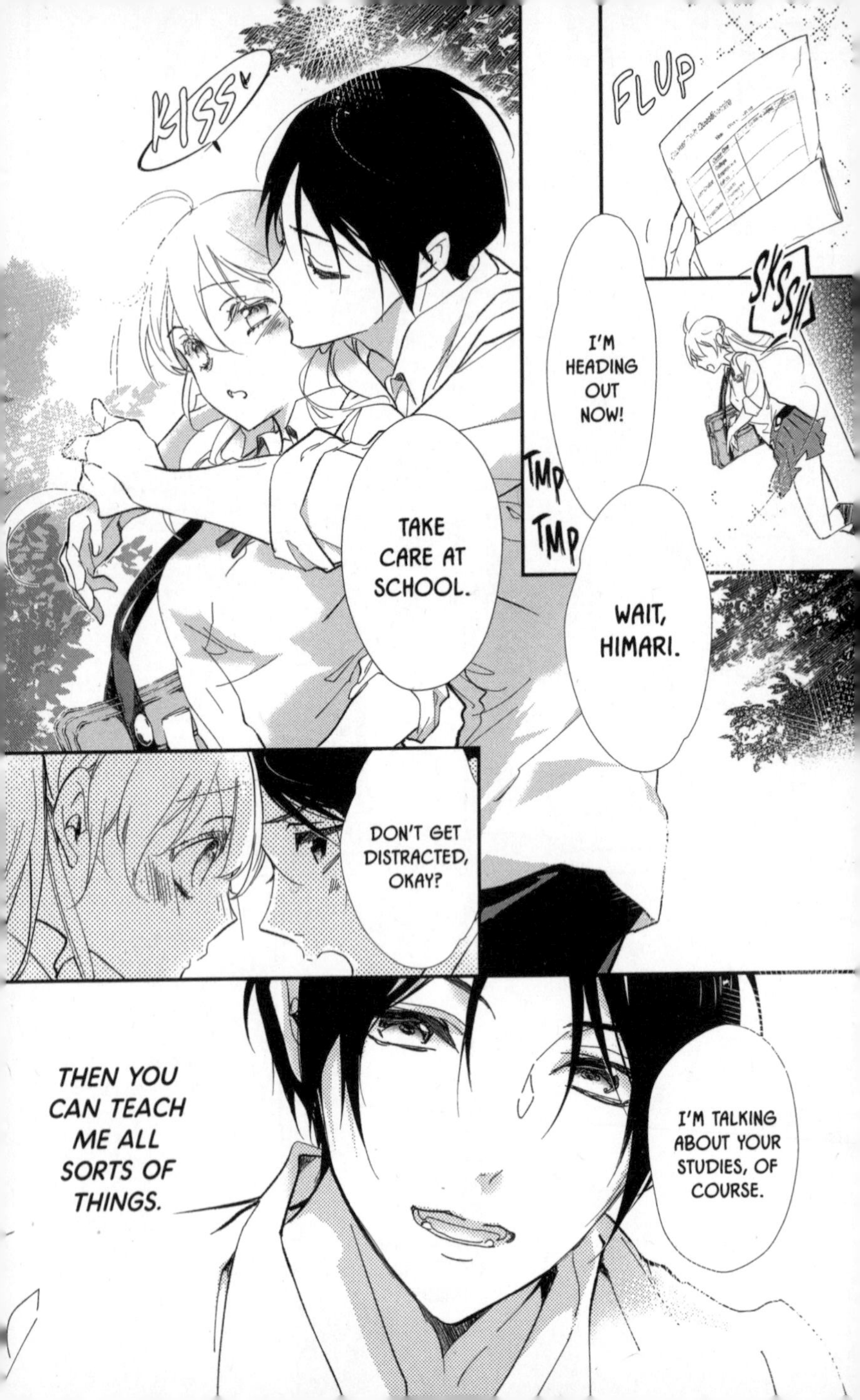
FLUP
SKSSH
I'M HEADING OUT NOW!
TMP TMP
WAIT, HIMARI.
KISS
TAKE CARE AT SCHOOL.
DON'T GET DISTRACTED, OKAY?
I'M TALKING ABOUT YOUR STUDIES, OF COURSE.
THEN YOU CAN TEACH ME ALL SORTS OF THINGS.

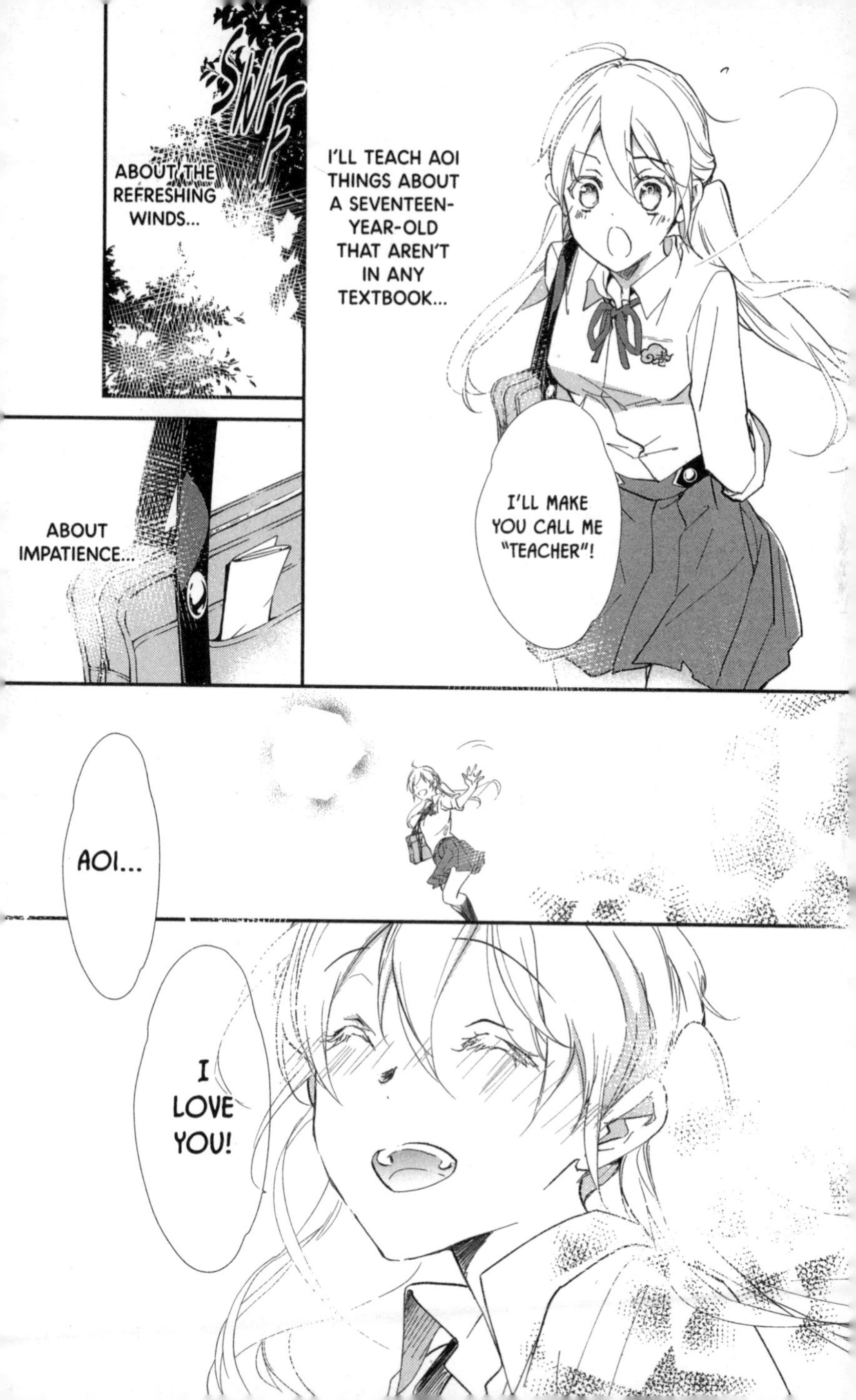
I'LL TEACH AOI THINGS ABOUT A SEVENTEEN-YEAR-OLD THAT AREN'T IN ANY TEXTBOOK...
I'LL MAKE YOU CALL ME "TEACHER"!
SWFF
ABOUT THE REFRESHING WINDS...
ABOUT IMPATIENCE...
AOI...
I LOVE YOU!

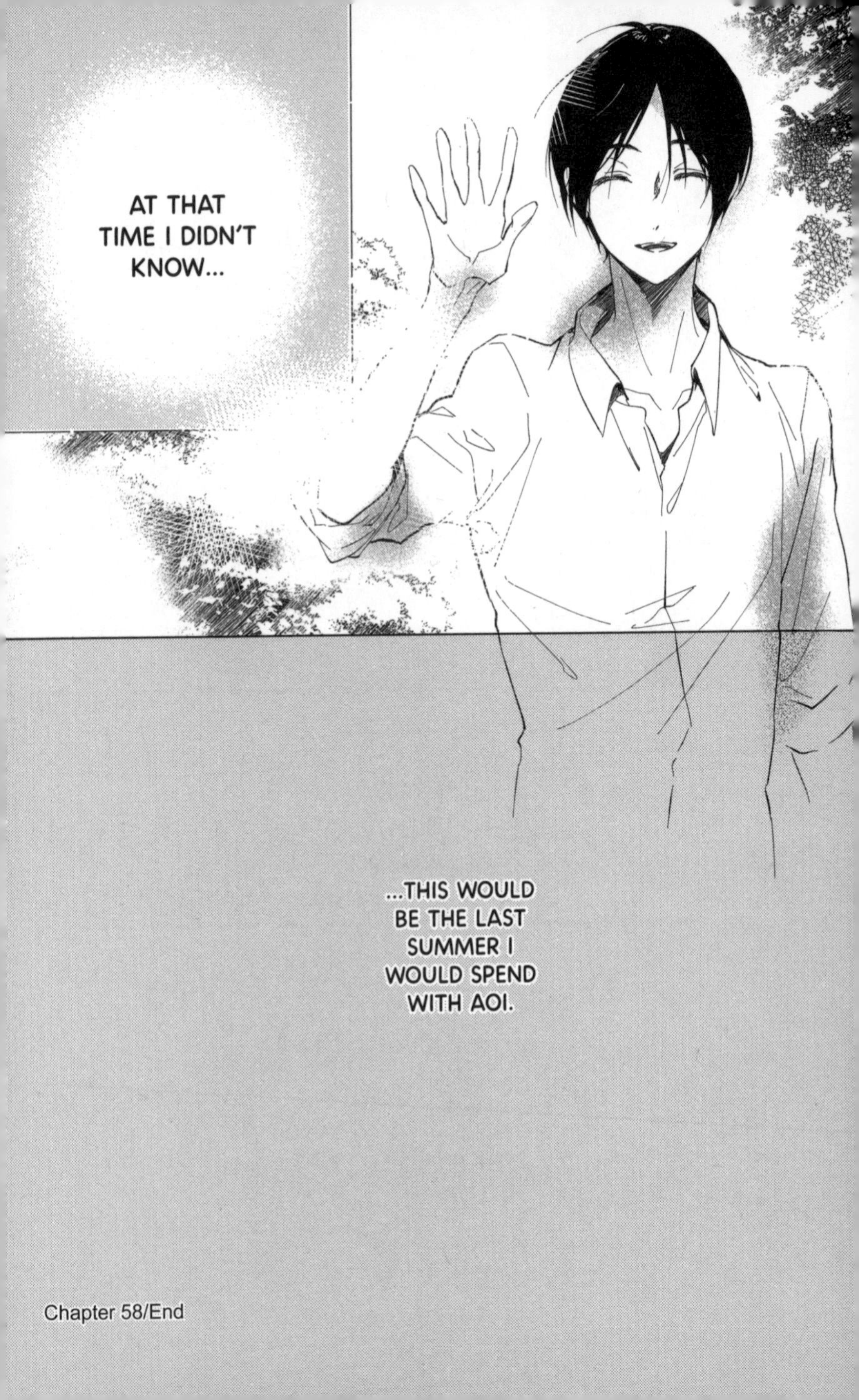
AT THAT TIME I DIDN'T KNOW...
...THIS WOULD BE THE LAST SUMMER I WOULD SPEND WITH AOI.
Chapter 58/End

the
DEMON
PRINCE
of MOMOCHI
HOUSE

The
DEMON
PRINCE
of MOMOCHI
HOUSE

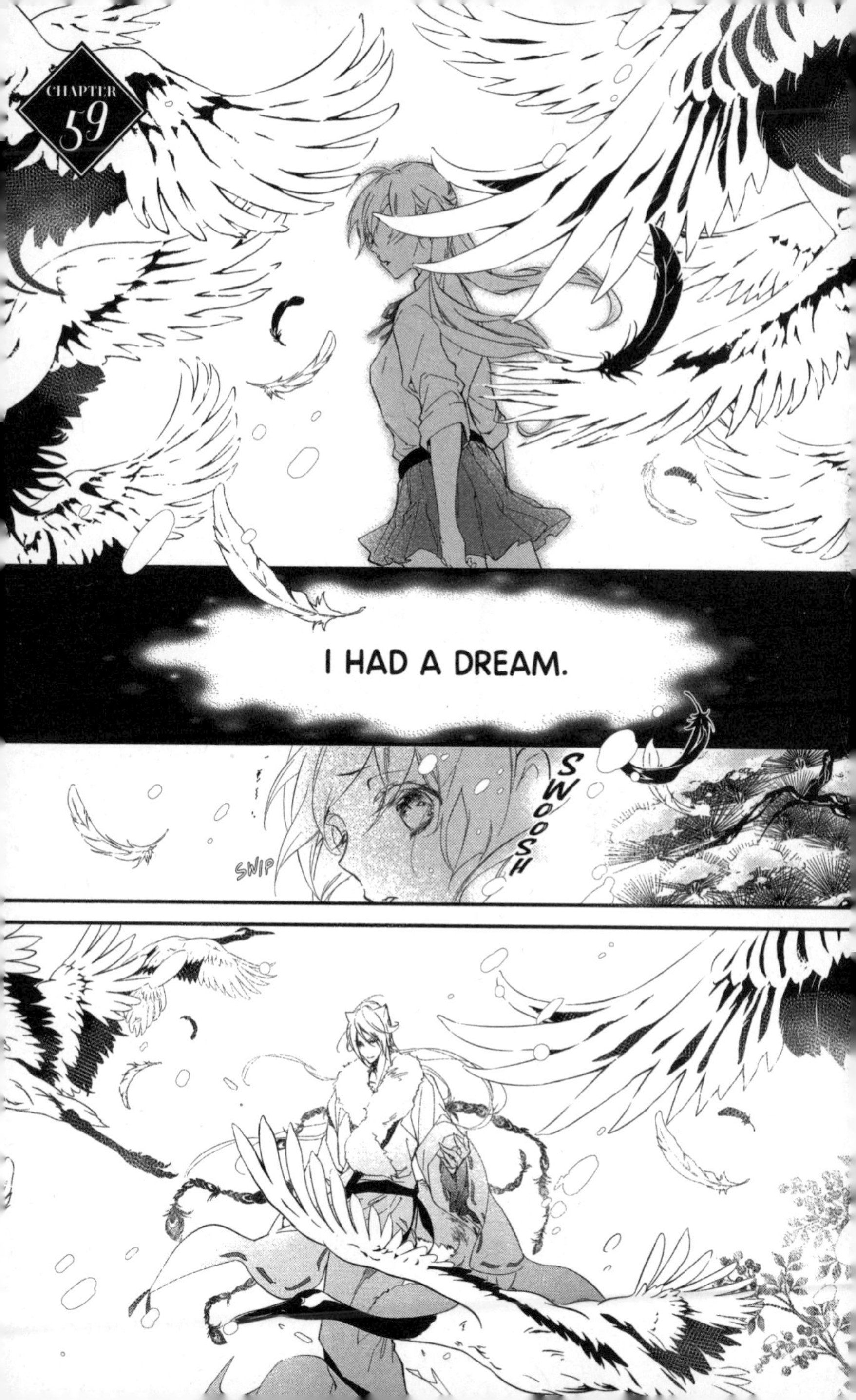
CHAPTER 59
I HAD A DREAM.
SWOOSH
...
SWIP

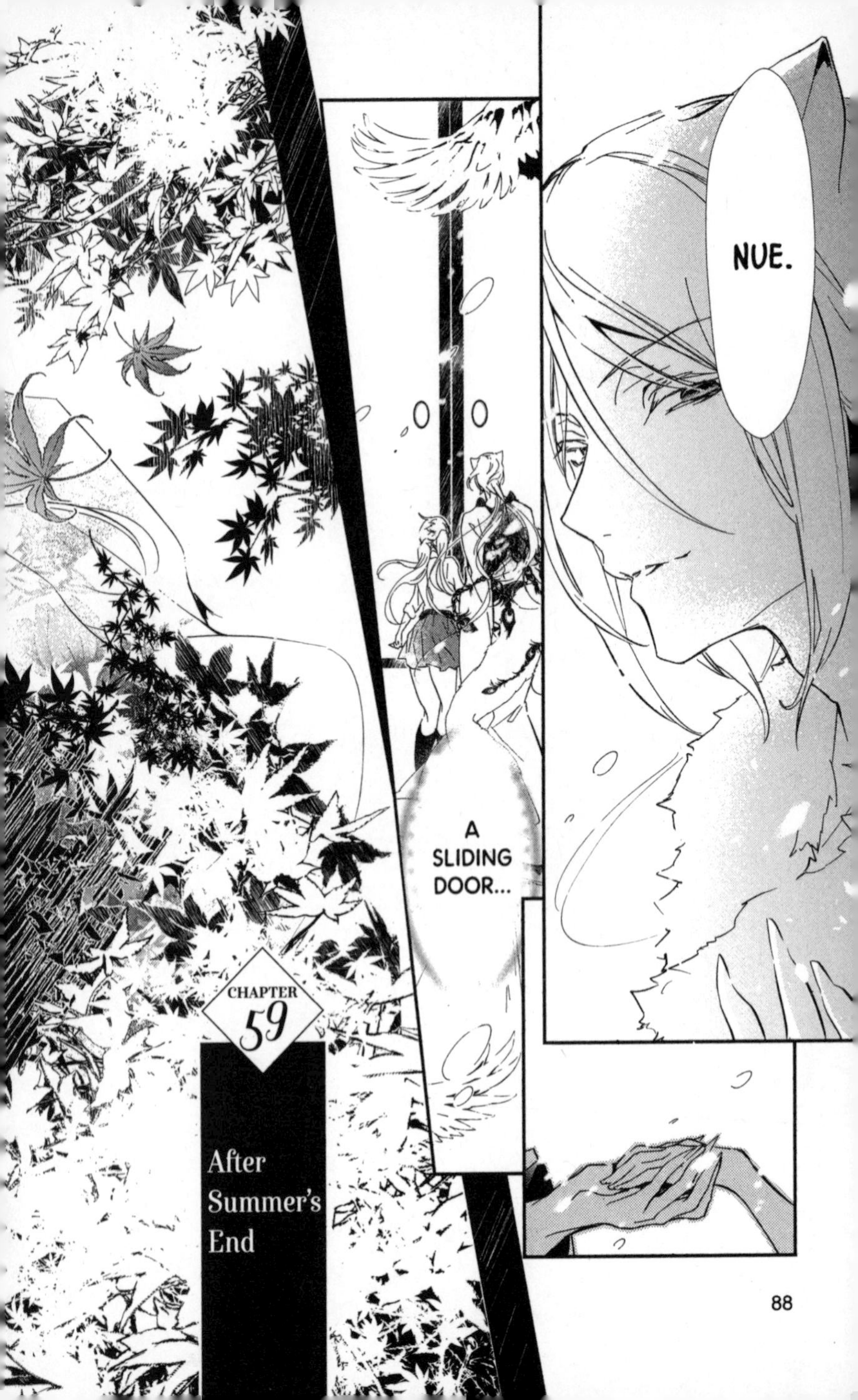
NUE.
A SLIDING DOOR...
CHAPTER 59
After Summer's End

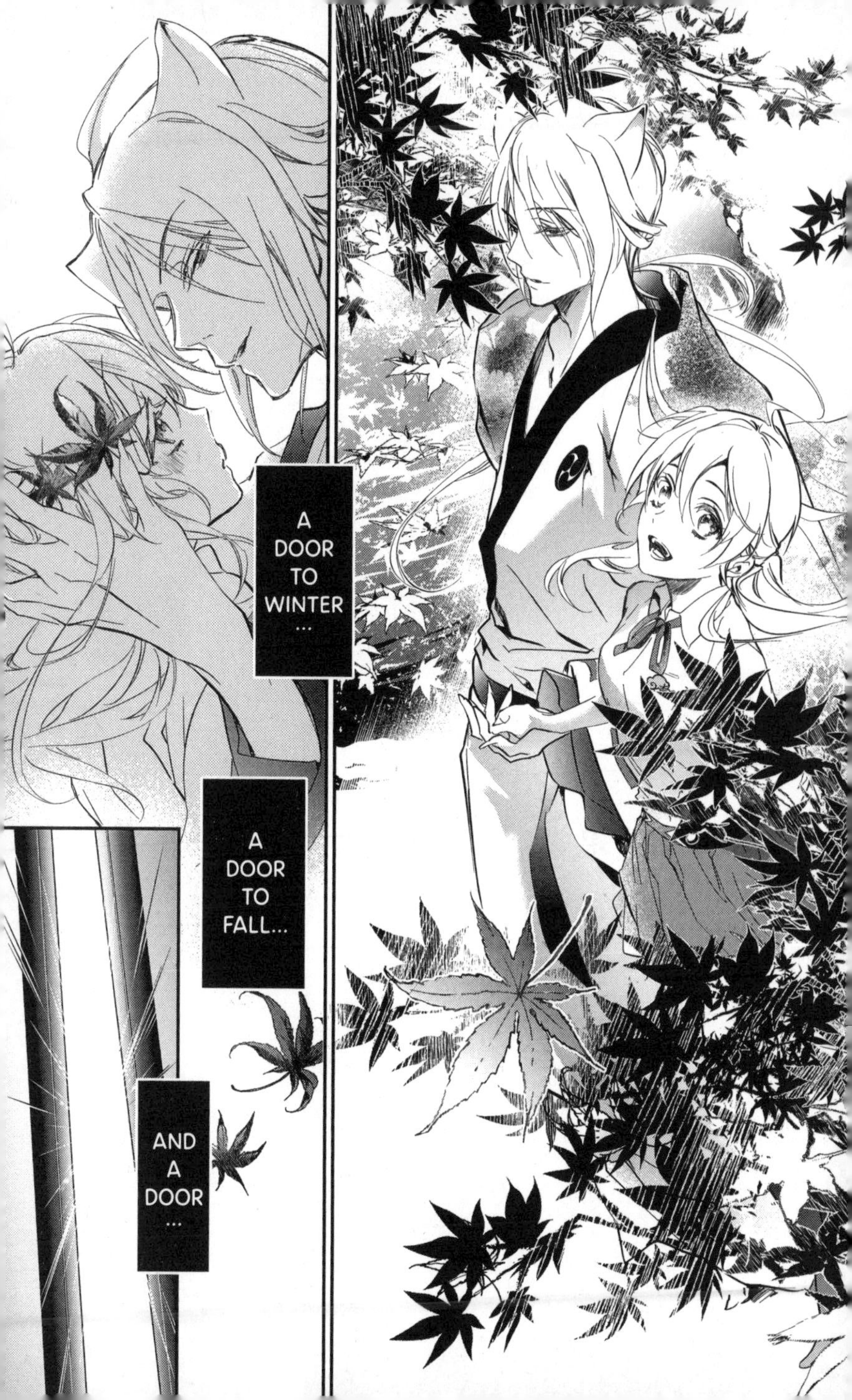
A DOOR TO WINTER...
A DOOR TO FALL...
AND A DOOR...

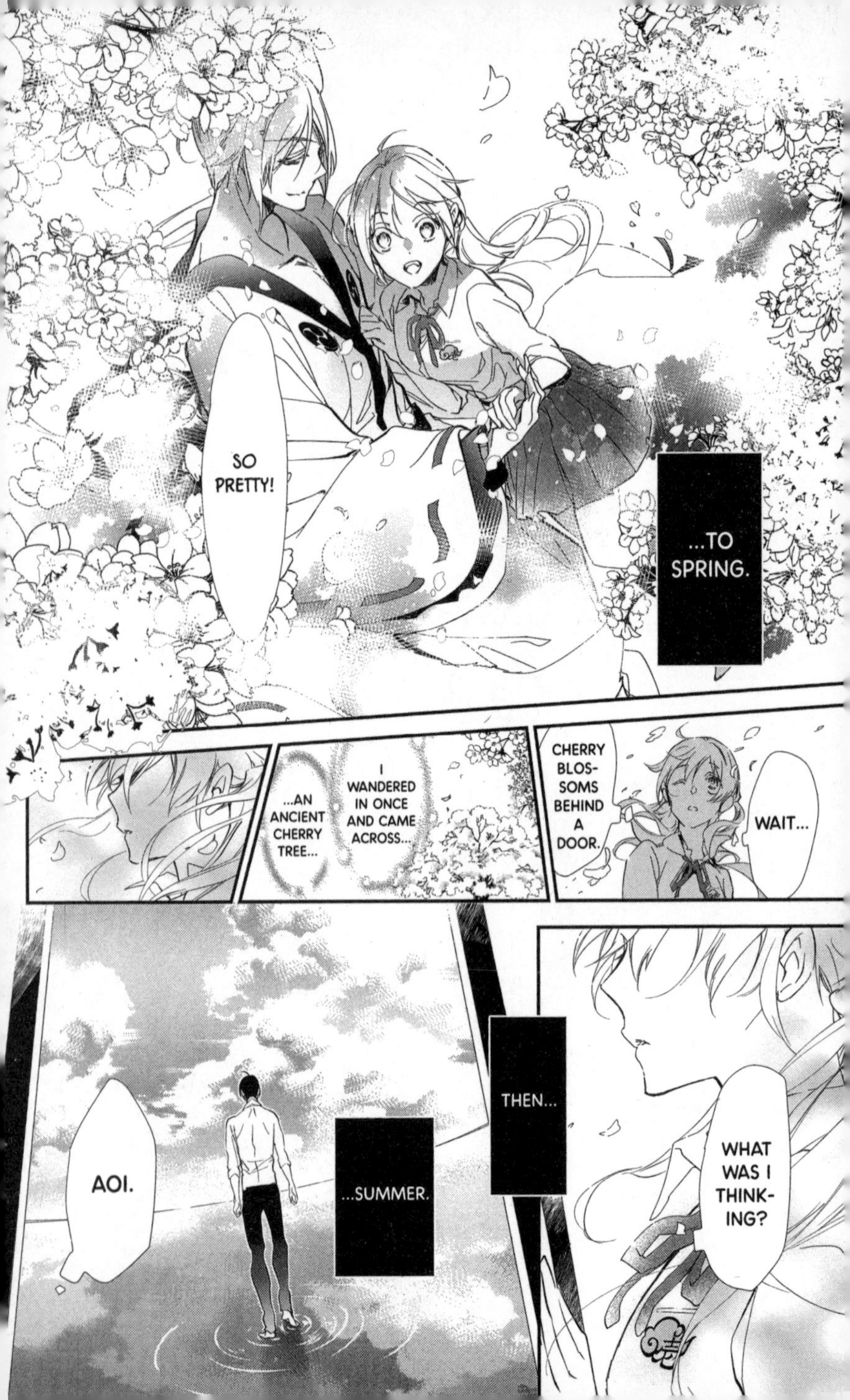

...TO SPRING.
SO PRETTY!
WAIT...
CHERRY BLOS-SOMS BEHIND A DOOR.
I WANDERED IN ONCE AND CAME ACROSS...
...AN ANCIENT CHERRY TREE...
WHAT WAS I THINK-ING?
THEN...
...SUMMER.
AOI.

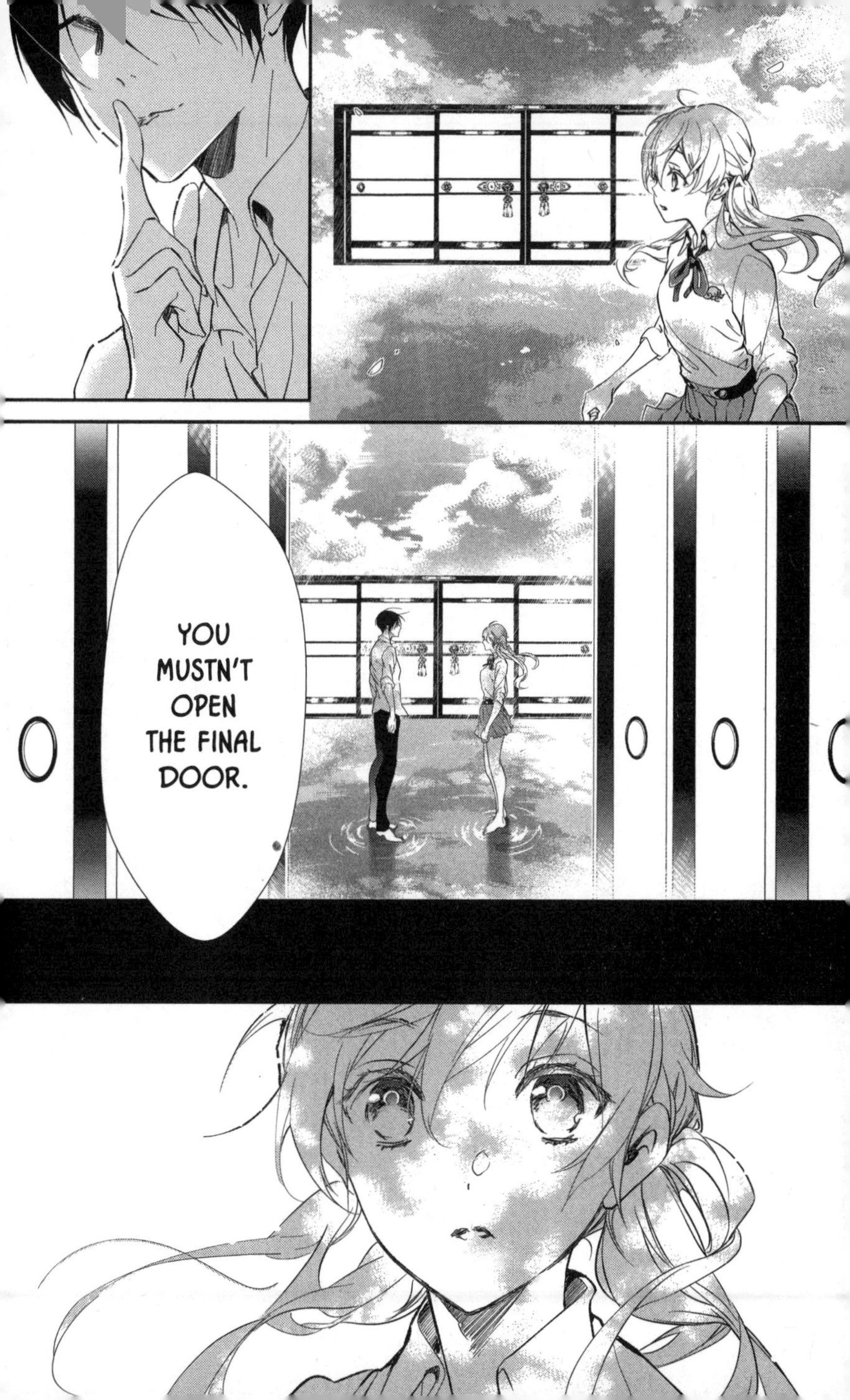
YOU MUSTN'T OPEN THE FINAL DOOR.

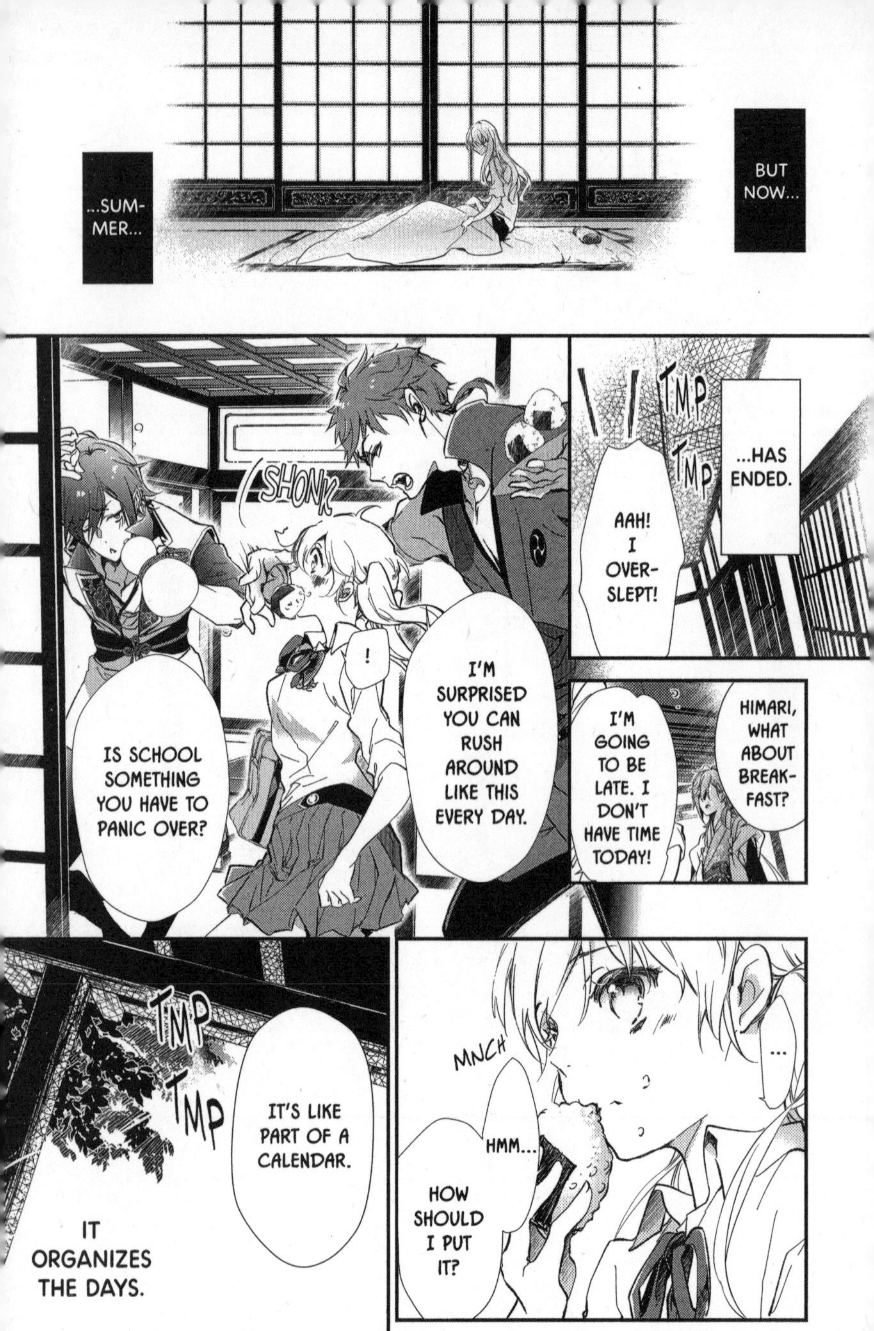
BUT NOW...
...SUM-MER...
TMP TMP
...HAS ENDED.
AAH! I OVER-SLEPT!
HIMARI, WHAT ABOUT BREAK-FAST?
I'M GOING TO BE LATE. I DON'T HAVE TIME TODAY!
SHONK
!
I'M SURPRISED YOU CAN RUSH AROUND LIKE THIS EVERY DAY.
IS SCHOOL SOMETHING YOU HAVE TO PANIC OVER?
...
MNCH
HMM...
HOW SHOULD I PUT IT?
TMP
TMP
IT'S LIKE PART OF A CALENDAR.
IT ORGANIZES THE DAYS.

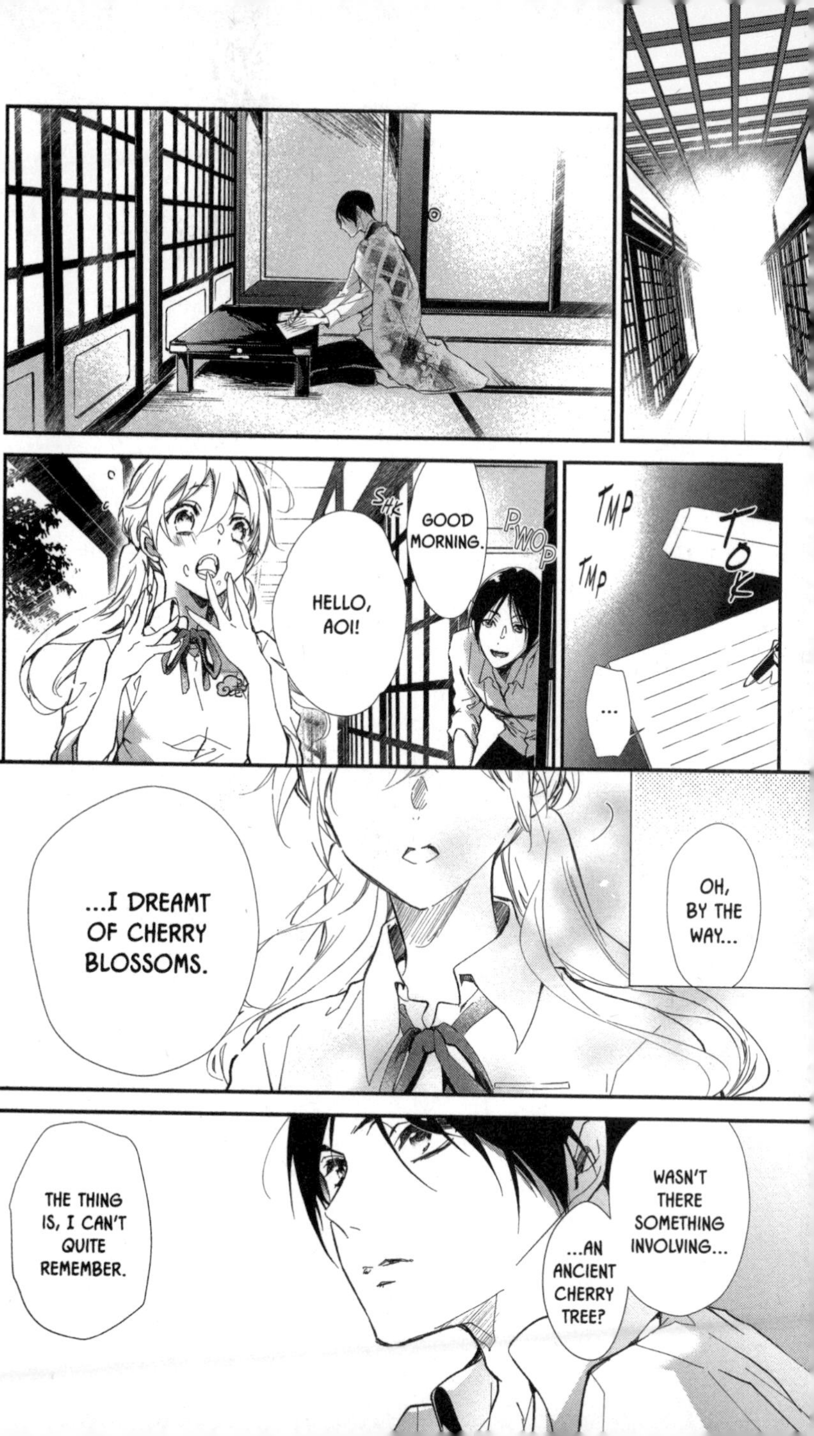
TMP
TOK
TMP
...
PWOP
GOOD MORNING.
SHK
HELLO, AOI!
OH, BY THE WAY...
...I DREAMT OF CHERRY BLOSSOMS.
WASN'T THERE SOMETHING INVOLVING...
...AN ANCIENT CHERRY TREE?
THE THING IS, I CAN'T QUITE REMEMBER.

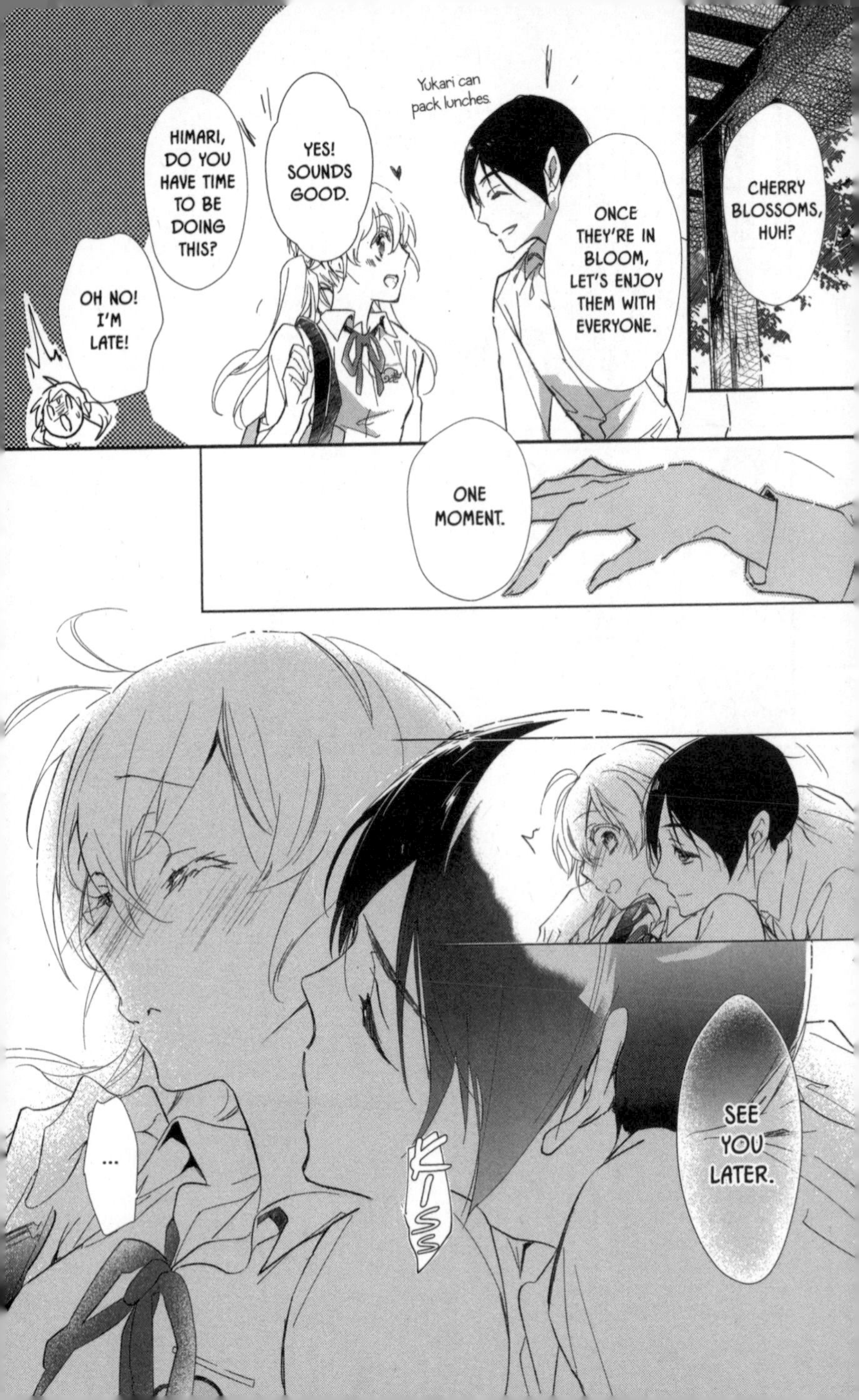
CHERRY BLOSSOMS, HUH?
ONCE THEY'RE IN BLOOM, LET'S ENJOY THEM WITH EVERYONE.
Yukari can pack lunches.
YES! SOUNDS GOOD.
HIMARI, DO YOU HAVE TIME TO BE DOING THIS?
OH NO! I'M LATE!
ONE MOMENT.
SEE YOU LATER.
KISS
...

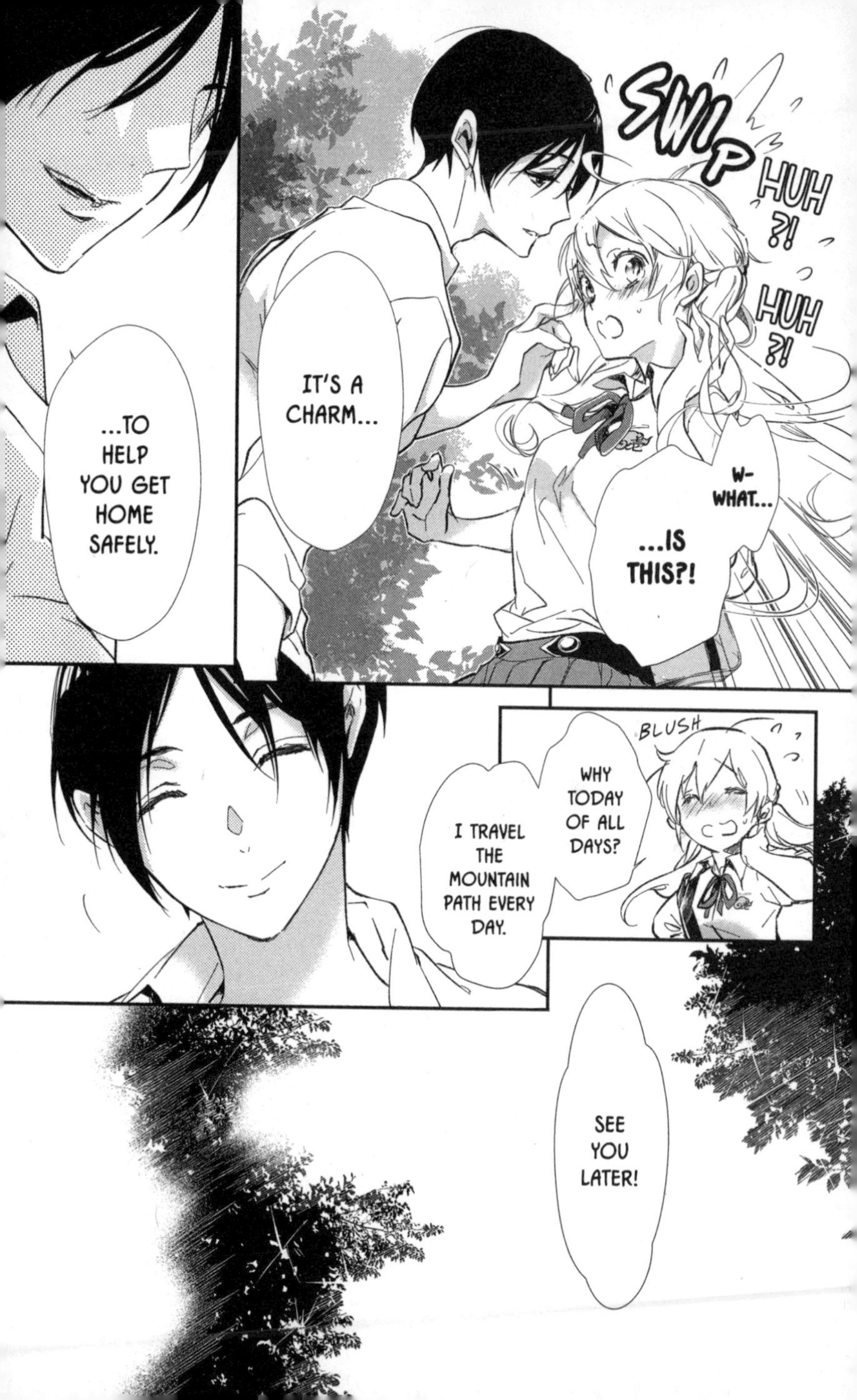
SWIP
HUH?!
HUH?!
W-WHAT...
...IS THIS?!
IT'S A CHARM...
...TO HELP YOU GET HOME SAFELY.
BLUSH
WHY TODAY OF ALL DAYS?
I TRAVEL THE MOUNTAIN PATH EVERY DAY.
SEE YOU LATER!

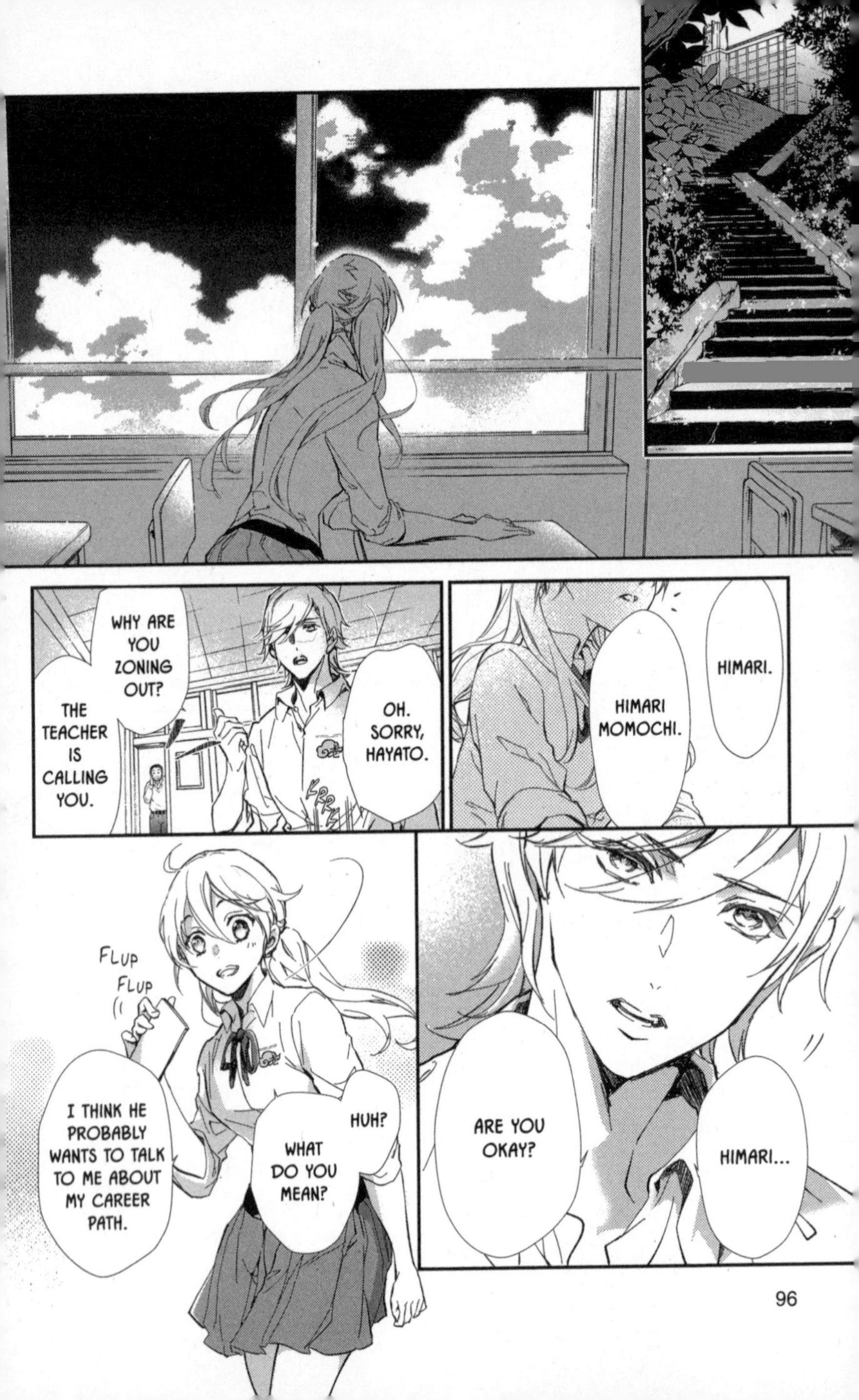
HIMARI.
HIMARI MOMOCHI.
WHY ARE YOU ZONING OUT?
THE TEACHER IS CALLING YOU.
OH. SORRY, HAYATO.
HIMARI...
ARE YOU OKAY?
HUH?
WHAT DO YOU MEAN?
I THINK HE PROBABLY WANTS TO TALK TO ME ABOUT MY CAREER PATH.
FLUP FLUP

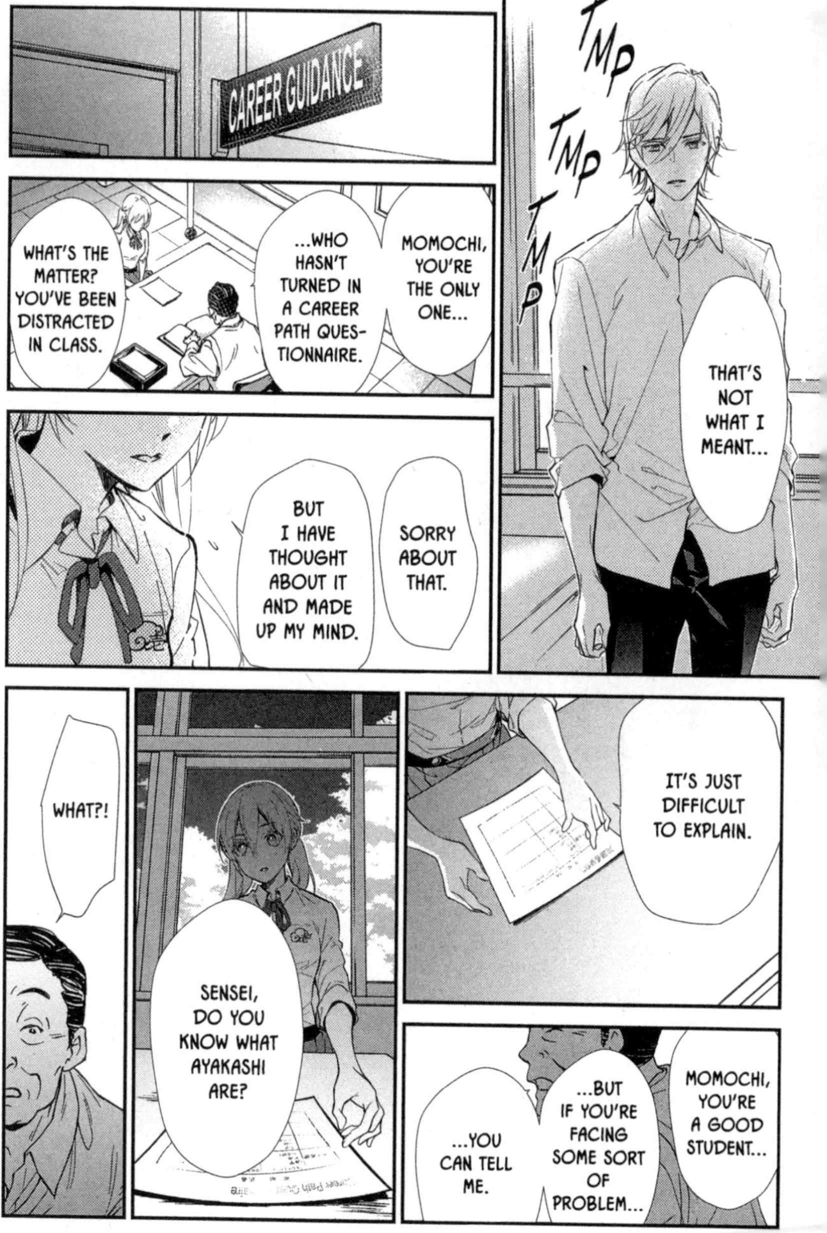
TMP
TMP
TMP
THAT'S JUST NOT WHAT I MEANT...
CAREER GUIDANCE
MOMOCHI, YOU'RE THE ONLY ONE...
...WHO HASN'T TURNED IN A CAREER PATH QUESTIONNAIRE.
WHAT'S THE MATTER? YOU'VE BEEN DISTRACTED IN CLASS.
SORRY ABOUT THAT.
BUT I HAVE THOUGHT ABOUT IT AND MADE UP MY MIND.
IT'S JUST DIFFICULT TO EXPLAIN.
MOMOCHI, YOU'RE A GOOD STUDENT...
...BUT IF YOU'RE FACING SOME SORT OF PROBLEM...
...YOU CAN TELL ME.
SENSEI, DO YOU KNOW WHAT AYAKASHI ARE?
WHAT?!

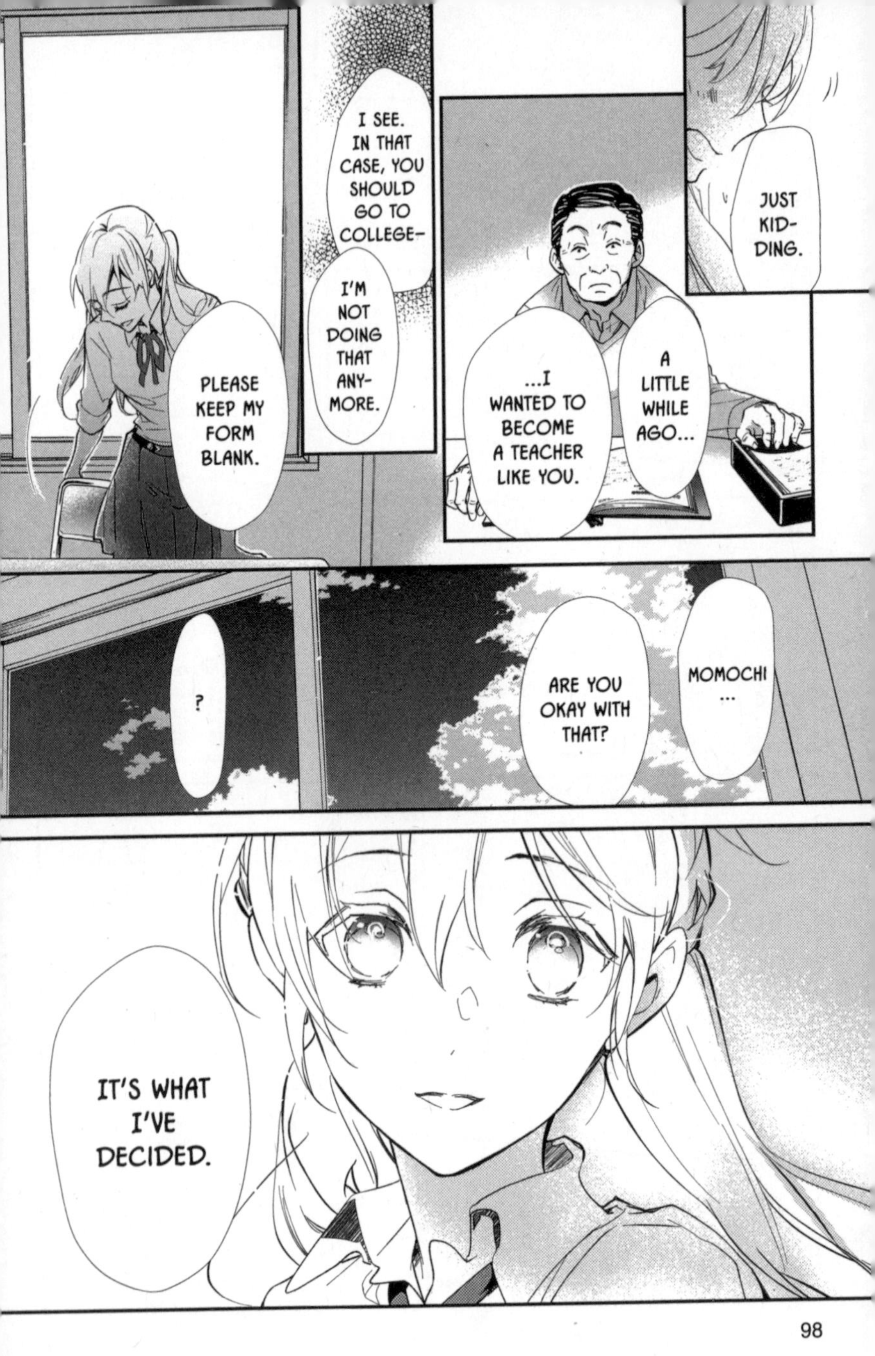
JUST KIDDING.
A LITTLE WHILE AGO...
...I WANTED TO BECOME A TEACHER LIKE YOU.
I SEE. IN THAT CASE, YOU SHOULD GO TO COLLEGE–
I'M NOT DOING THAT ANYMORE.
PLEASE KEEP MY FORM BLANK.
MOMOCHI...
ARE YOU OKAY WITH THAT?
?
IT'S WHAT I'VE DECIDED.

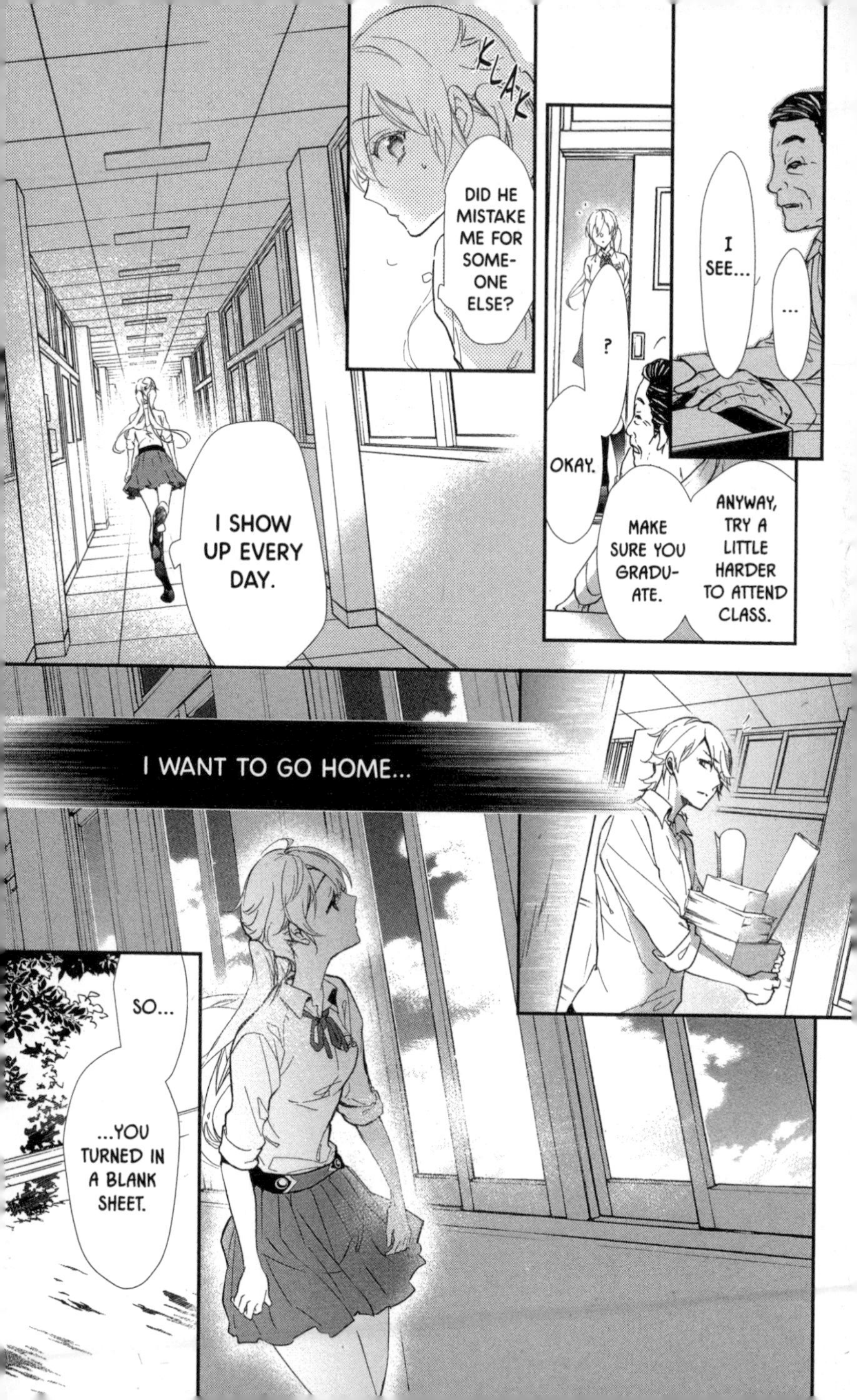
...
I SEE...
ANYWAY, TRY A LITTLE HARDER TO ATTEND CLASS.
MAKE SURE YOU GRADUATE.
?
OKAY.
KLAK
DID HE MISTAKE ME FOR SOMEONE ELSE?
I SHOW UP EVERY DAY.
I WANT TO GO HOME...
SO...
...YOU TURNED IN A BLANK SHEET.

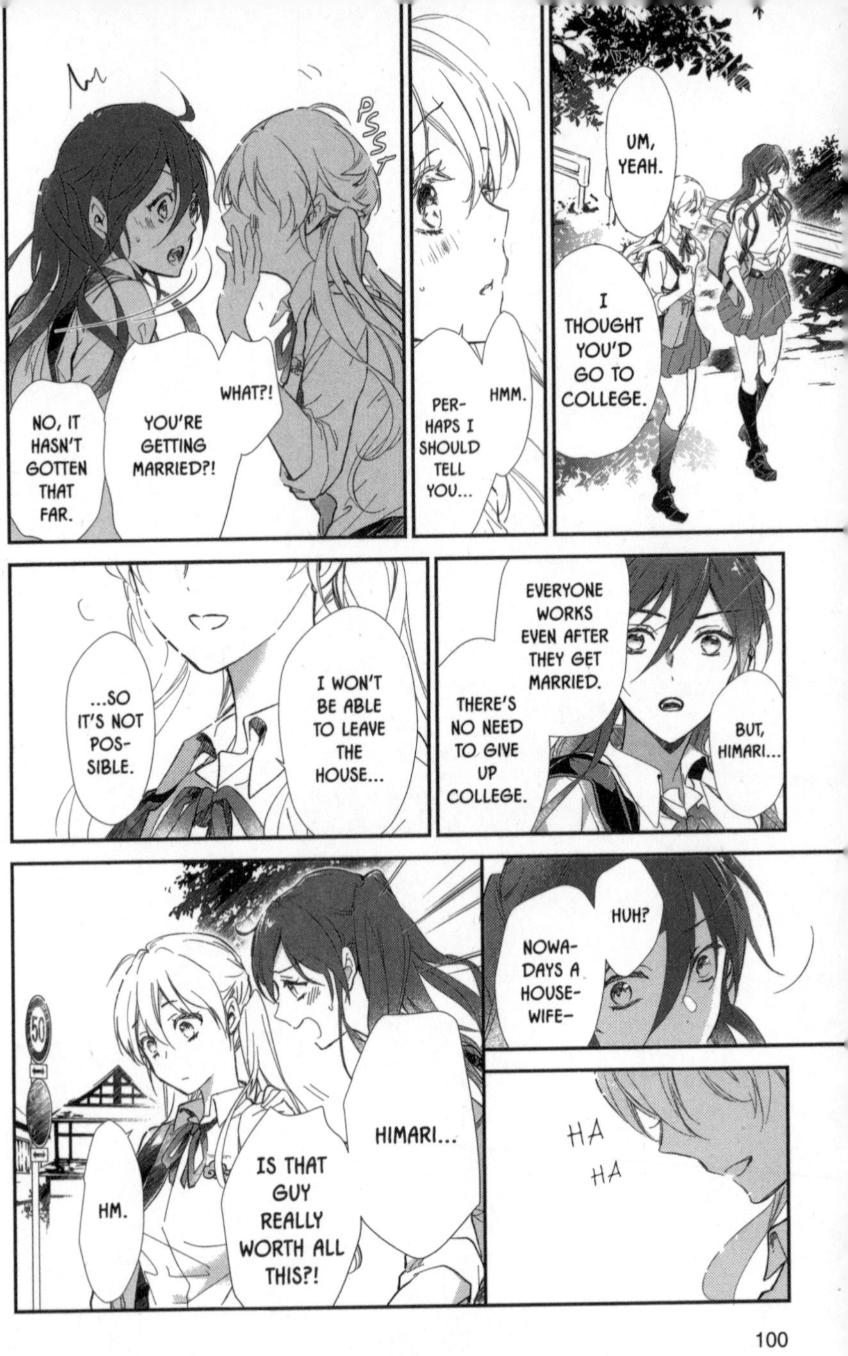
UM, YEAH.
I THOUGHT YOU'D GO TO COLLEGE.
HMM.
PER-HAPS I SHOULD TELL YOU...
PSST
WHAT?!
YOU'RE GETTING MARRIED?!
NO, IT HASN'T GOTTEN THAT FAR.
BUT, HIMARI...
EVERYONE WORKS EVEN AFTER THEY GET MARRIED.
THERE'S NO NEED TO GIVE UP COLLEGE.
I WON'T BE ABLE TO LEAVE THE HOUSE...
...SO IT'S NOT POS-SIBLE.
HUH?
NOWA-DAYS A HOUSE-WIFE-
HA HA
HIMARI...
IS THAT GUY REALLY WORTH ALL THIS?!
HM.

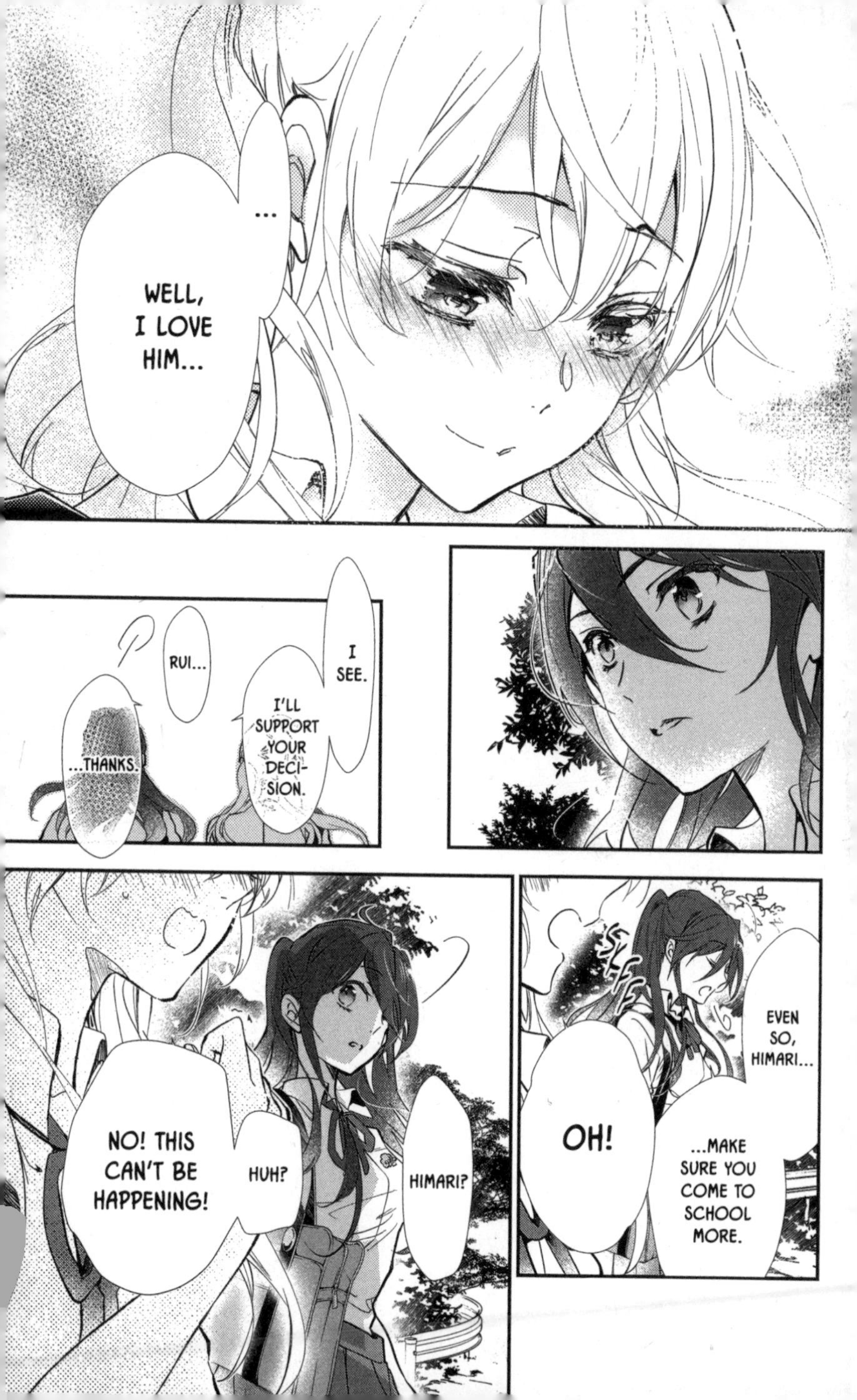
...
WELL, I LOVE HIM...
I SEE.
I'LL SUPPORT YOUR DECISION.
RUI...
...THANKS.
EVEN SO, HIMARI...
...MAKE SURE YOU COME TO SCHOOL MORE.
OH!
HIMARI?
HUH?
NO! THIS CAN'T BE HAPPENING!

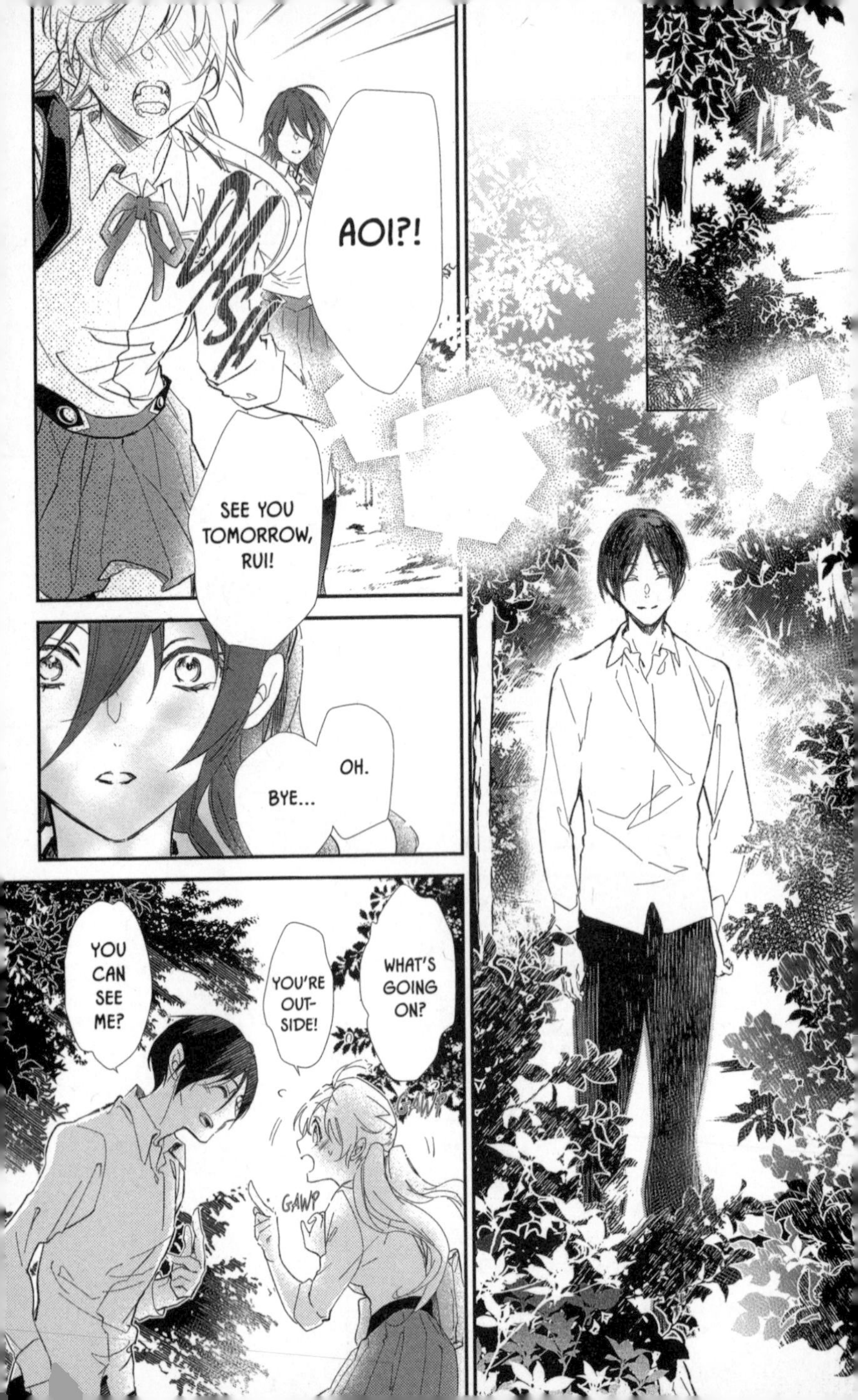
AOI?!
SEE YOU TOMORROW, RUI!
OH.
BYE...
WHAT'S GOING ON?
YOU'RE OUT-SIDE!
YOU CAN SEE ME?
GAWP
GAWP

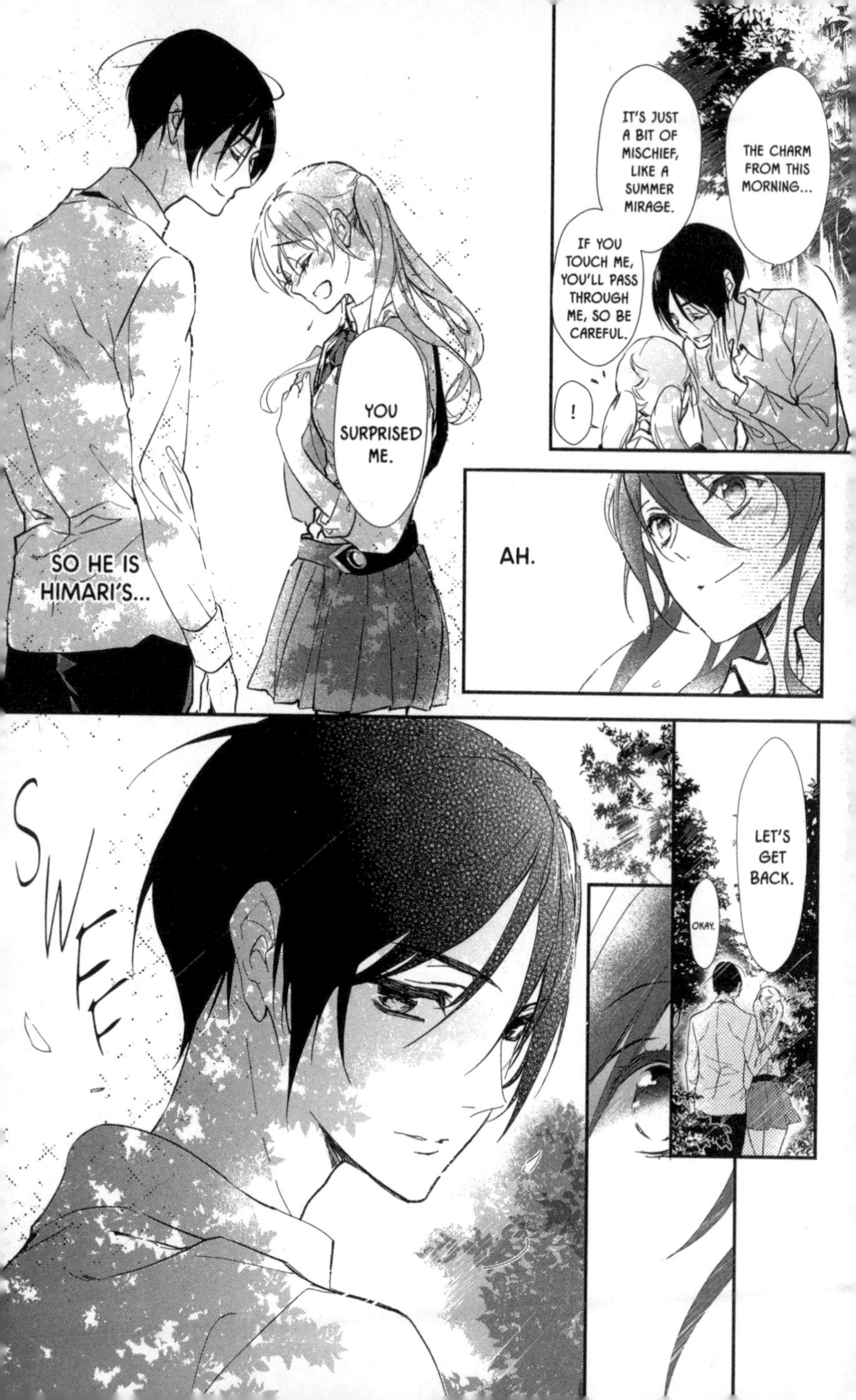
THE CHARM FROM THIS MORNING...
IT'S JUST A BIT OF MISCHIEF, LIKE A SUMMER MIRAGE.
IF YOU TOUCH ME, YOU'LL PASS THROUGH ME, SO BE CAREFUL.
!
AH.
YOU SURPRISED ME.
SO HE IS HIMARI'S...
LET'S GET BACK.
OKAY.
SWEFF

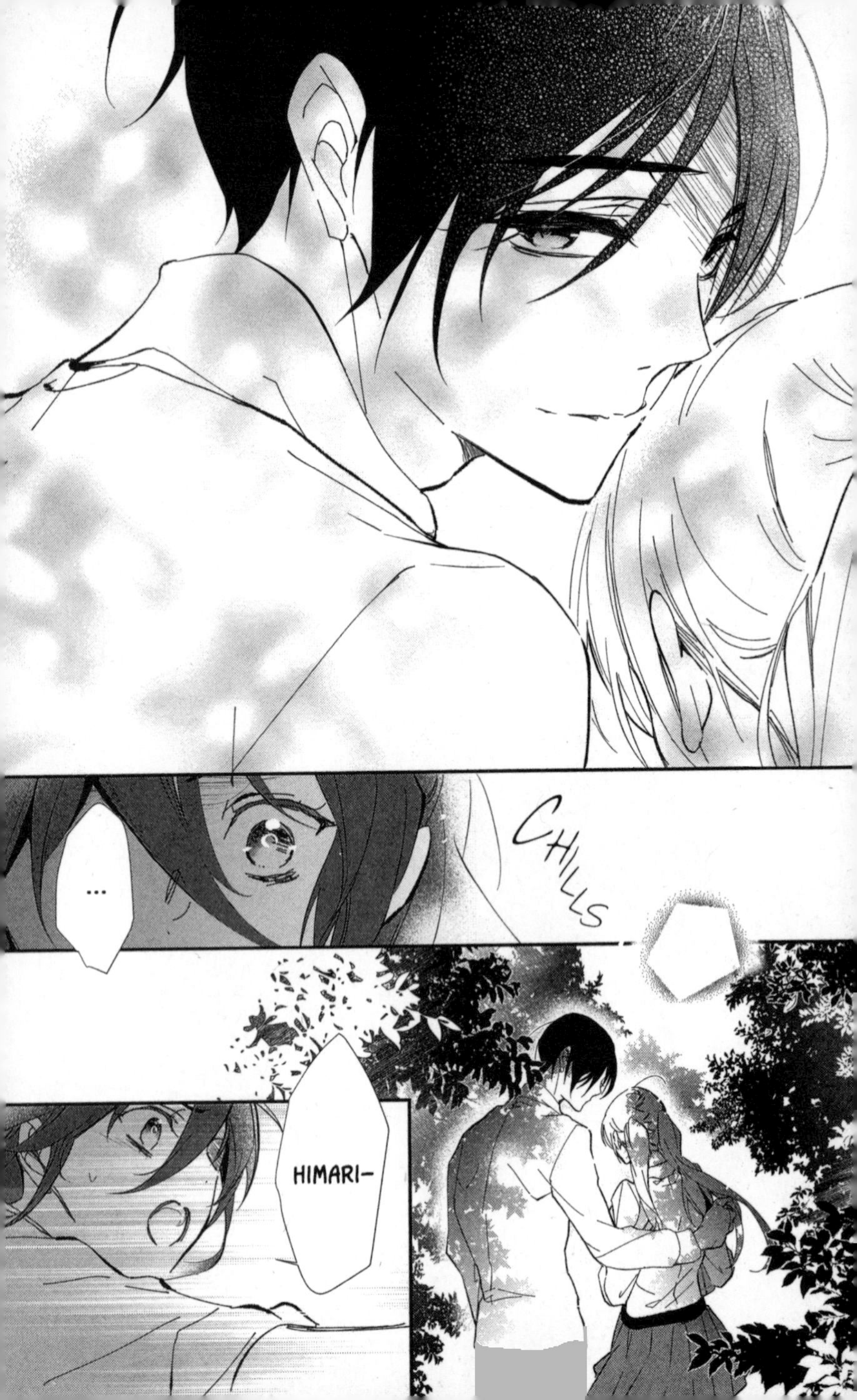

CHILLS
...
HIMARI-

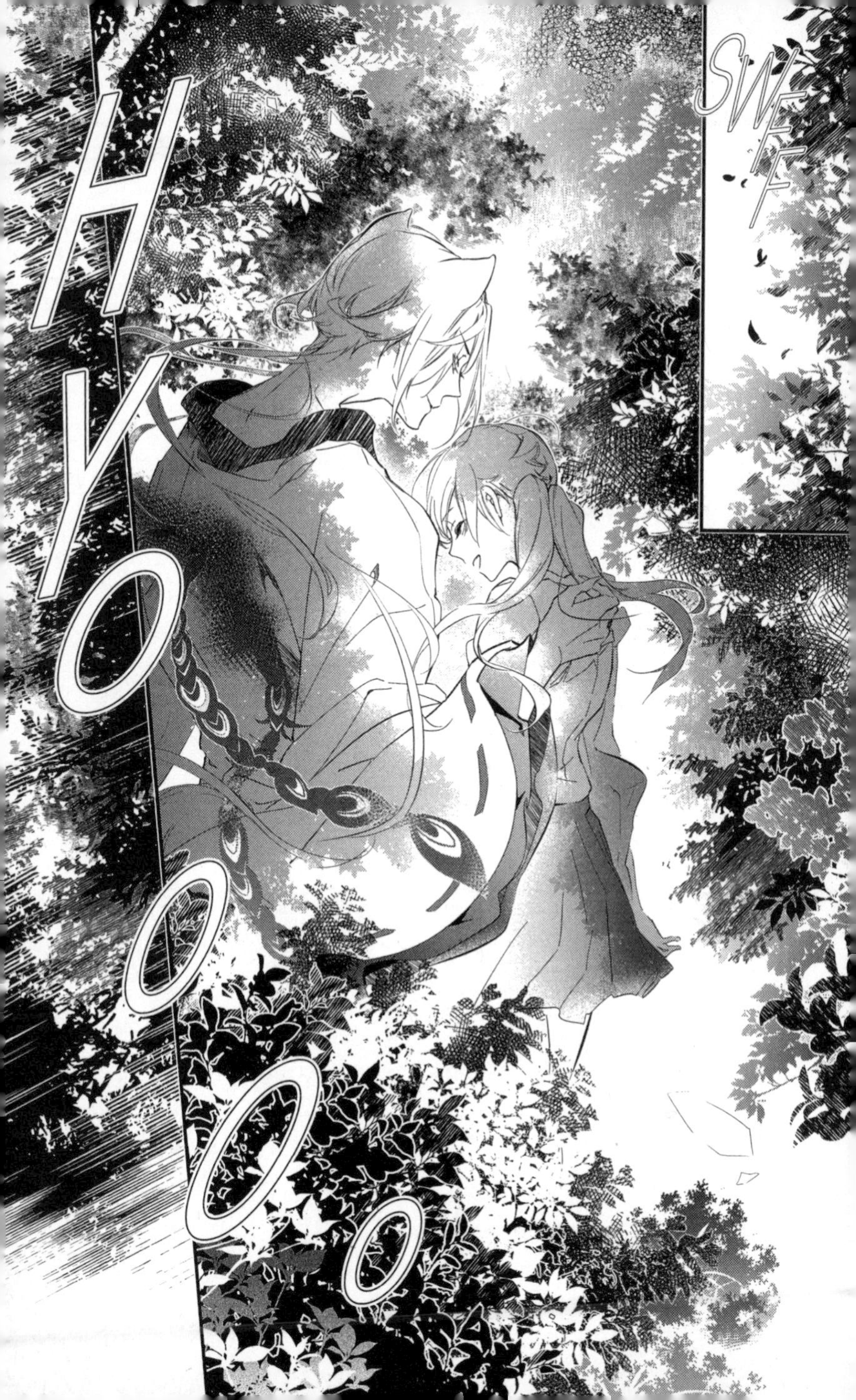
SWFF
HYOOOOO

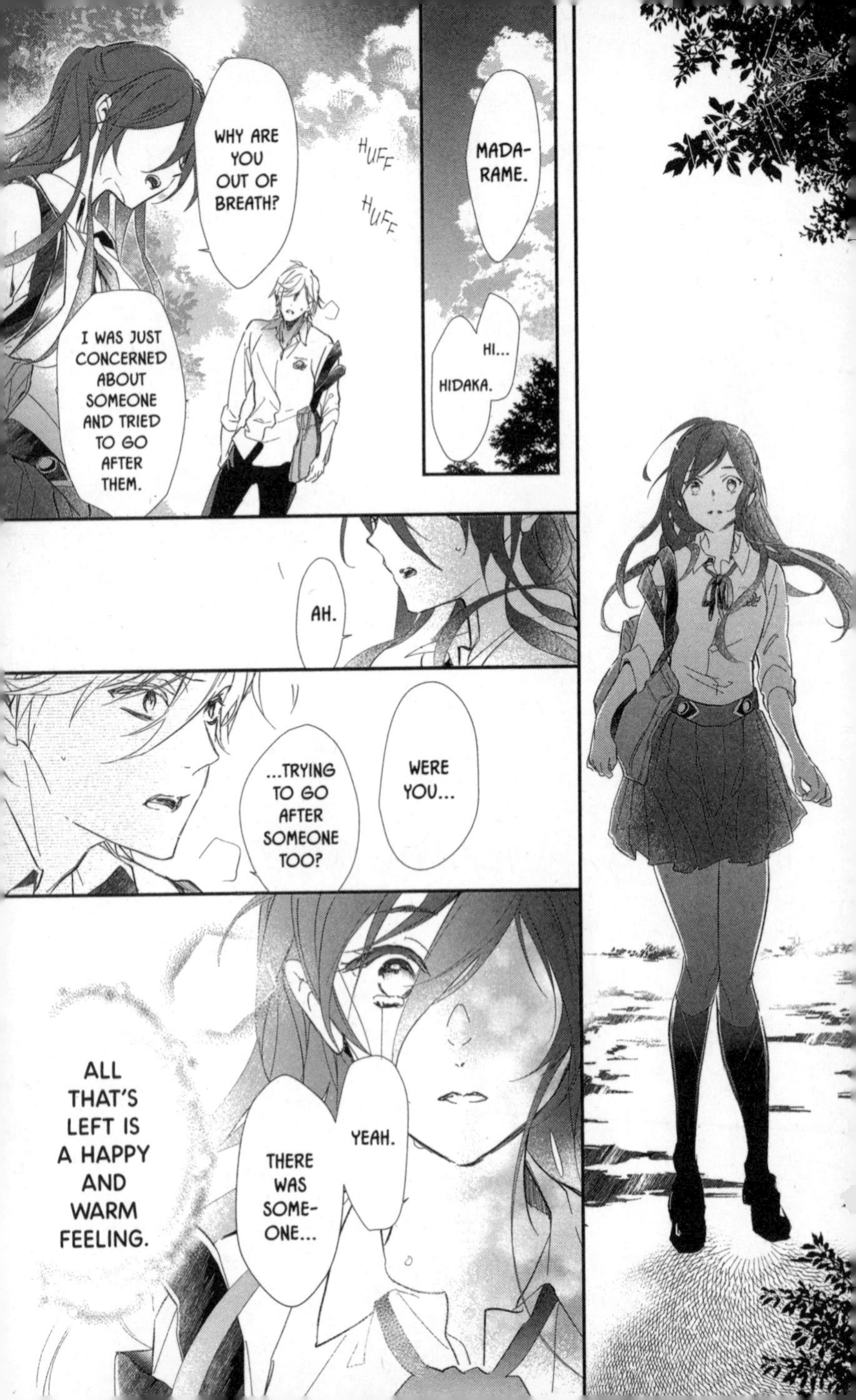
MADA-RAME.
HI... HIDAKA.
WHY ARE YOU OUT OF BREATH?
HUFF
HUFF
I WAS JUST CONCERNED ABOUT SOMEONE AND TRIED TO GO AFTER THEM.
AH.
WERE YOU...
...TRYING TO GO AFTER SOMEONE TOO?
YEAH.
THERE WAS SOME-ONE...
ALL THAT'S LEFT IS A HAPPY AND WARM FEELING.

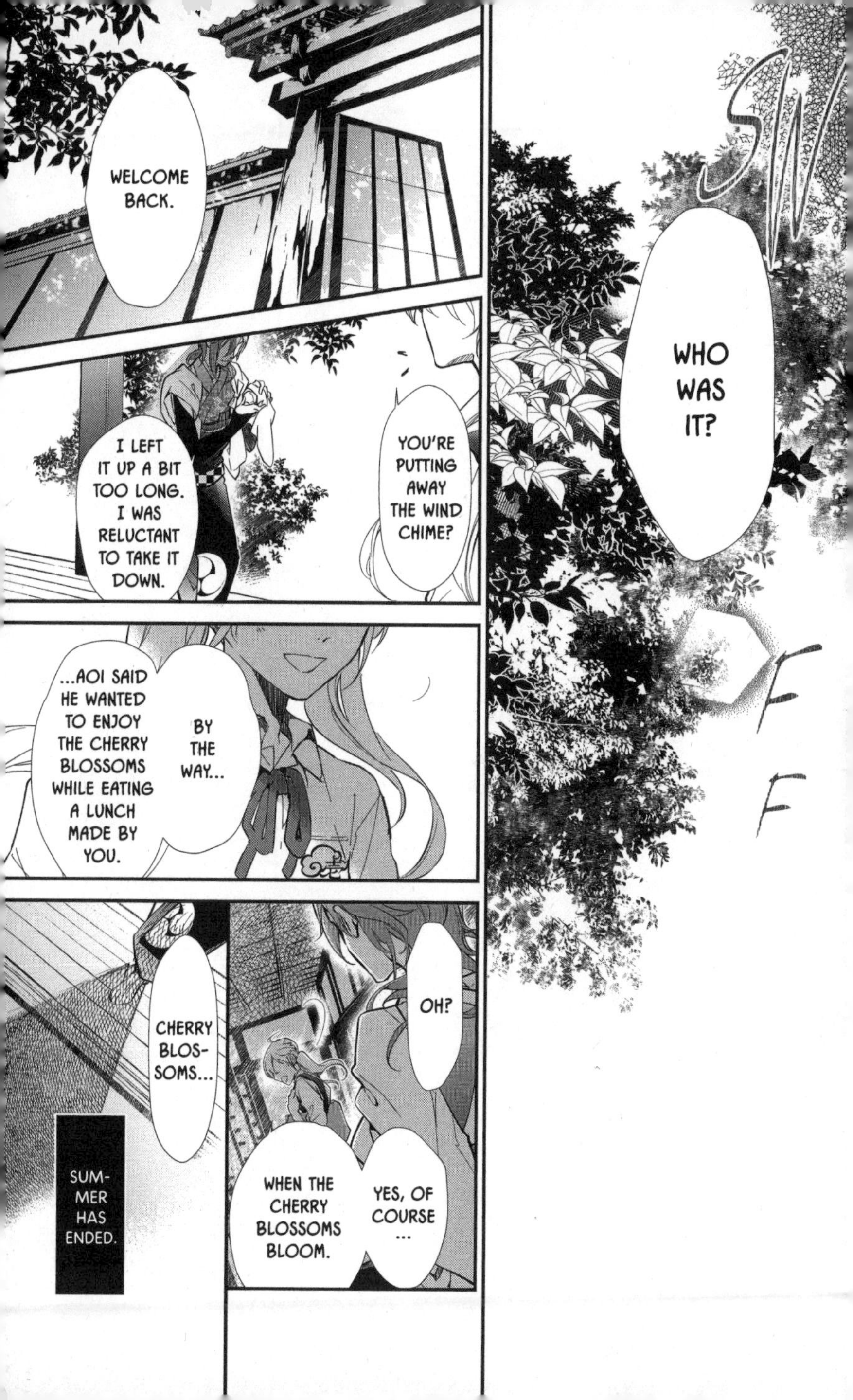
SW
WHO WAS IT?
FF
WELCOME BACK.
YOU'RE PUTTING AWAY THE WIND CHIME?
I LEFT IT UP A BIT TOO LONG. I WAS RELUCTANT TO TAKE IT DOWN.
BY THE WAY...
...AOI SAID HE WANTED TO ENJOY THE CHERRY BLOSSOMS WHILE EATING A LUNCH MADE BY YOU.
OH?
YES, OF COURSE...
WHEN THE CHERRY BLOSSOMS BLOOM.
CHERRY BLOSSOMS...
SUMMER HAS ENDED.

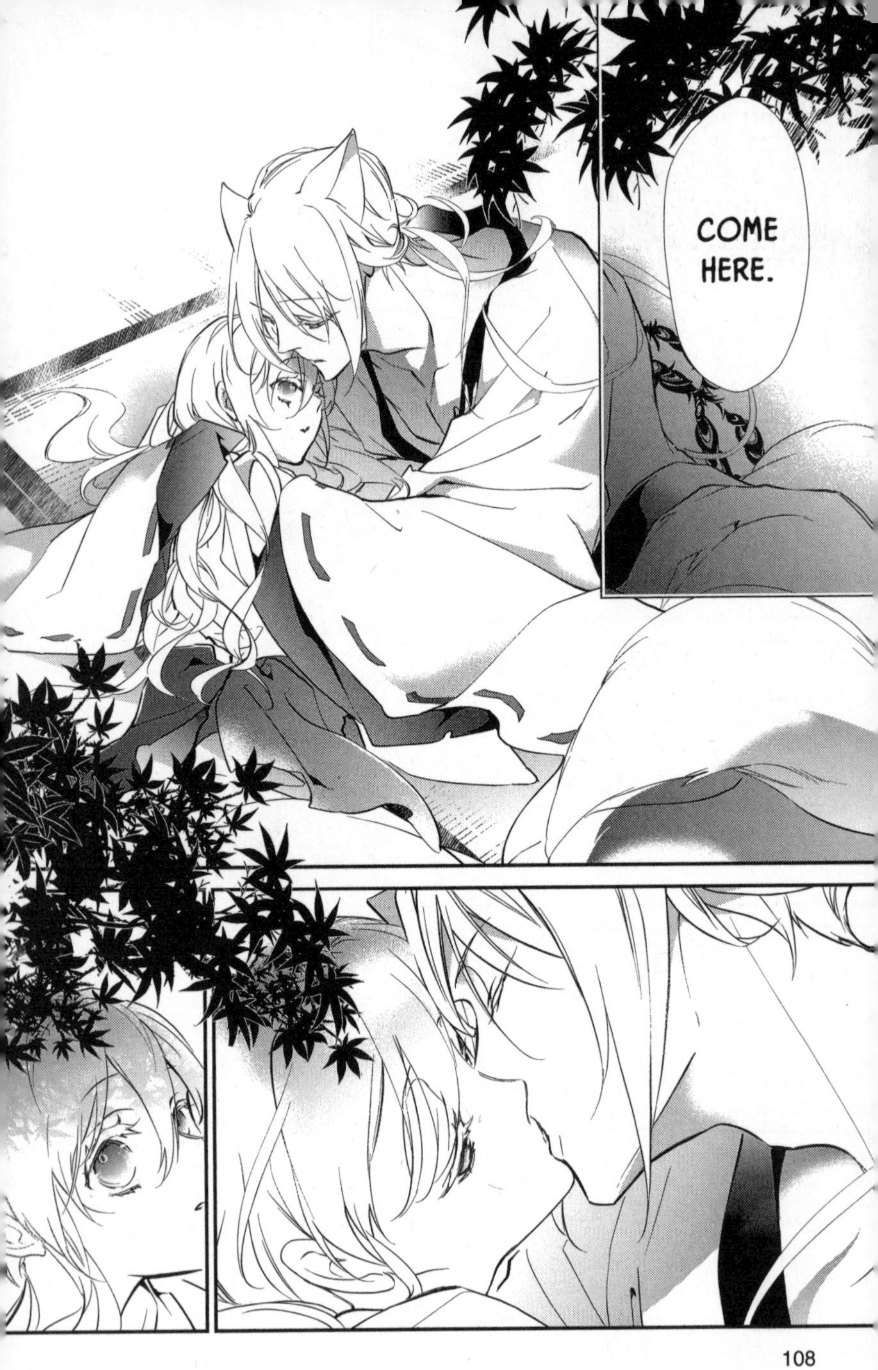
COME HERE.

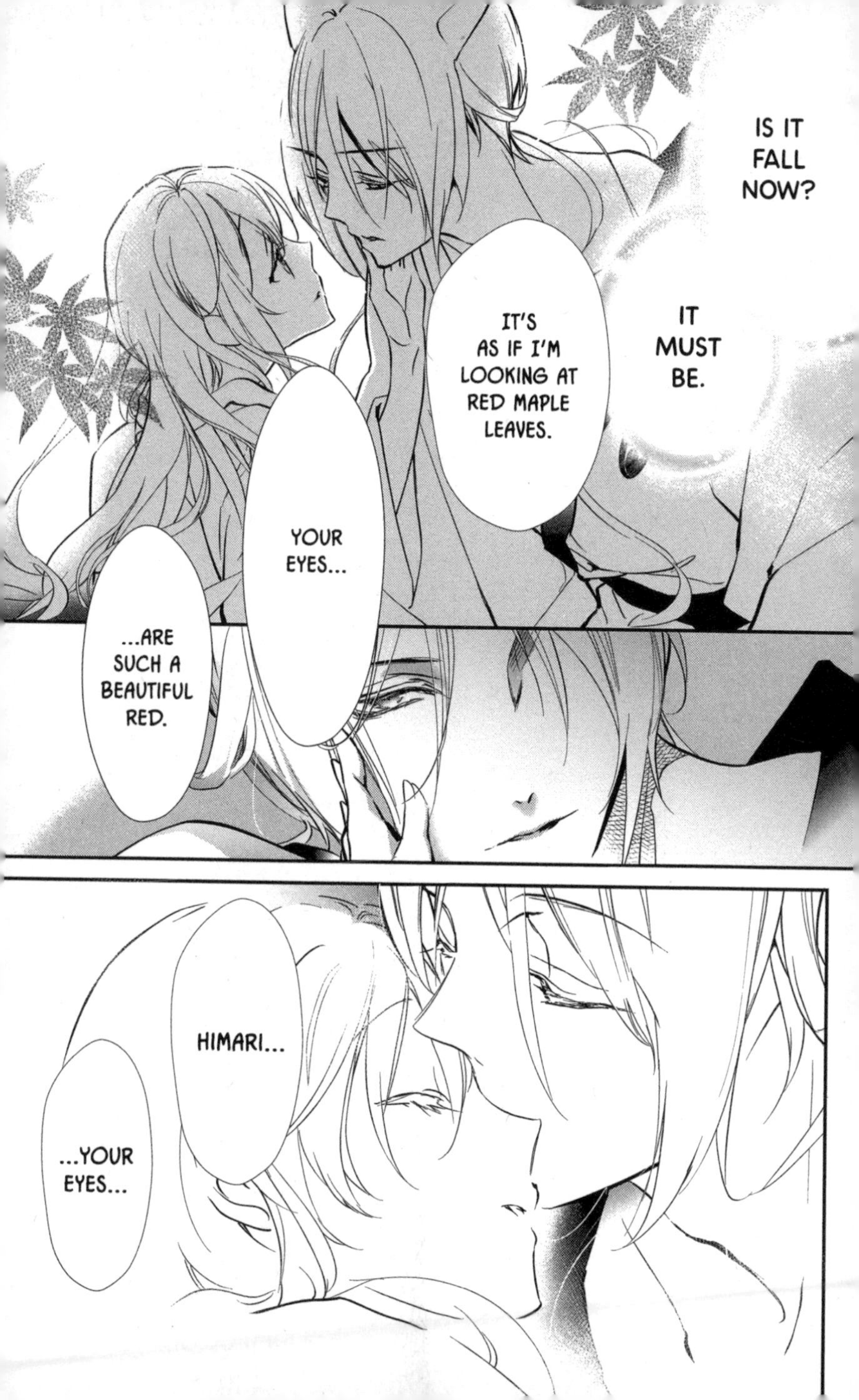
IS IT FALL NOW?
IT MUST BE.
IT'S AS IF I'M LOOKING AT RED MAPLE LEAVES.
YOUR EYES...
...ARE SUCH A BEAUTIFUL RED.
HIMARI...
...YOUR EYES...

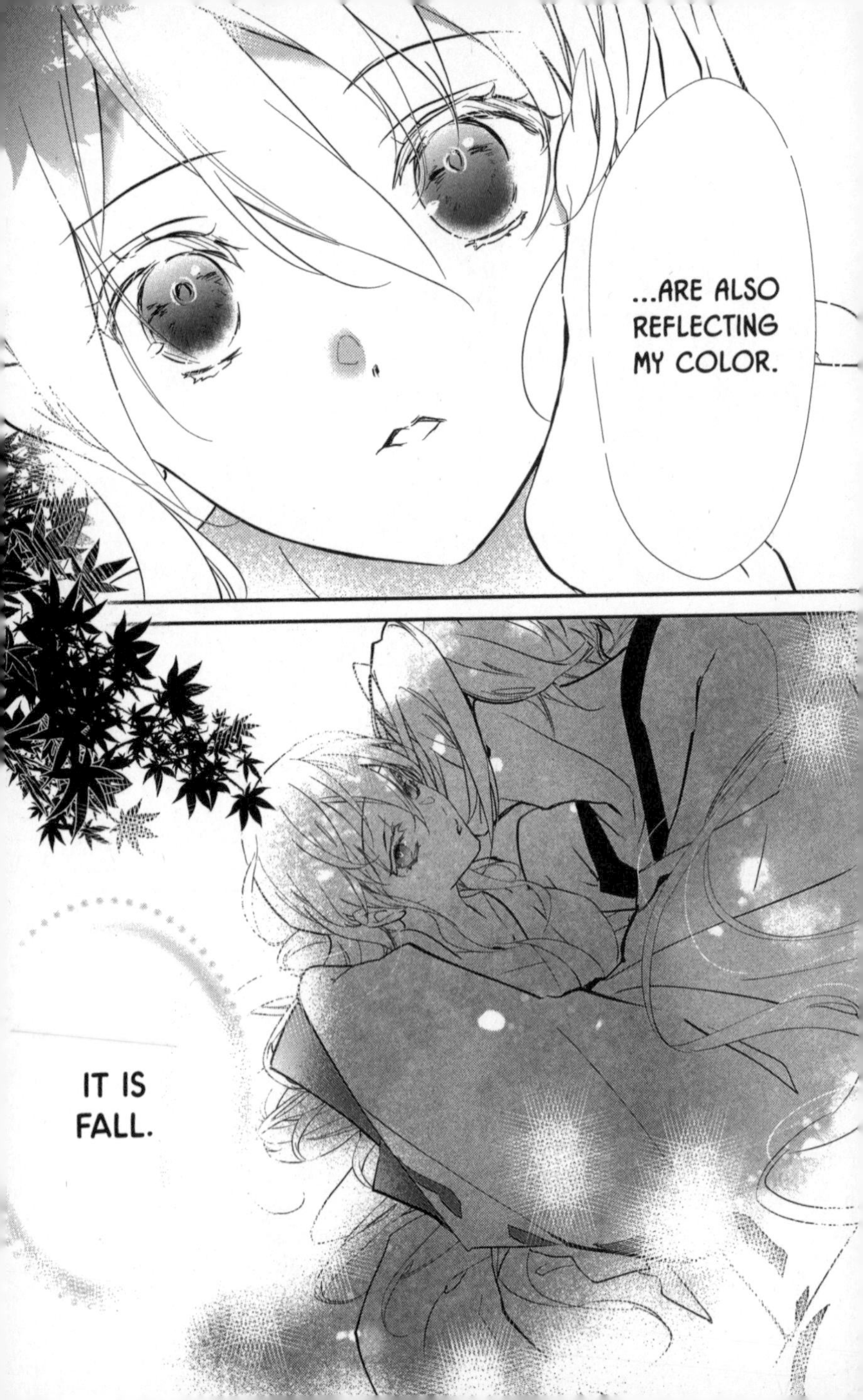
...ARE ALSO
REFLECTING
MY COLOR.
IT IS
FALL.

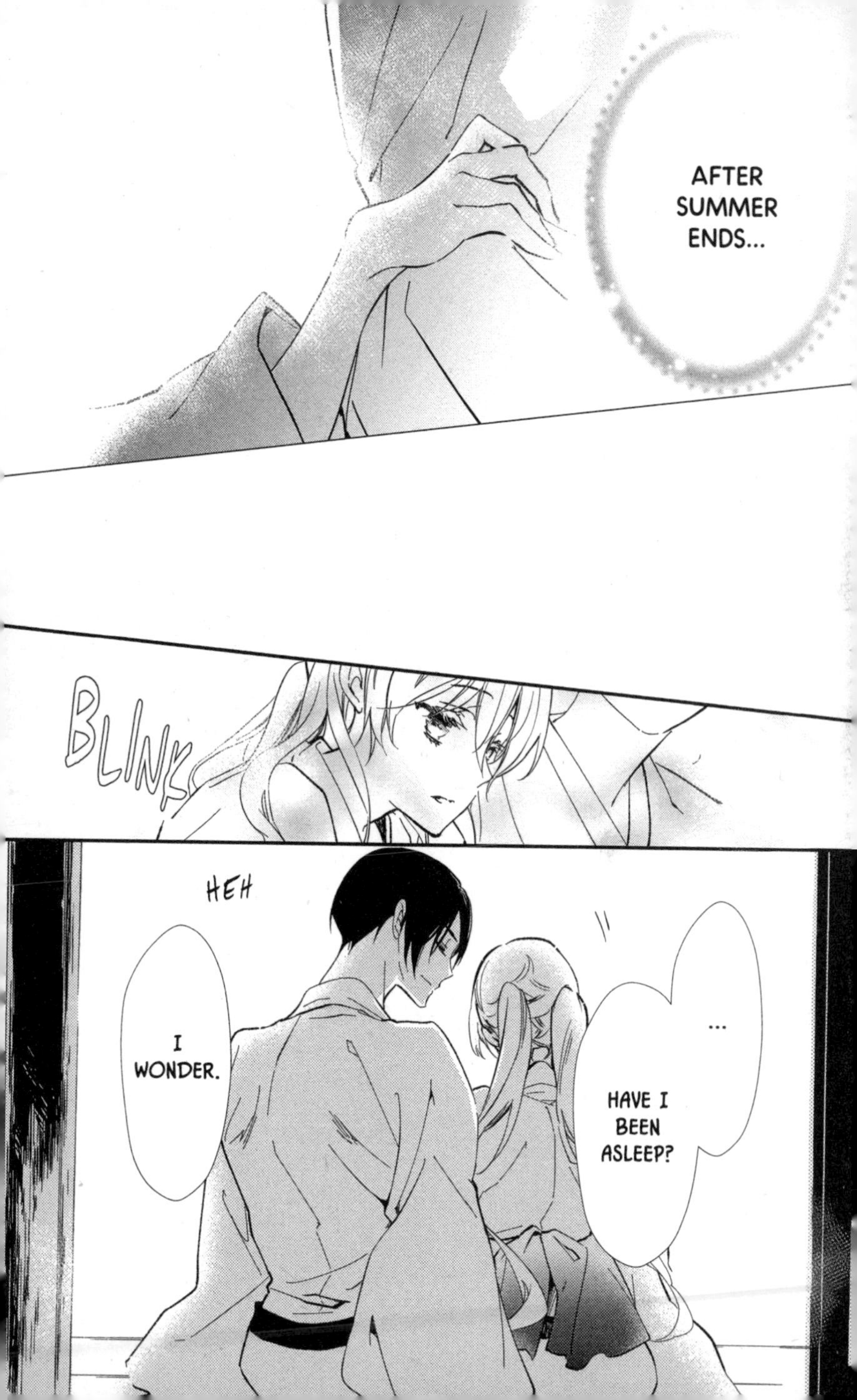
AFTER SUMMER ENDS...
BLINK
... HAVE I BEEN ASLEEP?
HEH
I WONDER.

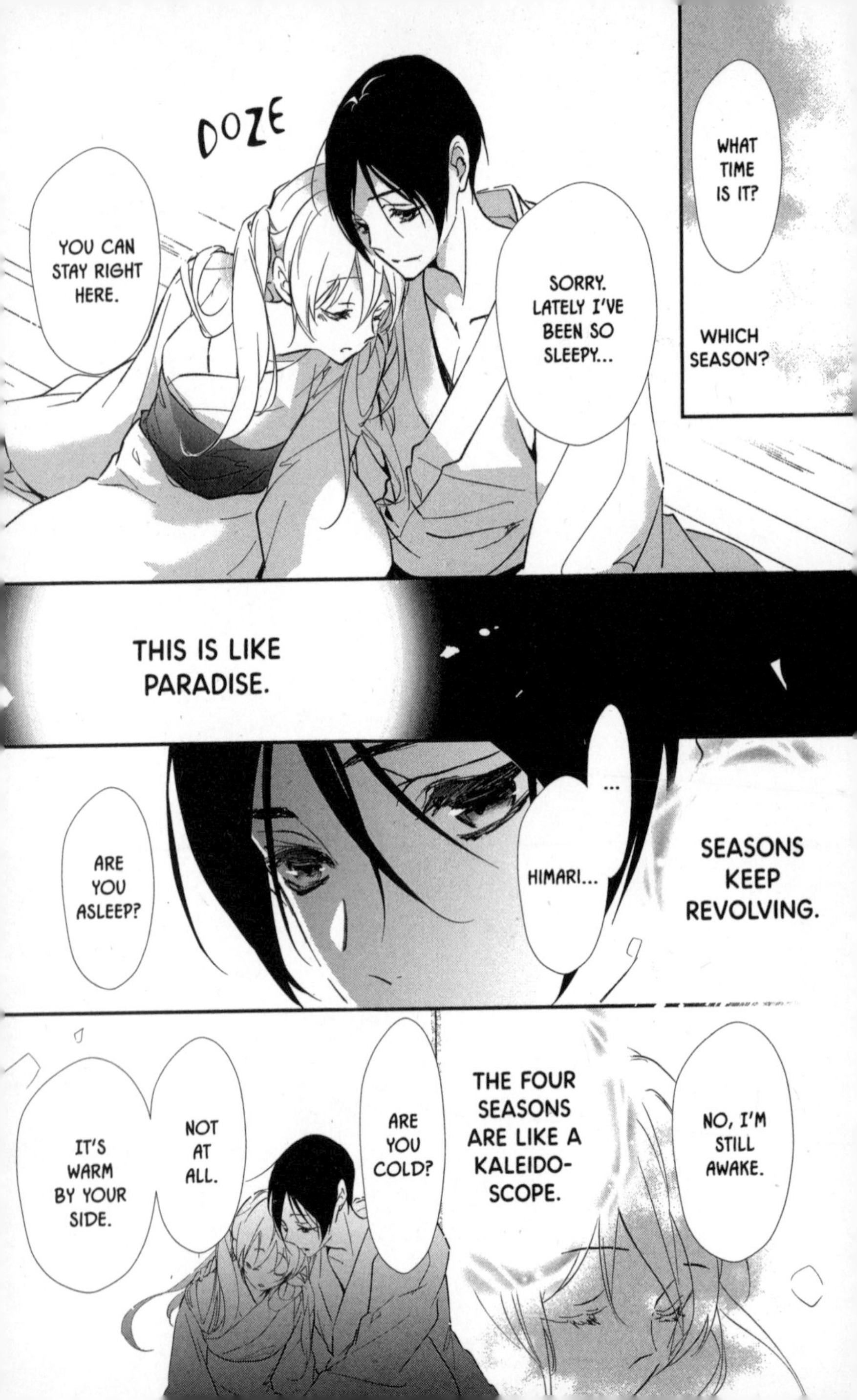
WHAT TIME IS IT?
WHICH SEASON?
SORRY. LATELY I'VE BEEN SO SLEEPY...
DOZE
YOU CAN STAY RIGHT HERE.
THIS IS LIKE PARADISE.
SEASONS KEEP REVOLVING.
...
HIMARI...
ARE YOU ASLEEP?
NO, I'M STILL AWAKE.
THE FOUR SEASONS ARE LIKE A KALEIDO-SCOPE.
ARE YOU COLD?
NOT AT ALL.
IT'S WARM BY YOUR SIDE.

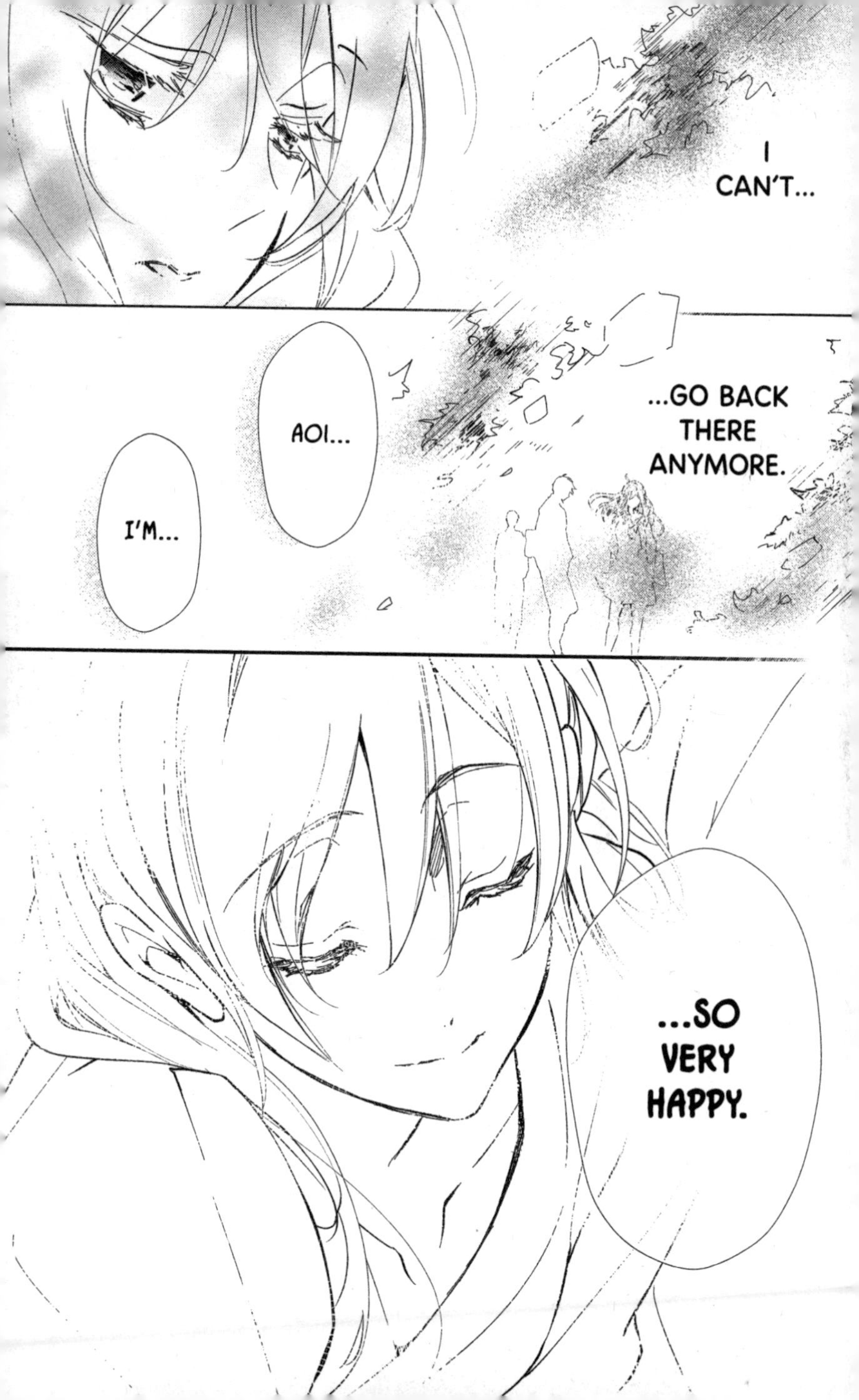
I CAN'T...
...GO BACK THERE ANYMORE.
AOI...
I'M...
...SO VERY HAPPY.

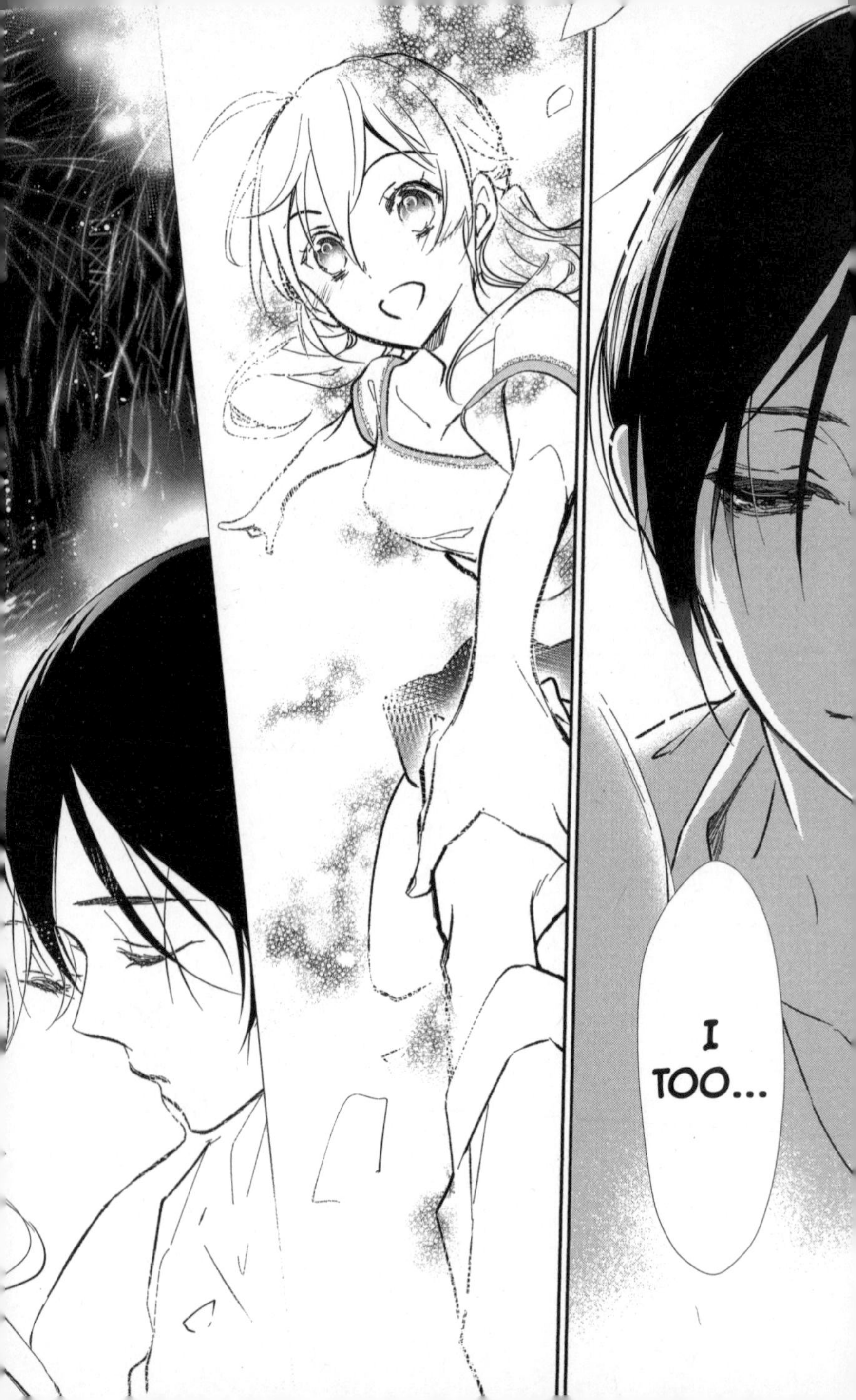
I TOO...

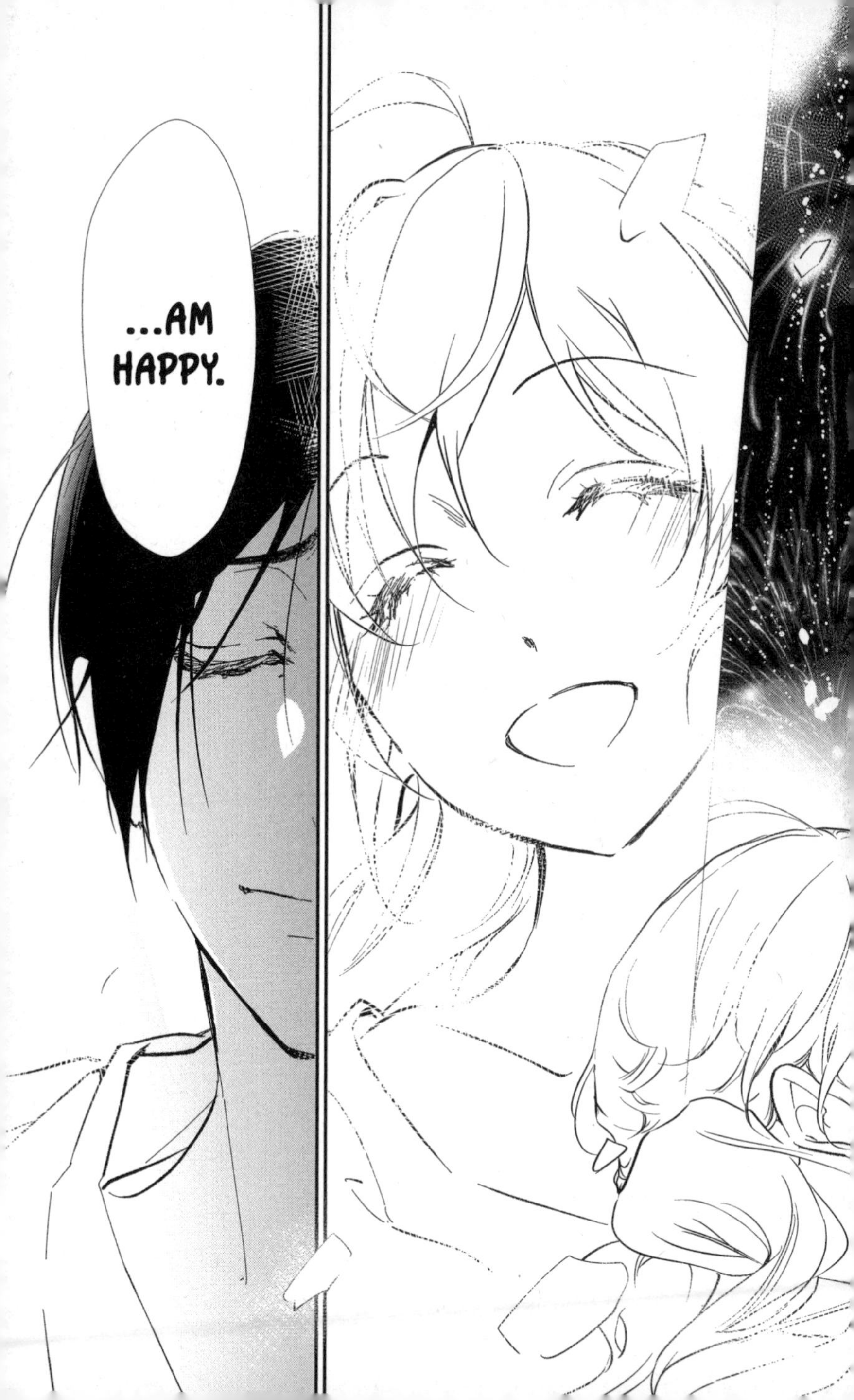
...AM HAPPY.

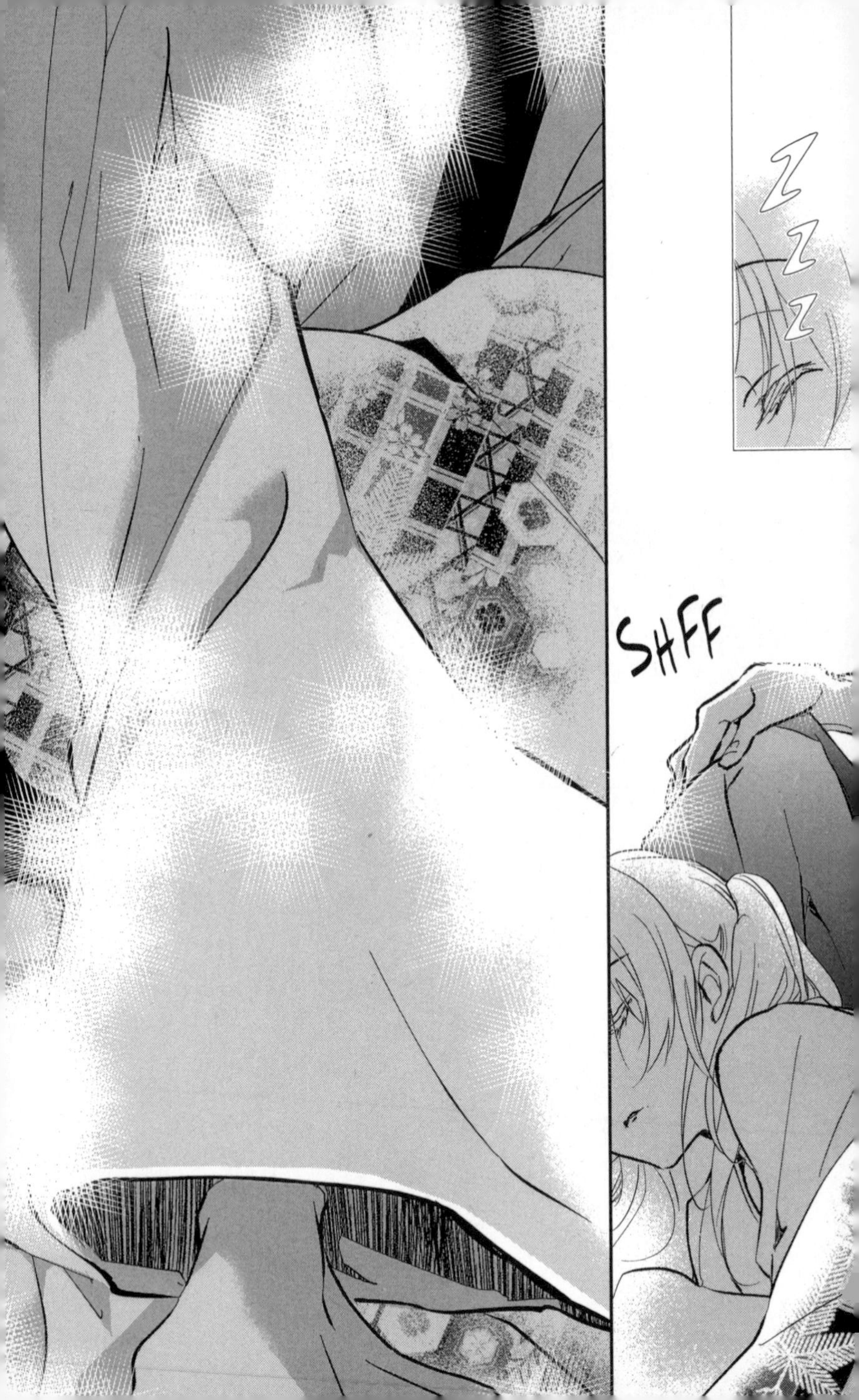
Z Z Z
SHFF

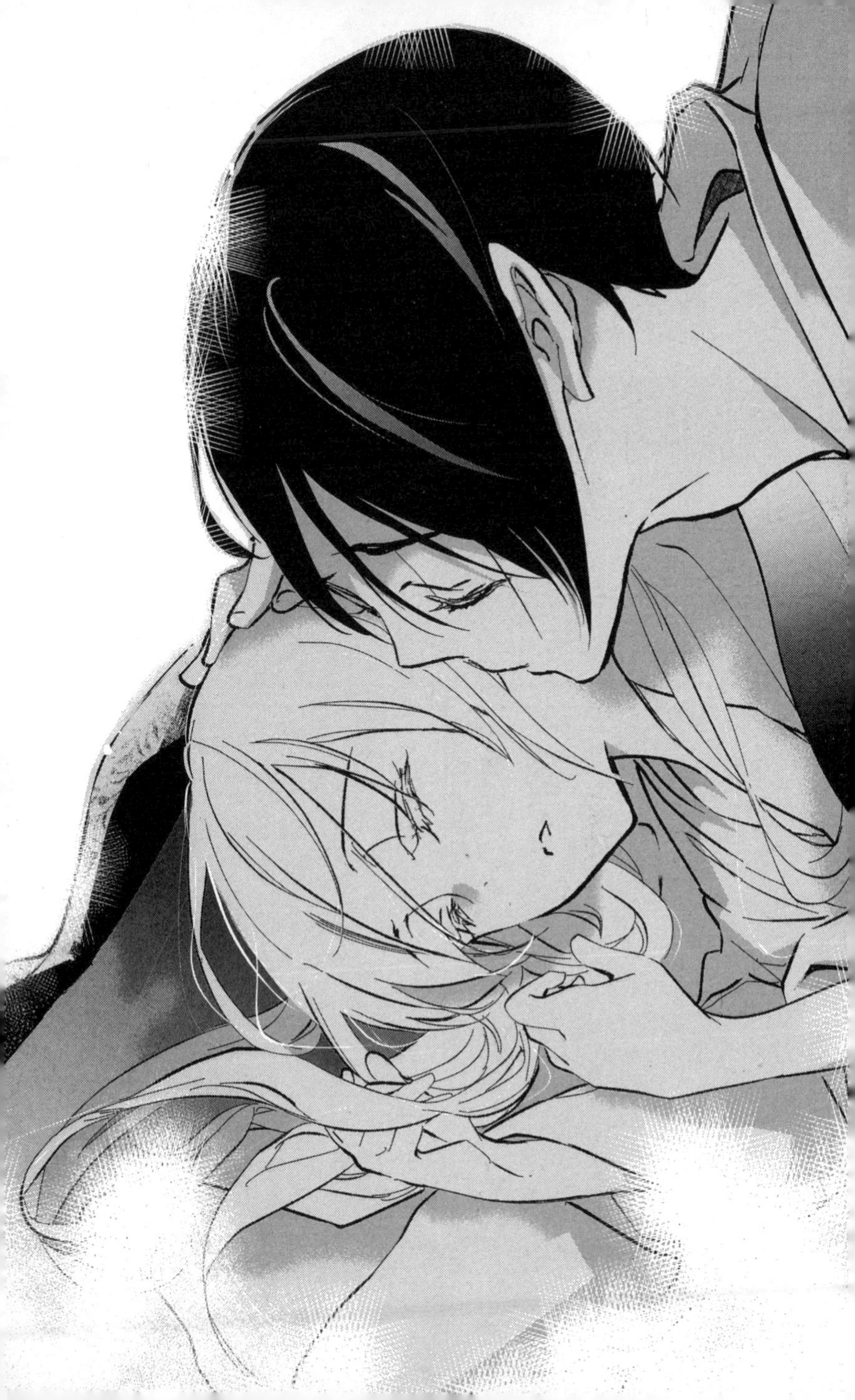

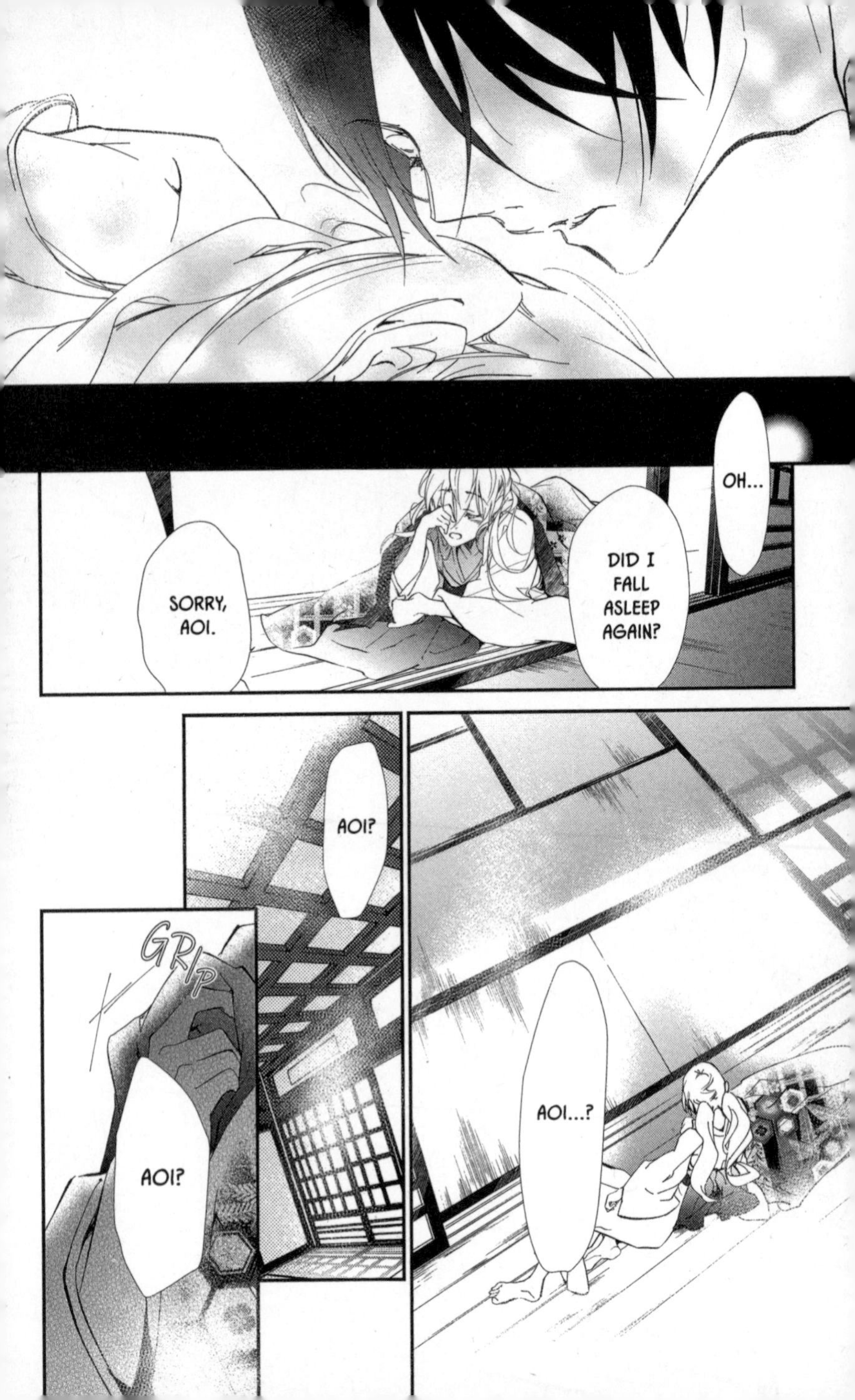
OH...
DID I FALL ASLEEP AGAIN?
SORRY, AOI.
AOI...?
AOI?
GRIP
AOI?

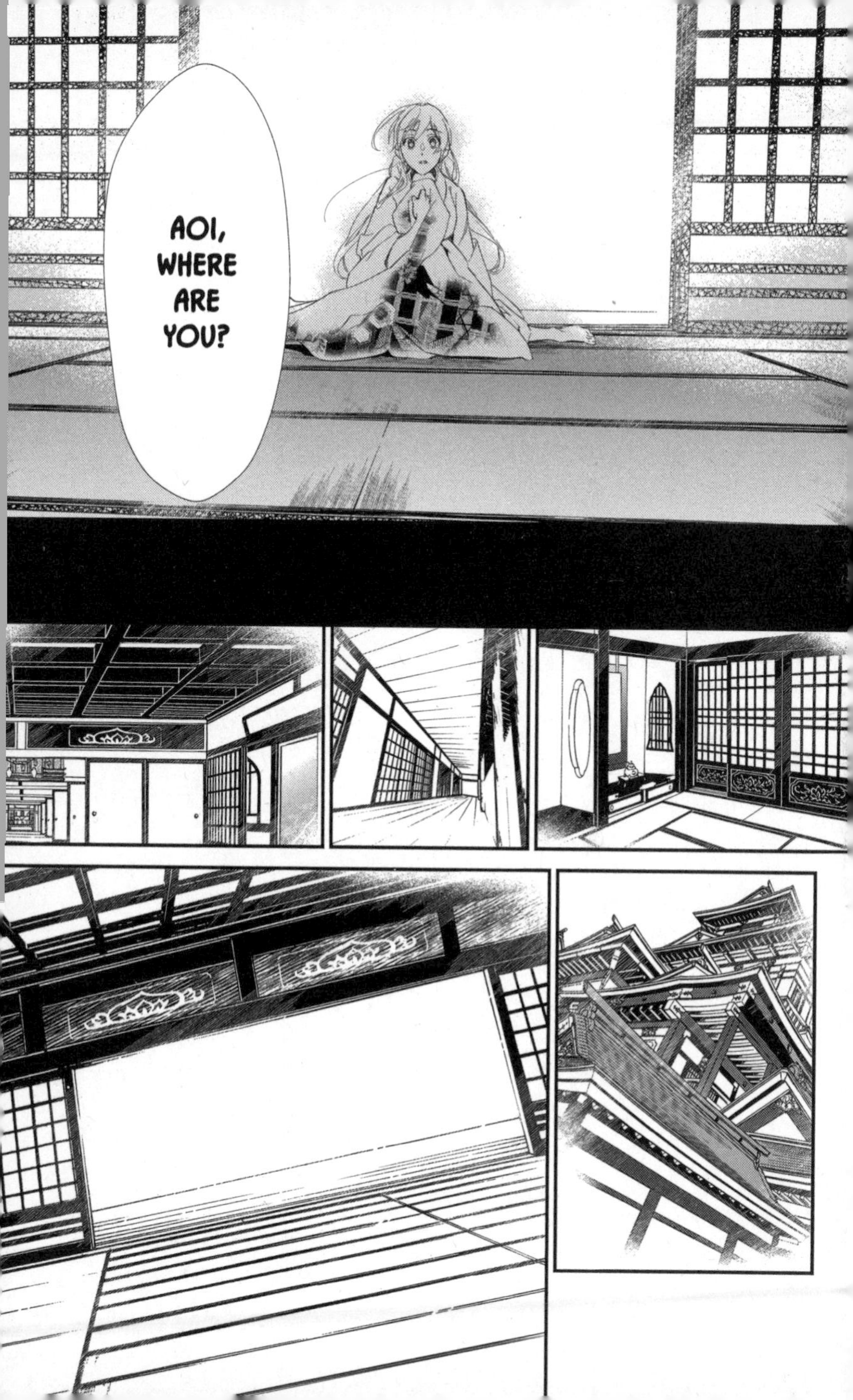
AOI, WHERE ARE YOU?

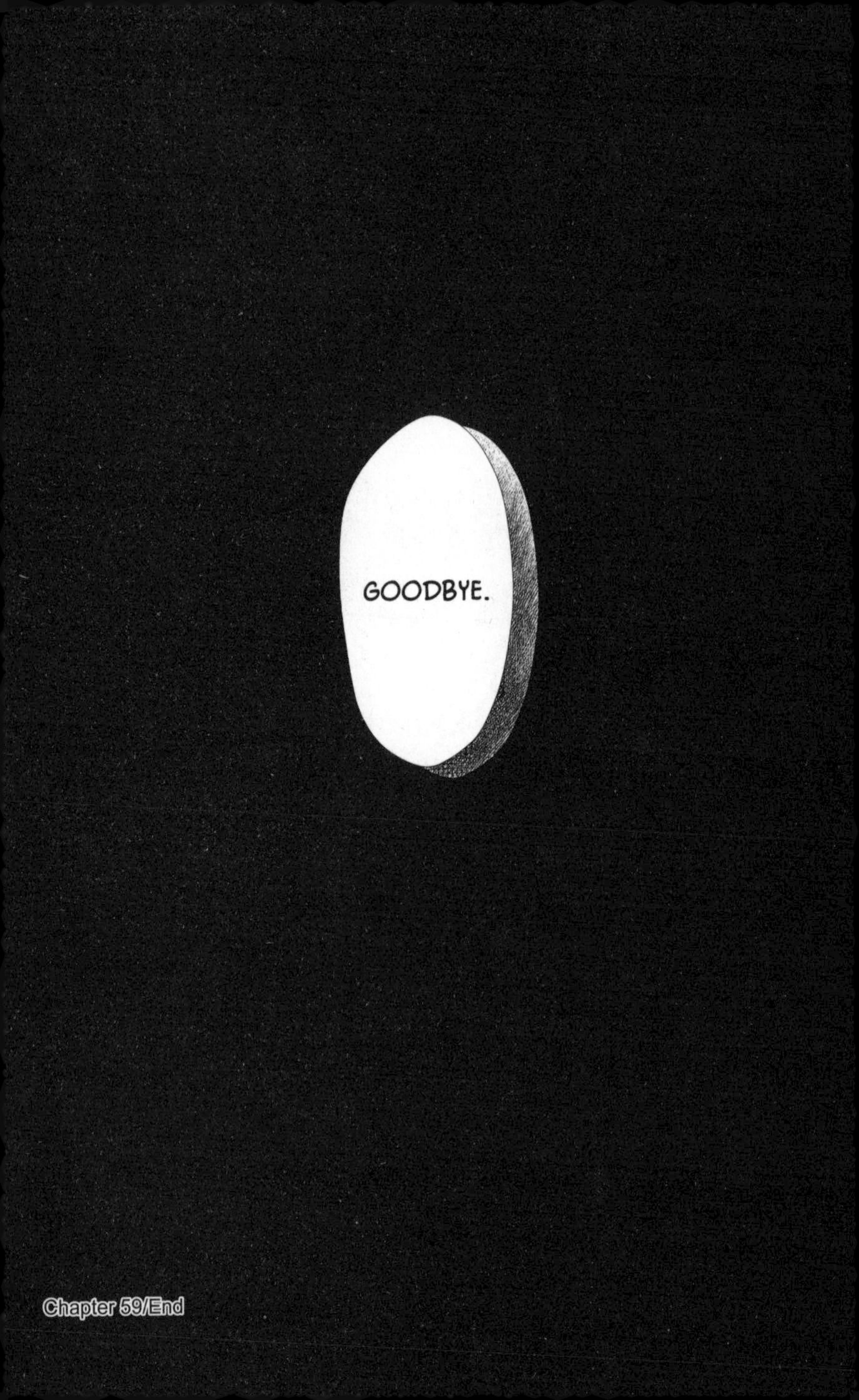
GOODBYE.
Chapter 59/End

The
DEMON
PRINCE
of MOMOCHI
HOUSE

The
DEMON
PRINCE
of MOMOCHI
HOUSE

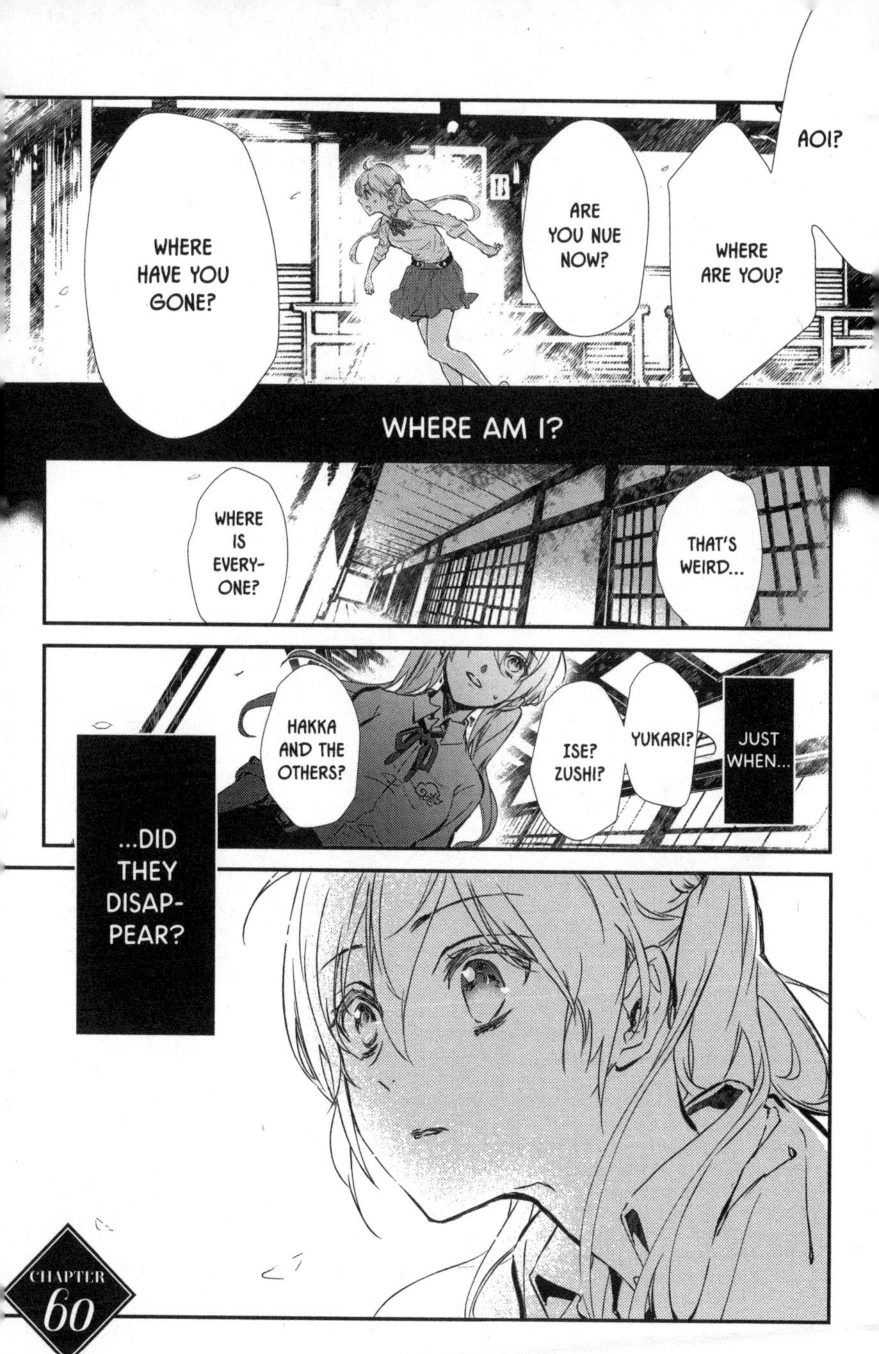
AOI?
WHERE ARE YOU?
ARE YOU NUE NOW?
WHERE HAVE YOU GONE?
WHERE AM I?
THAT'S WEIRD...
WHERE IS EVERY-ONE?
JUST WHEN...
YUKARI?
ISE? ZUSHI?
HAKKA AND THE OTHERS?
...DID THEY DISAP-PEAR?
CHAPTER 60

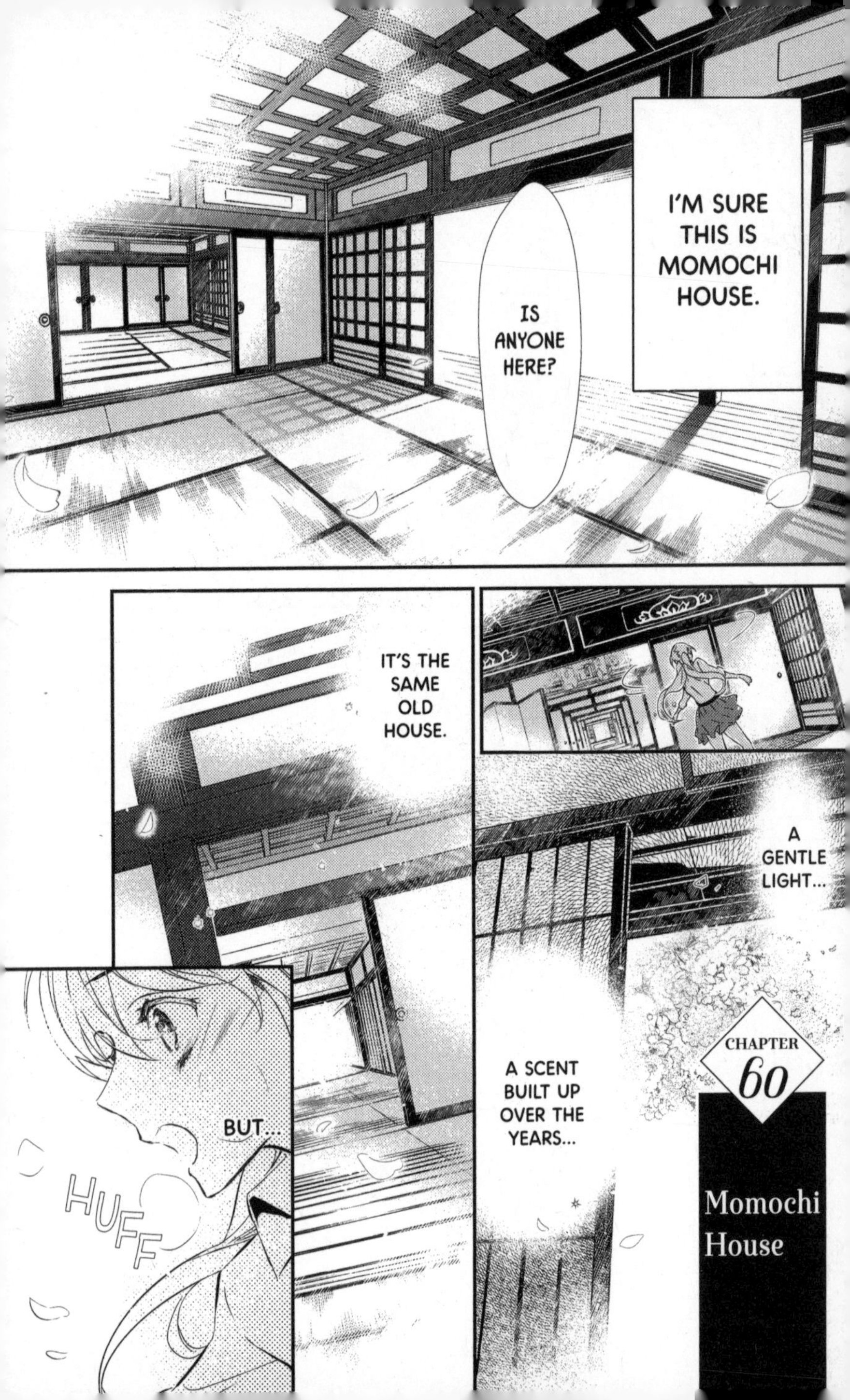
I'M SURE THIS IS MOMOCHI HOUSE.
IS ANYONE HERE?
A GENTLE LIGHT...
A SCENT BUILT UP OVER THE YEARS...
CHAPTER 60
Momochi House
IT'S THE SAME OLD HOUSE.
BUT...
HUFF

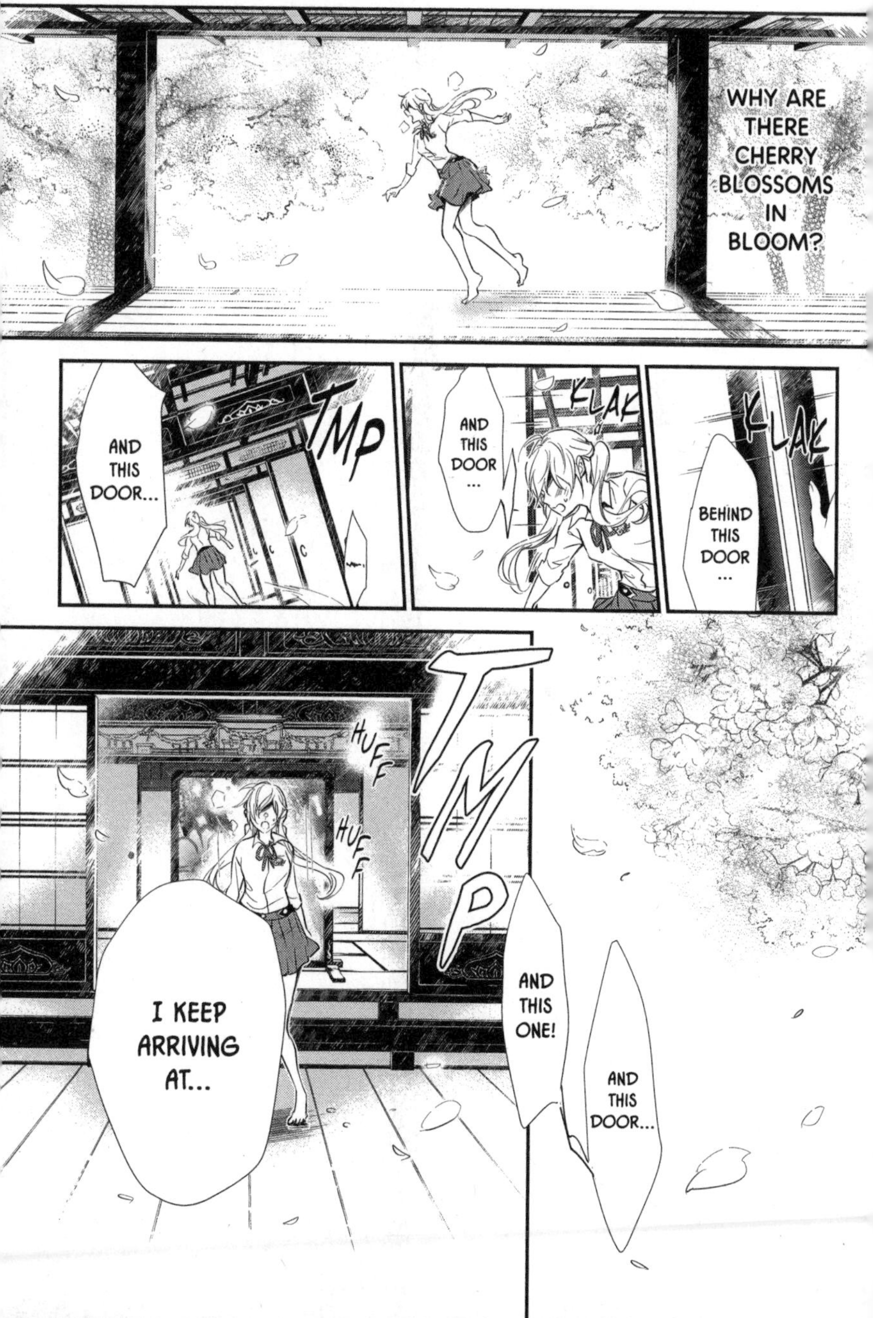

WHY ARE THERE CHERRY BLOSSOMS IN BLOOM?
KLAK
BEHIND THIS DOOR...
KLAK
AND THIS DOOR...
TMP
AND THIS DOOR...
AND THIS DOOR...
AND THIS ONE!
TMP
HUFF
HUFF
I KEEP ARRIVING AT...

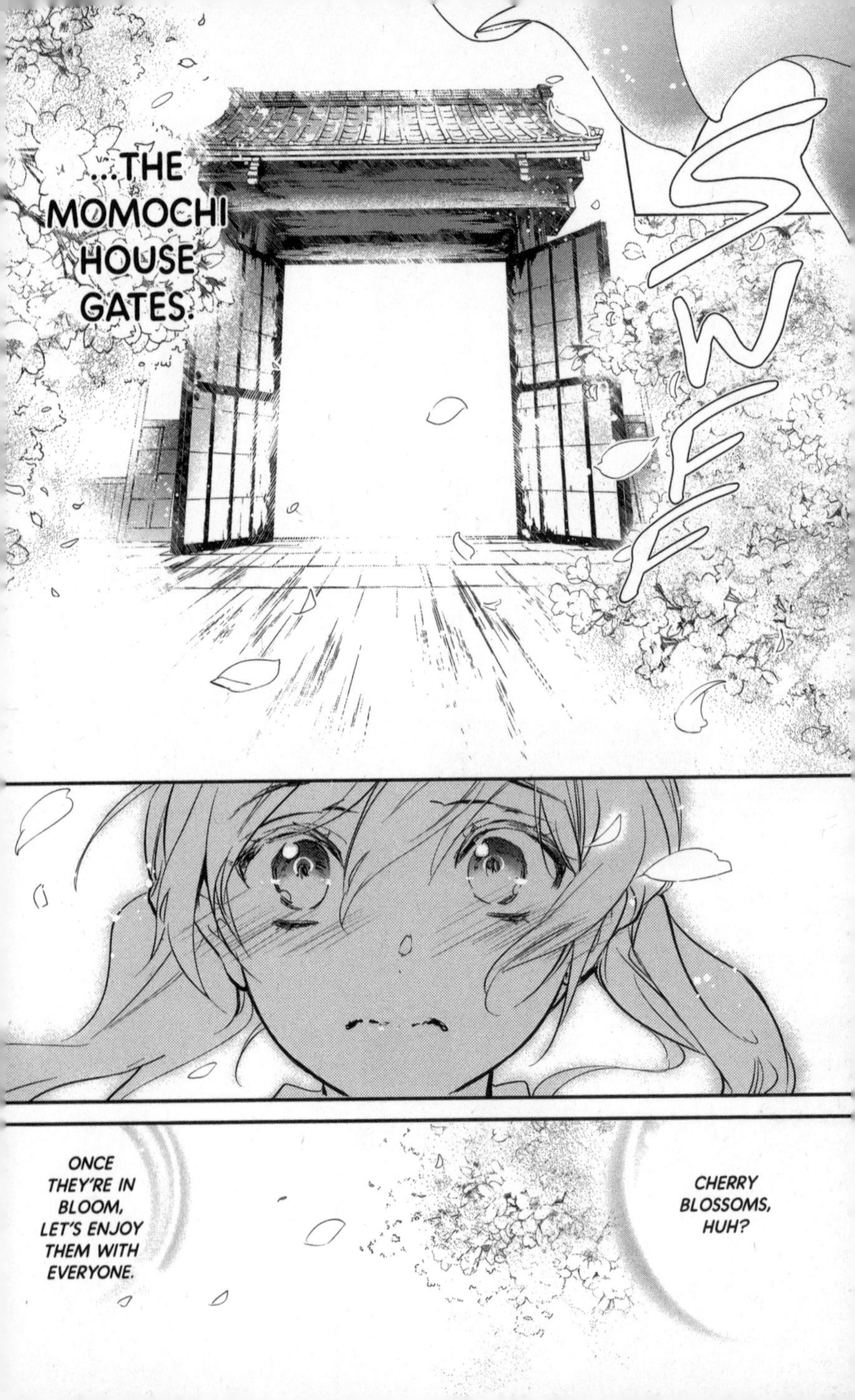
SWFF
...THE MOMOCHI HOUSE GATES.
CHERRY BLOSSOMS, HUH?
ONCE THEY'RE IN BLOOM, LET'S ENJOY THEM WITH EVERYONE.

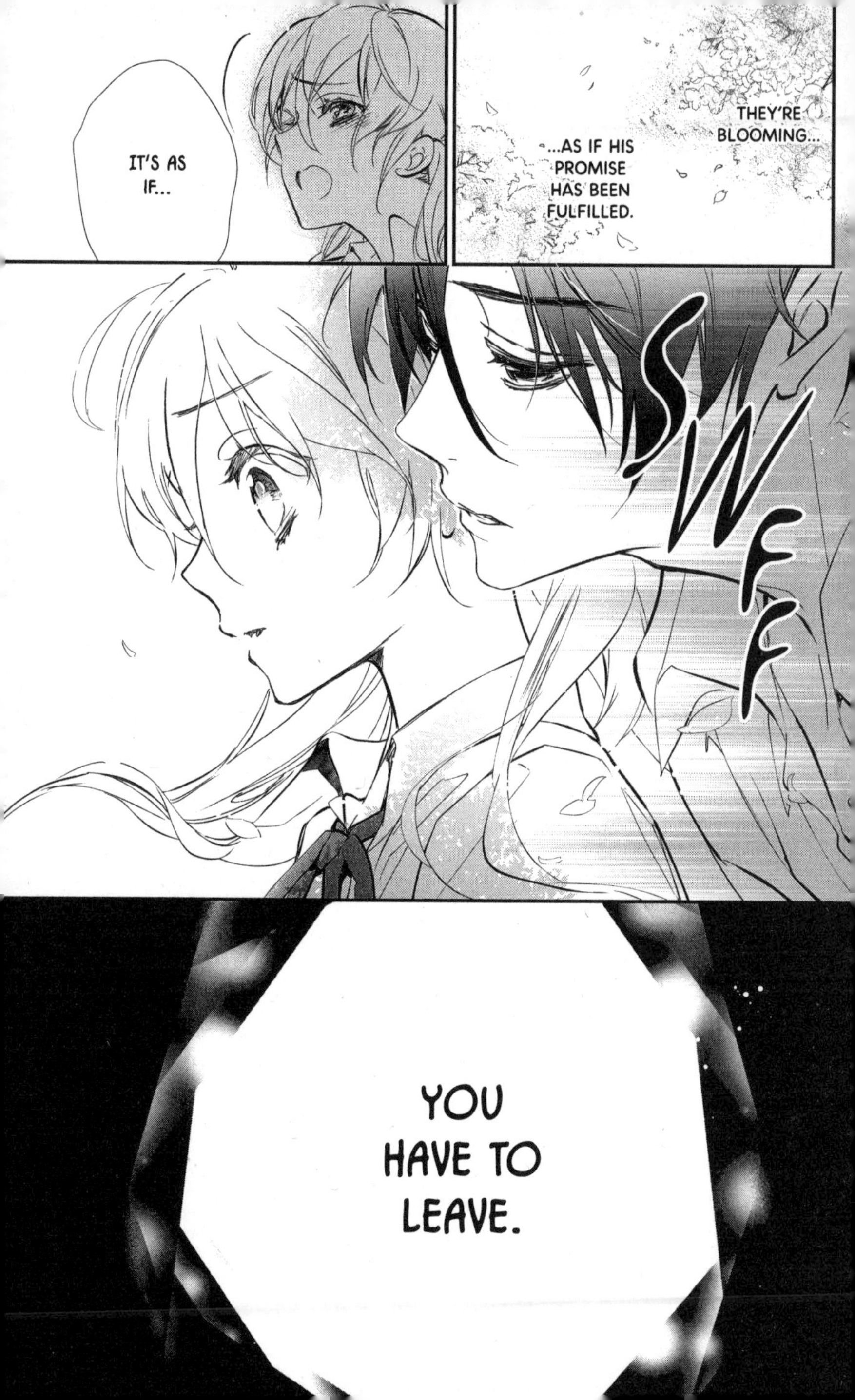
THEY'RE BLOOMING...
...AS IF HIS PROMISE HAS BEEN FULFILLED.
IT'S AS IF...
SWFFF
YOU HAVE TO LEAVE.

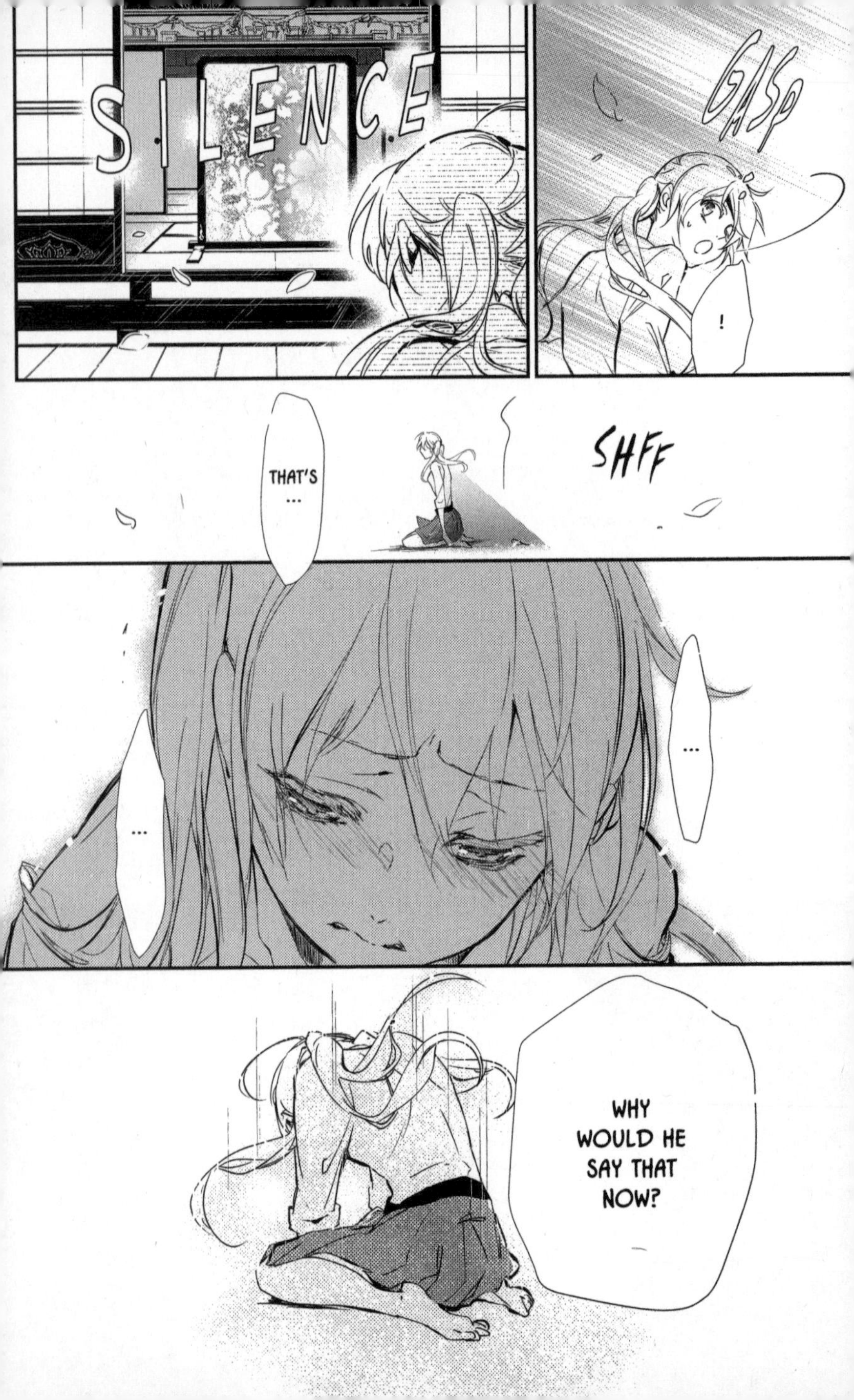
GASP
!
SILENCE
SHFF
THAT'S ...
...
...
WHY WOULD HE SAY THAT NOW?

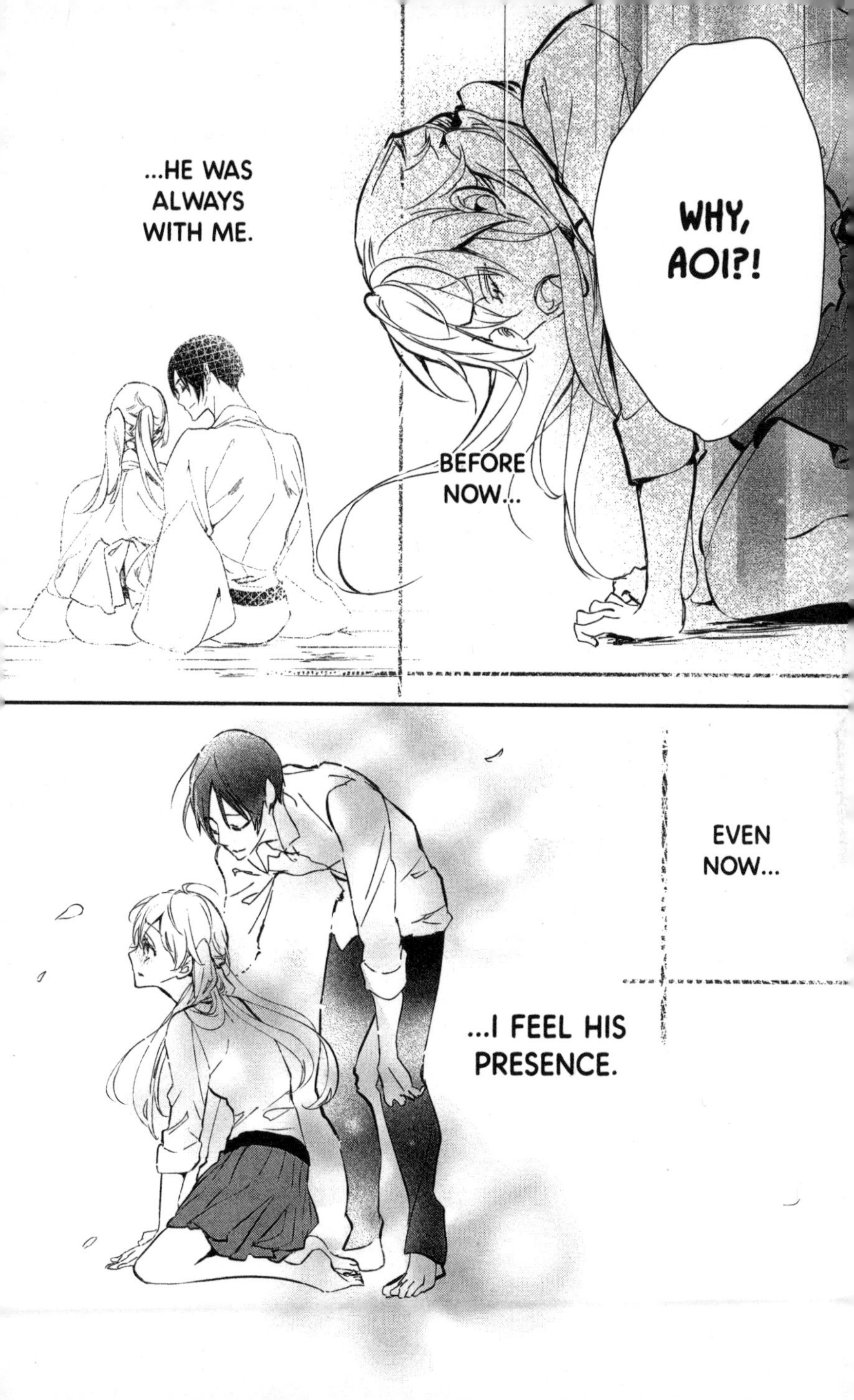
WHY, AOI?!
BEFORE NOW...
...HE WAS ALWAYS WITH ME.
EVEN NOW...
...I FEEL HIS PRESENCE.

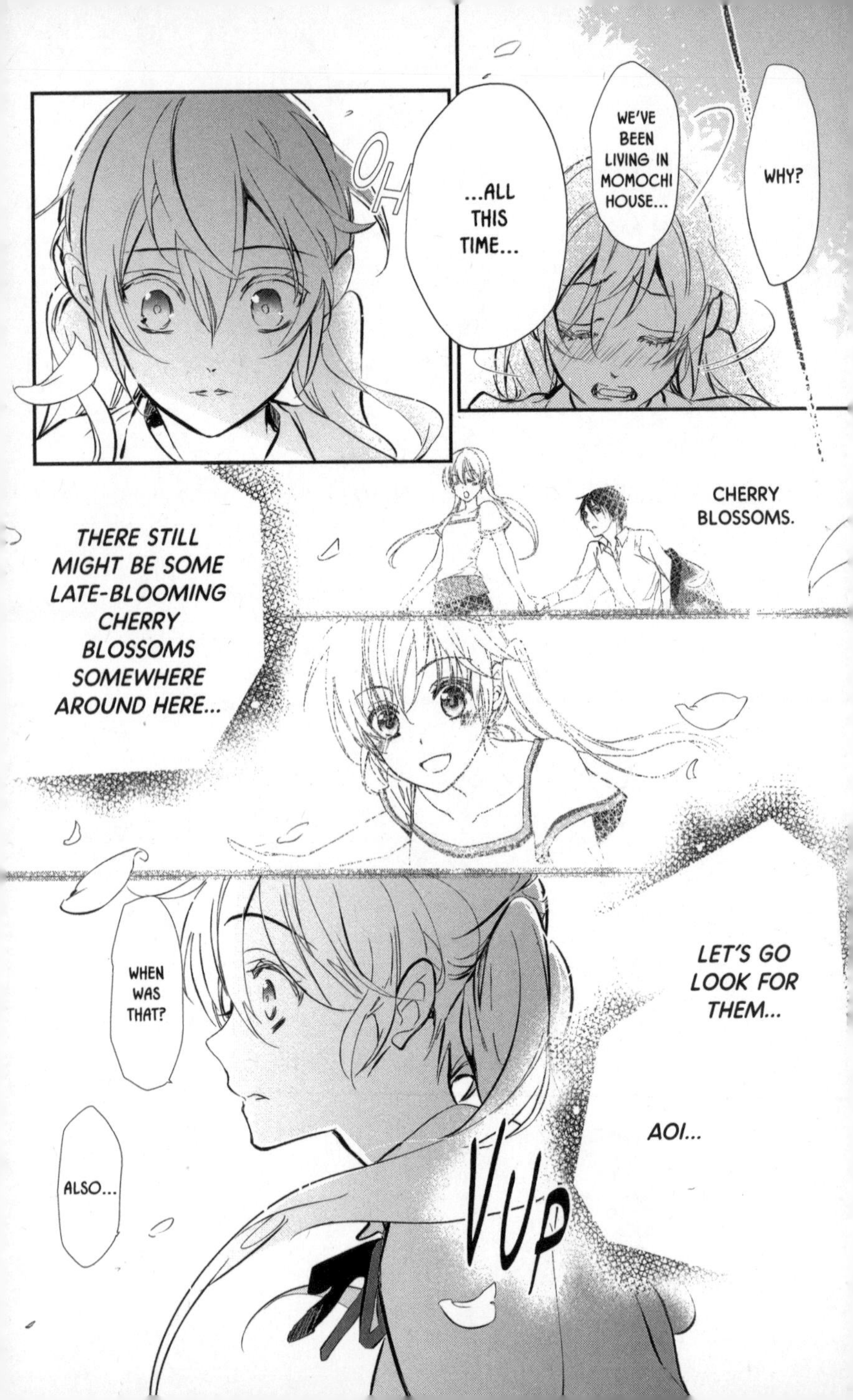
WHY?
WE'VE BEEN LIVING IN MOMOCHI HOUSE...
...ALL THIS TIME...
OH
CHERRY BLOSSOMS.
THERE STILL MIGHT BE SOME LATE-BLOOMING CHERRY BLOSSOMS SOMEWHERE AROUND HERE...
LET'S GO LOOK FOR THEM...
WHEN WAS THAT?
AOI...
ALSO...
VUP

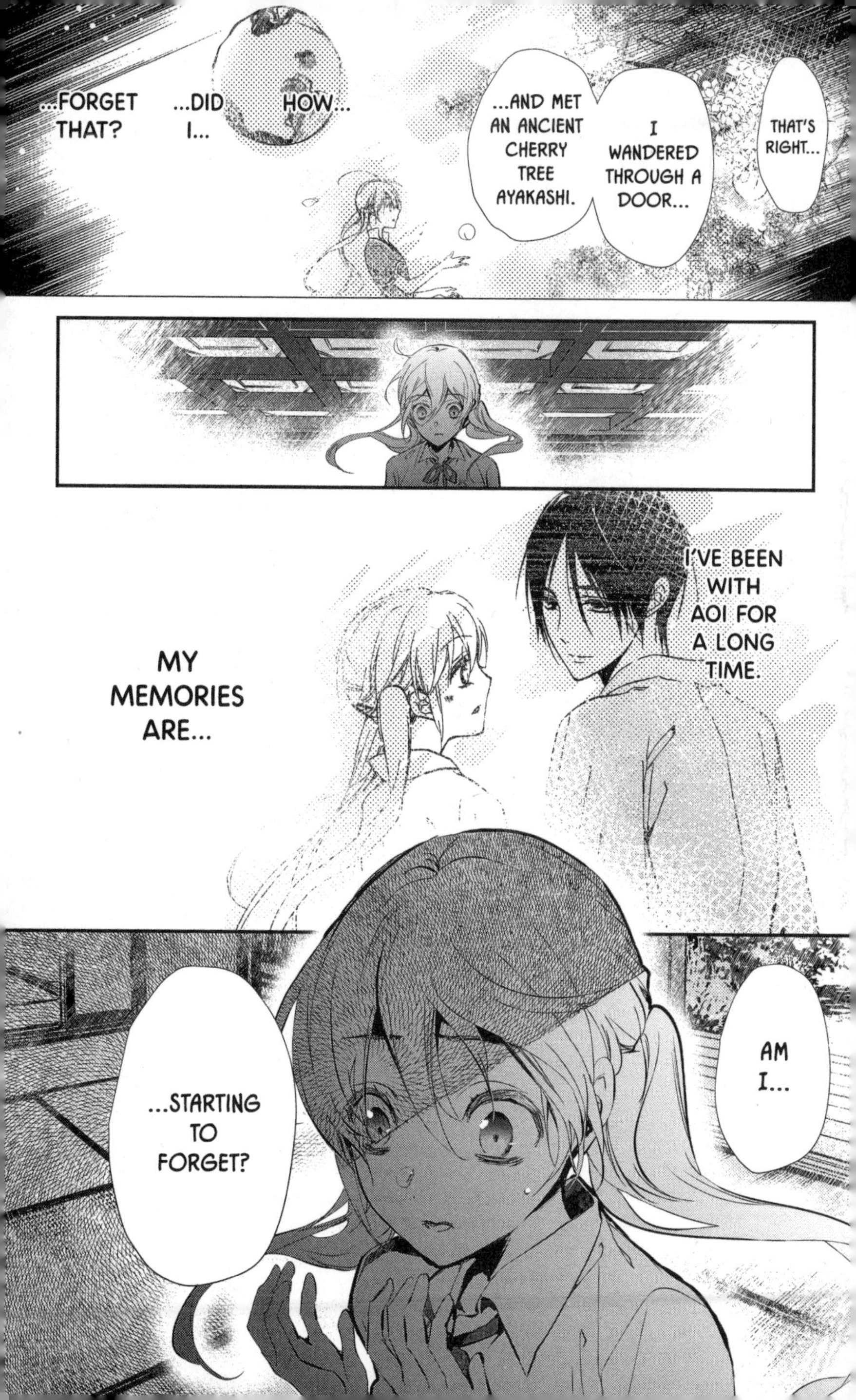
THAT'S RIGHT...
I WANDERED THROUGH A DOOR...
...AND MET AN ANCIENT CHERRY TREE AYAKASHI.
HOW...
...DID I...
...FORGET THAT?
I'VE BEEN WITH AOI FOR A LONG TIME.
MY MEMORIES ARE...
AM I...
...STARTING TO FORGET?

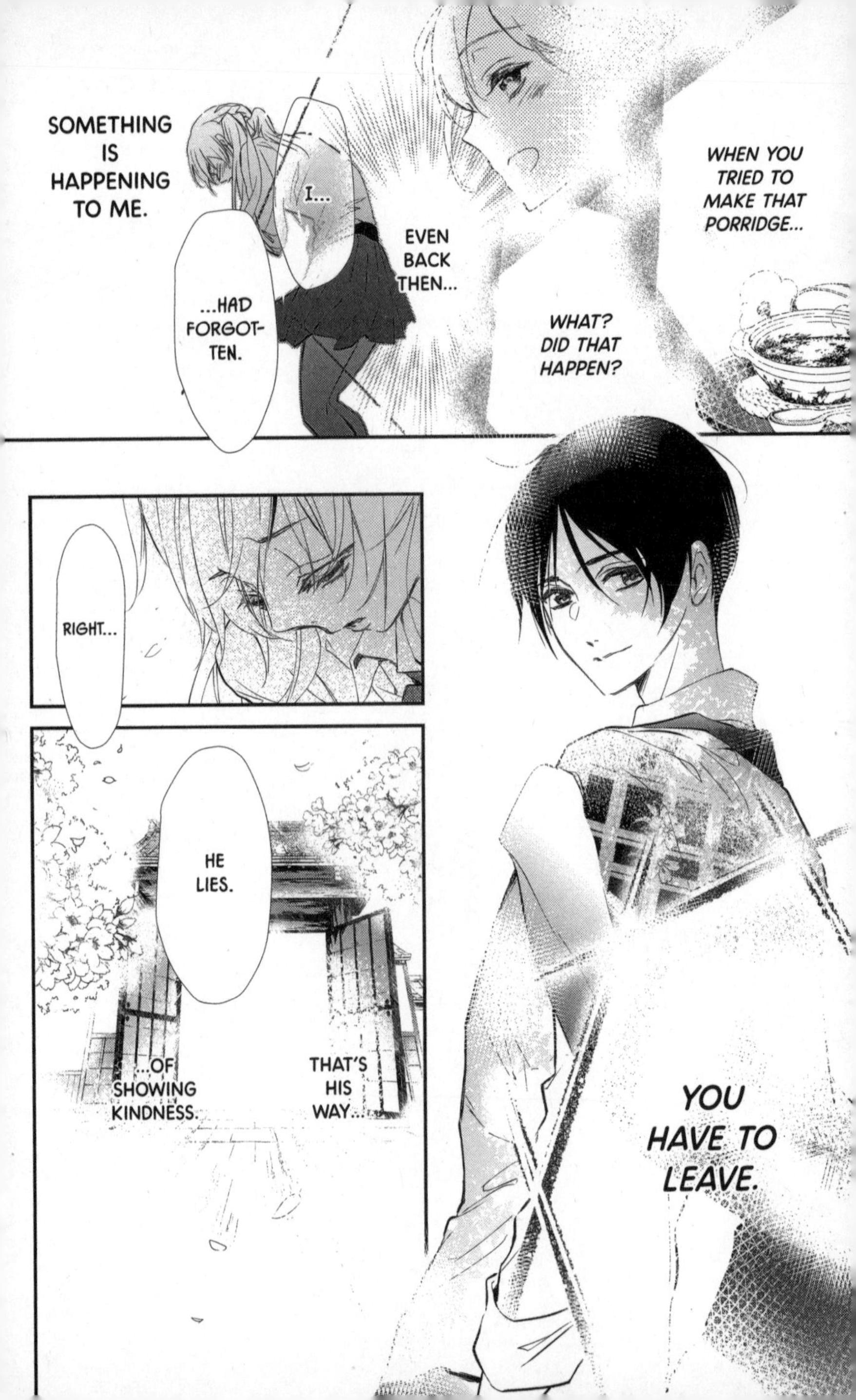
WHEN YOU TRIED TO MAKE THAT PORRIDGE...
WHAT? DID THAT HAPPEN?
EVEN BACK THEN...
I...
...HAD FORGOT-TEN.
SOMETHING IS HAPPENING TO ME.
YOU HAVE TO LEAVE.
RIGHT...
HE LIES.
THAT'S HIS WAY...
...OF SHOWING KINDNESS.

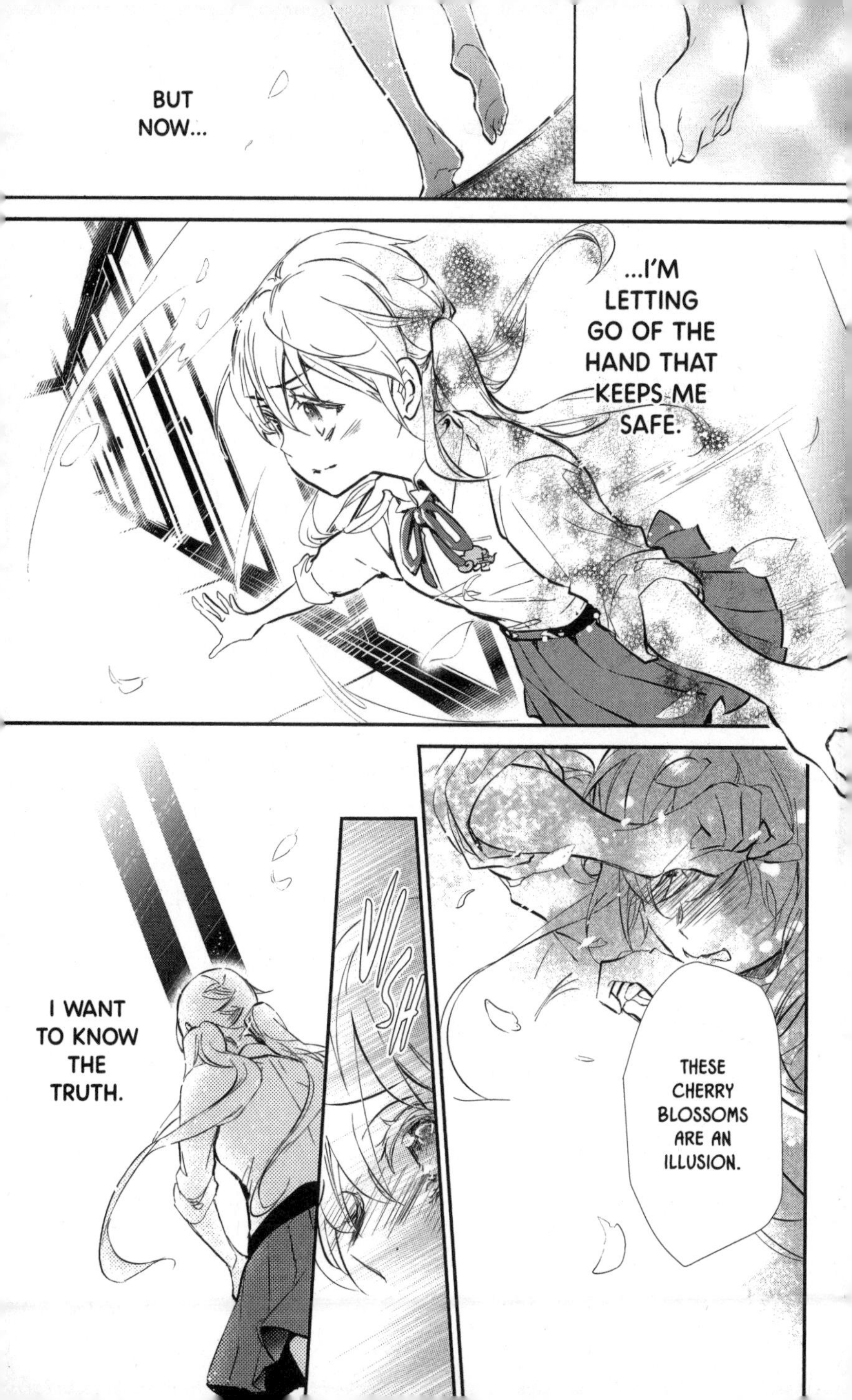
BUT NOW...
...I'M LETTING GO OF THE HAND THAT KEEPS ME SAFE.
THESE CHERRY BLOSSOMS ARE AN ILLUSION.
VISH
I WANT TO KNOW THE TRUTH.

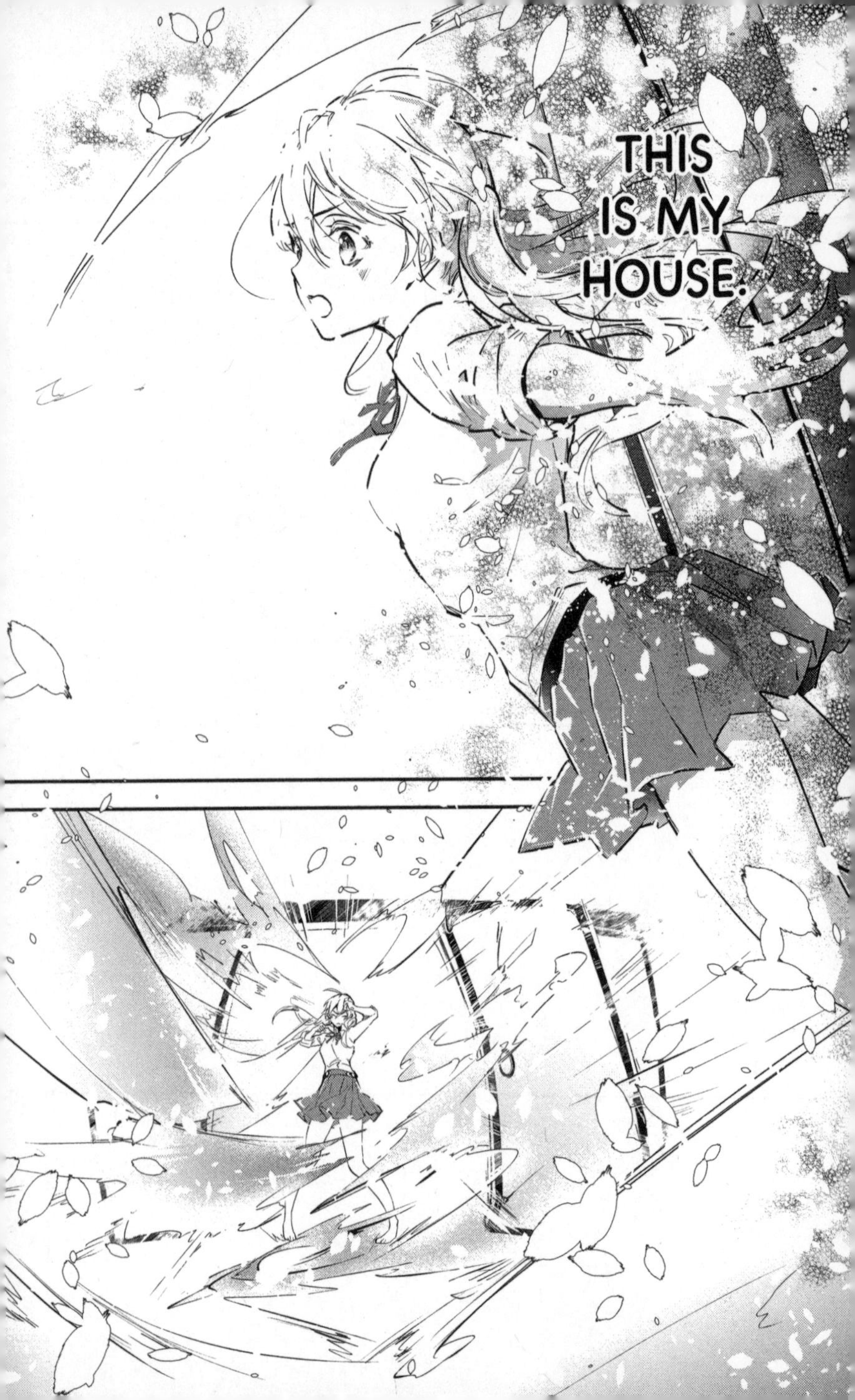
THIS IS MY HOUSE.

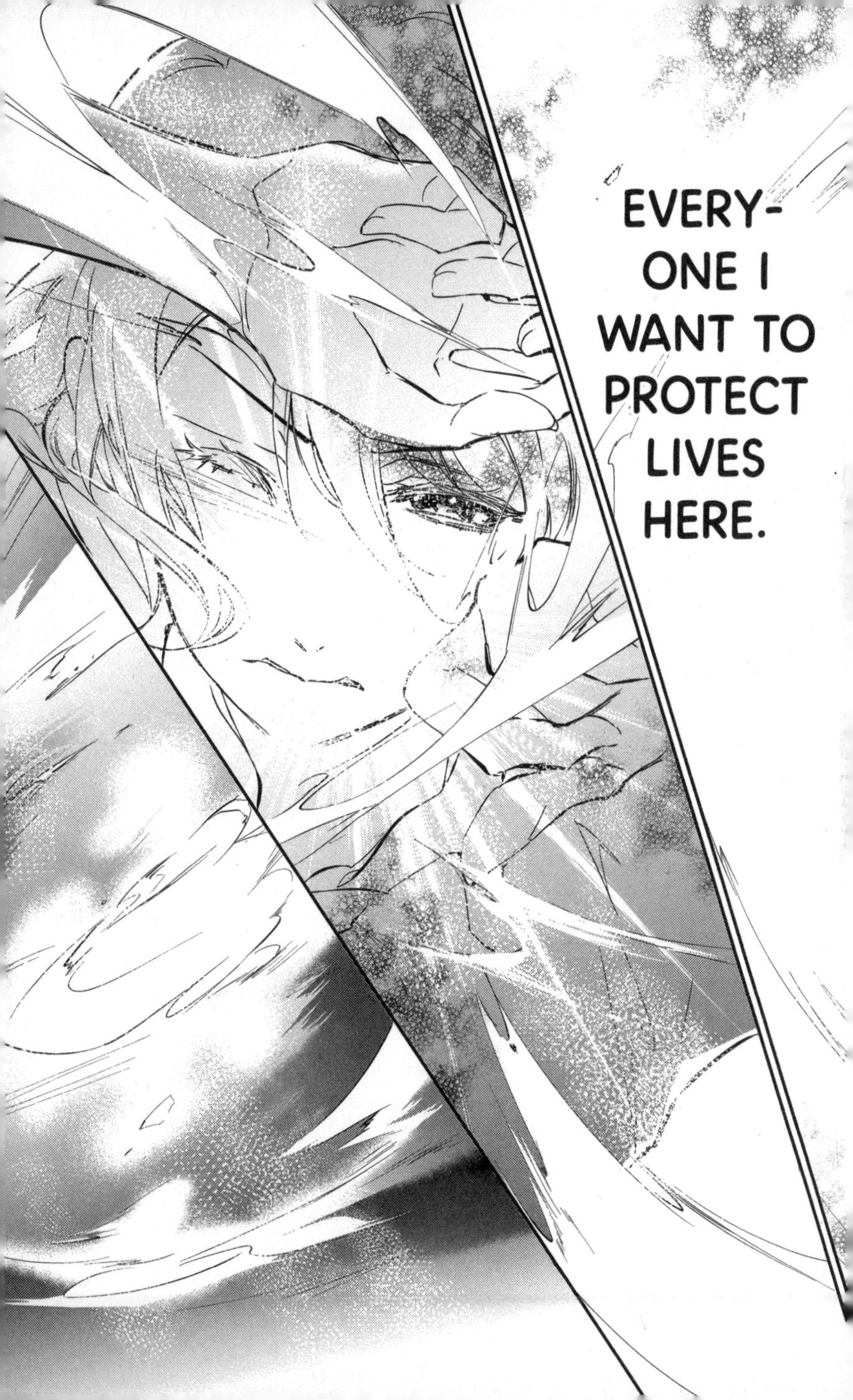
EVERY-ONE I WANT TO PROTECT LIVES HERE.

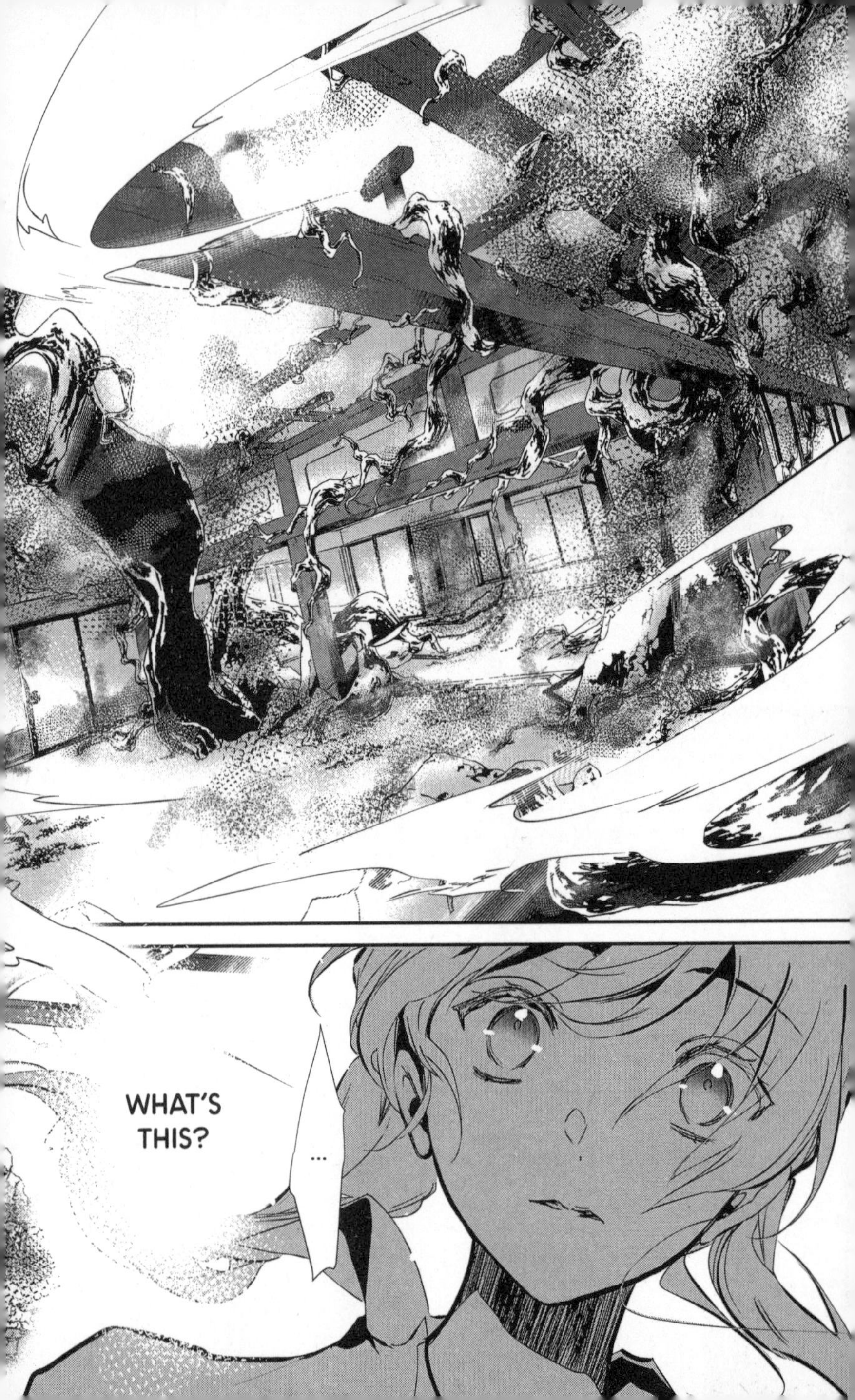
...
WHAT'S THIS?

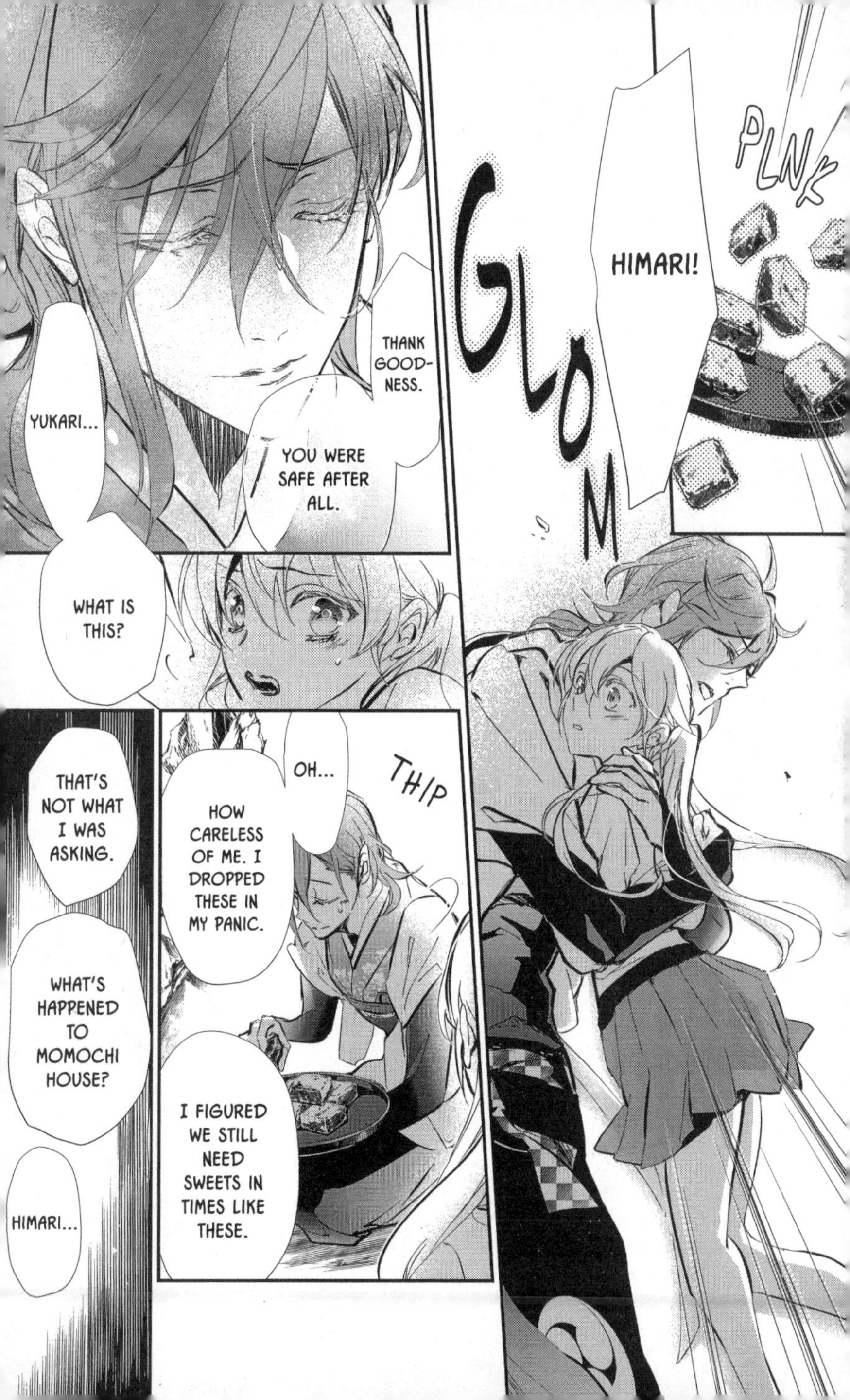
PLNK
HIMARI!
GLOMM
THANK GOODNESS.
YOU WERE SAFE AFTER ALL.
YUKARI...
WHAT IS THIS?
OH...
THIP
HOW CARELESS OF ME. I DROPPED THESE IN MY PANIC.
I FIGURED WE STILL NEED SWEETS IN TIMES LIKE THESE.
THAT'S NOT WHAT I WAS ASKING.
WHAT'S HAPPENED TO MOMOCHI HOUSE?
HIMARI...

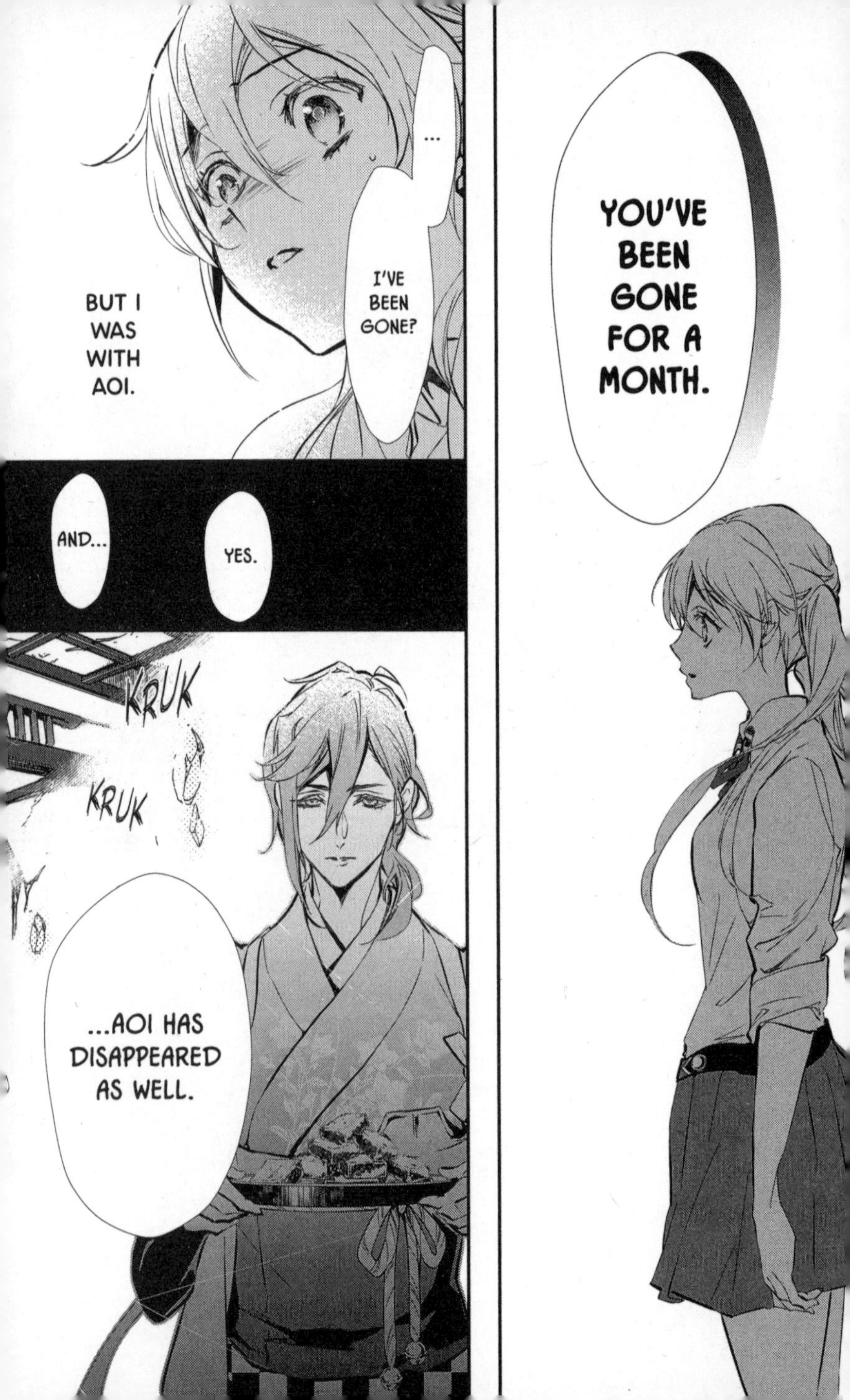
YOU'VE BEEN GONE FOR A MONTH.
...
I'VE BEEN GONE?
BUT I WAS WITH AOI.
YES.
AND...
KRUK
KRUK
...AOI HAS DISAPPEARED AS WELL.

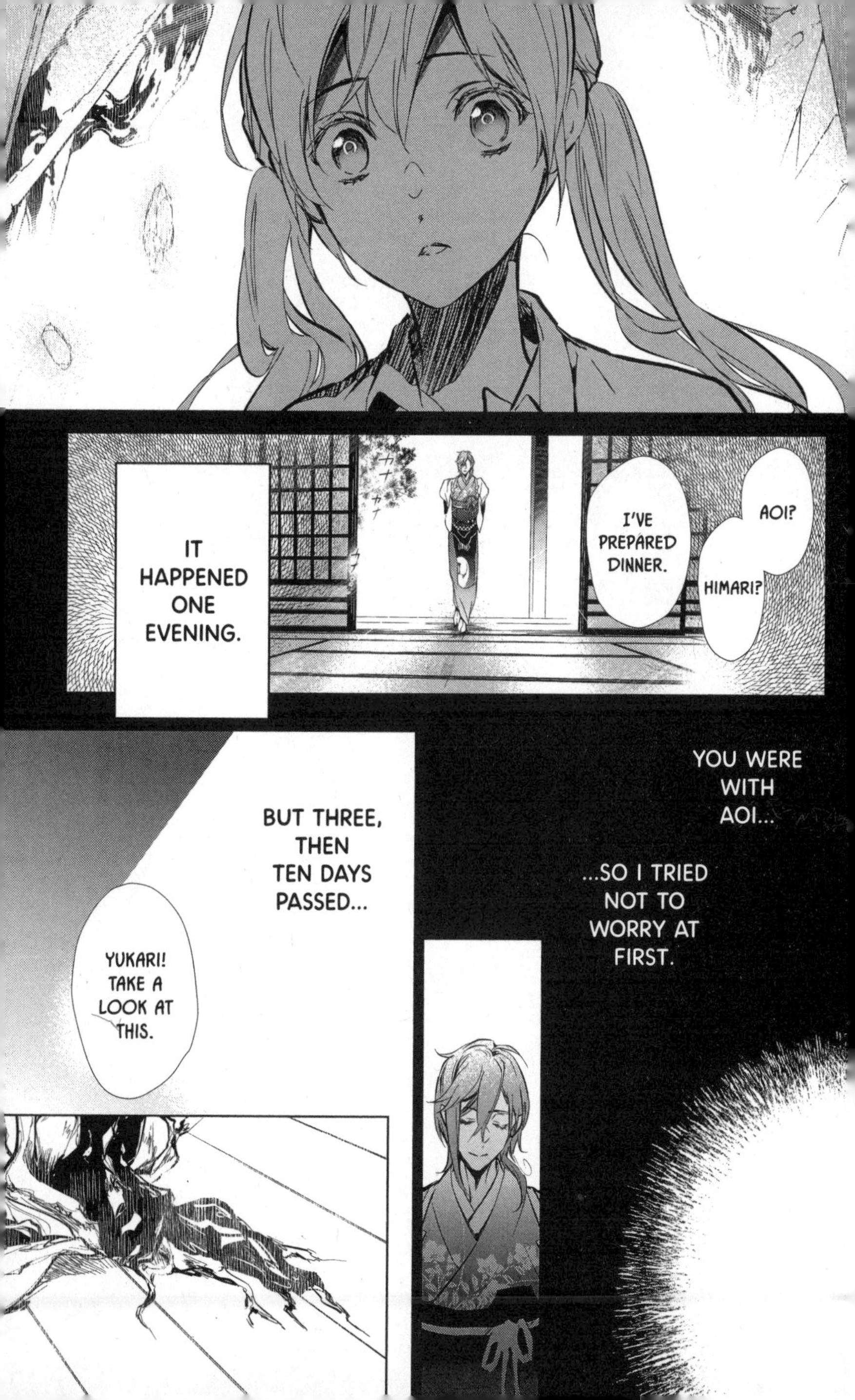
AOI?
HIMARI?
I'VE PREPARED DINNER.
IT HAPPENED ONE EVENING.
YOU WERE WITH AOI...
...SO I TRIED NOT TO WORRY AT FIRST.
BUT THREE, THEN TEN DAYS PASSED...
YUKARI! TAKE A LOOK AT THIS.

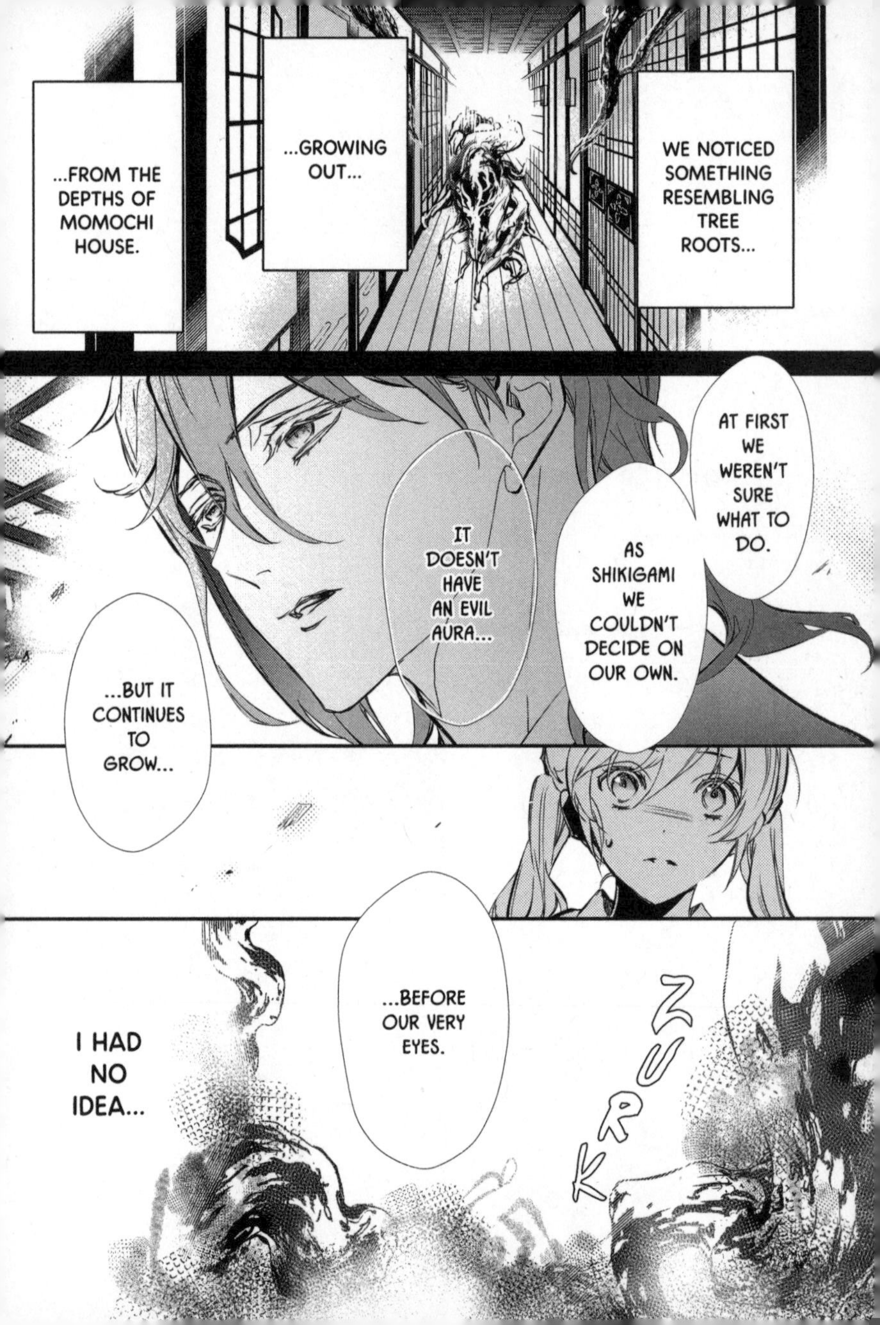
WE NOTICED SOMETHING RESEMBLING TREE ROOTS...
...GROWING OUT...
...FROM THE DEPTHS OF MOMOCHI HOUSE.
AT FIRST WE WEREN'T SURE WHAT TO DO.
AS SHIKIGAMI WE COULDN'T DECIDE ON OUR OWN.
IT DOESN'T HAVE AN EVIL AURA...
...BUT IT CONTINUES TO GROW...
ZURK
...BEFORE OUR VERY EYES.
I HAD NO IDEA...

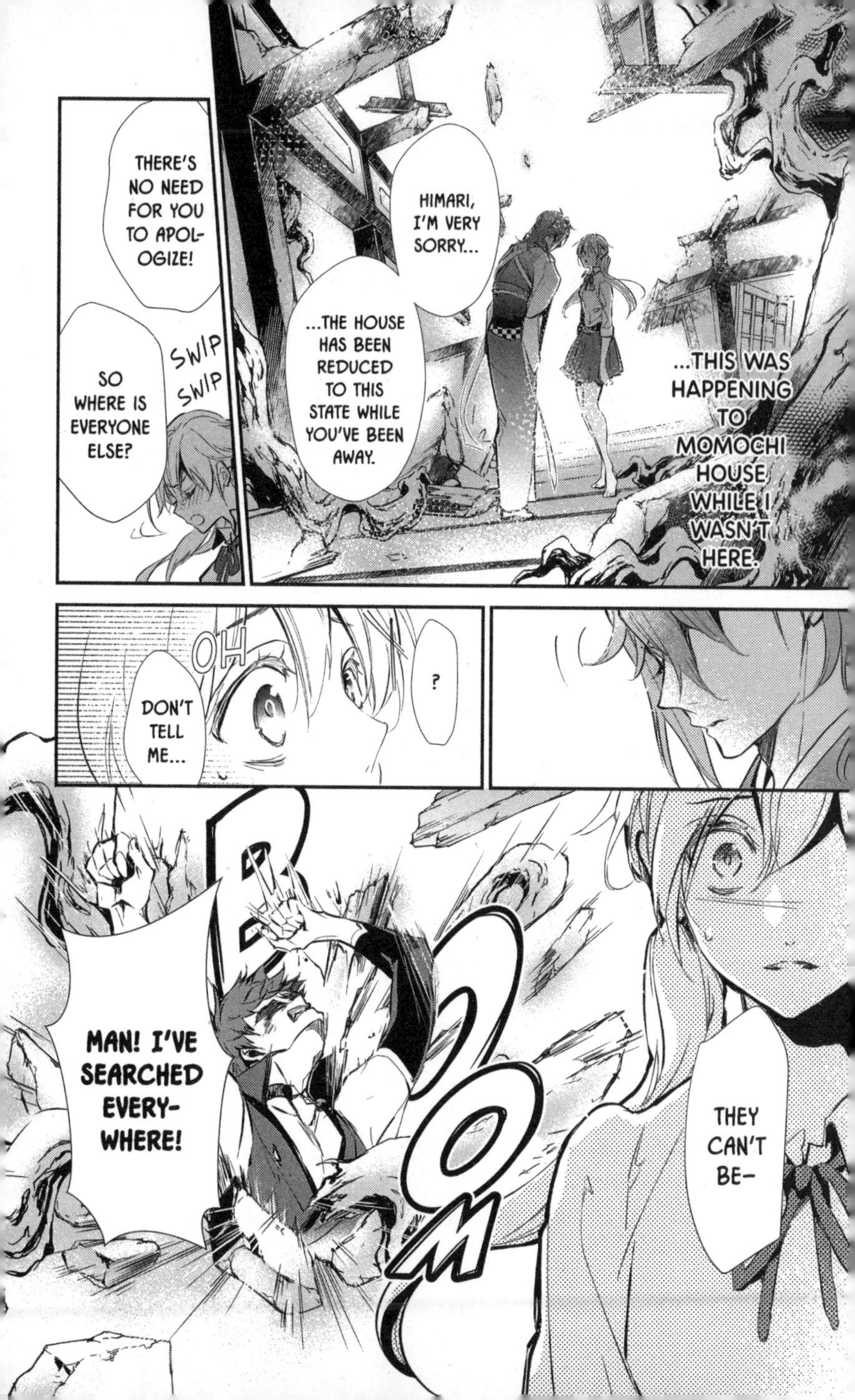
HIMARI, I'M VERY SORRY...
...THE HOUSE HAS BEEN REDUCED TO THIS STATE WHILE YOU'VE BEEN AWAY.
...THIS WAS HAPPENING TO MOMOCHI HOUSE WHILE I WASN'T HERE.
THERE'S NO NEED FOR YOU TO APOL-OGIZE!
SWIP SWIP
SO WHERE IS EVERYONE ELSE?
?
OH
DON'T TELL ME...
THEY CAN'T BE–
BOOM
MAN! I'VE SEARCHED EVERY-WHERE!

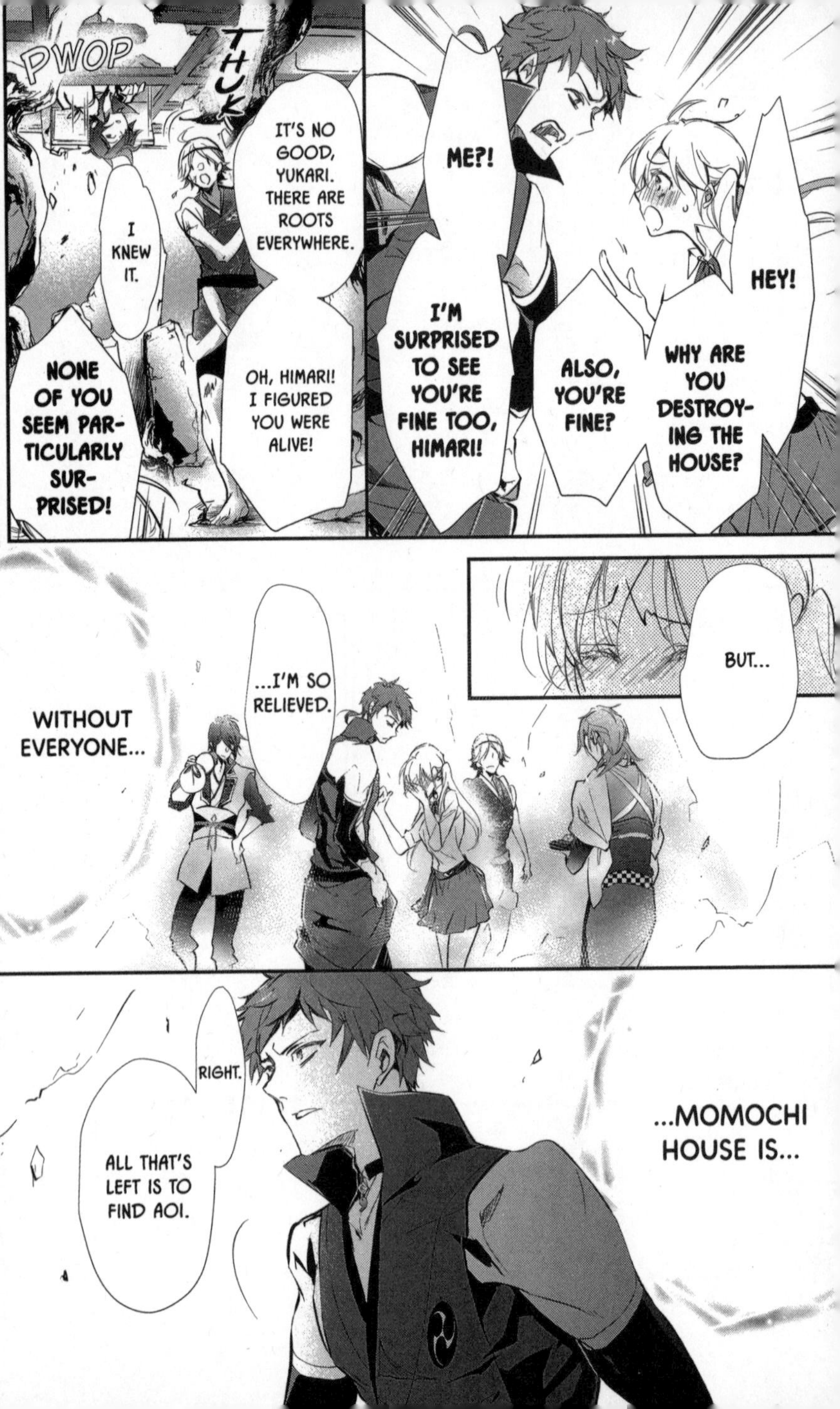
HEY!
WHY ARE YOU DESTROYING THE HOUSE?
ME?!
ALSO, YOU'RE FINE?
I'M SURPRISED TO SEE YOU'RE FINE TOO, HIMARI!
PWOP
THUK
IT'S NO GOOD, YUKARI. THERE ARE ROOTS EVERYWHERE.
I KNEW IT.
OH, HIMARI! I FIGURED YOU WERE ALIVE!
NONE OF YOU SEEM PARTICULARLY SURPRISED!
BUT...
...I'M SO RELIEVED.
WITHOUT EVERYONE...
...MOMOCHI HOUSE IS...
RIGHT.
ALL THAT'S LEFT IS TO FIND AOI.

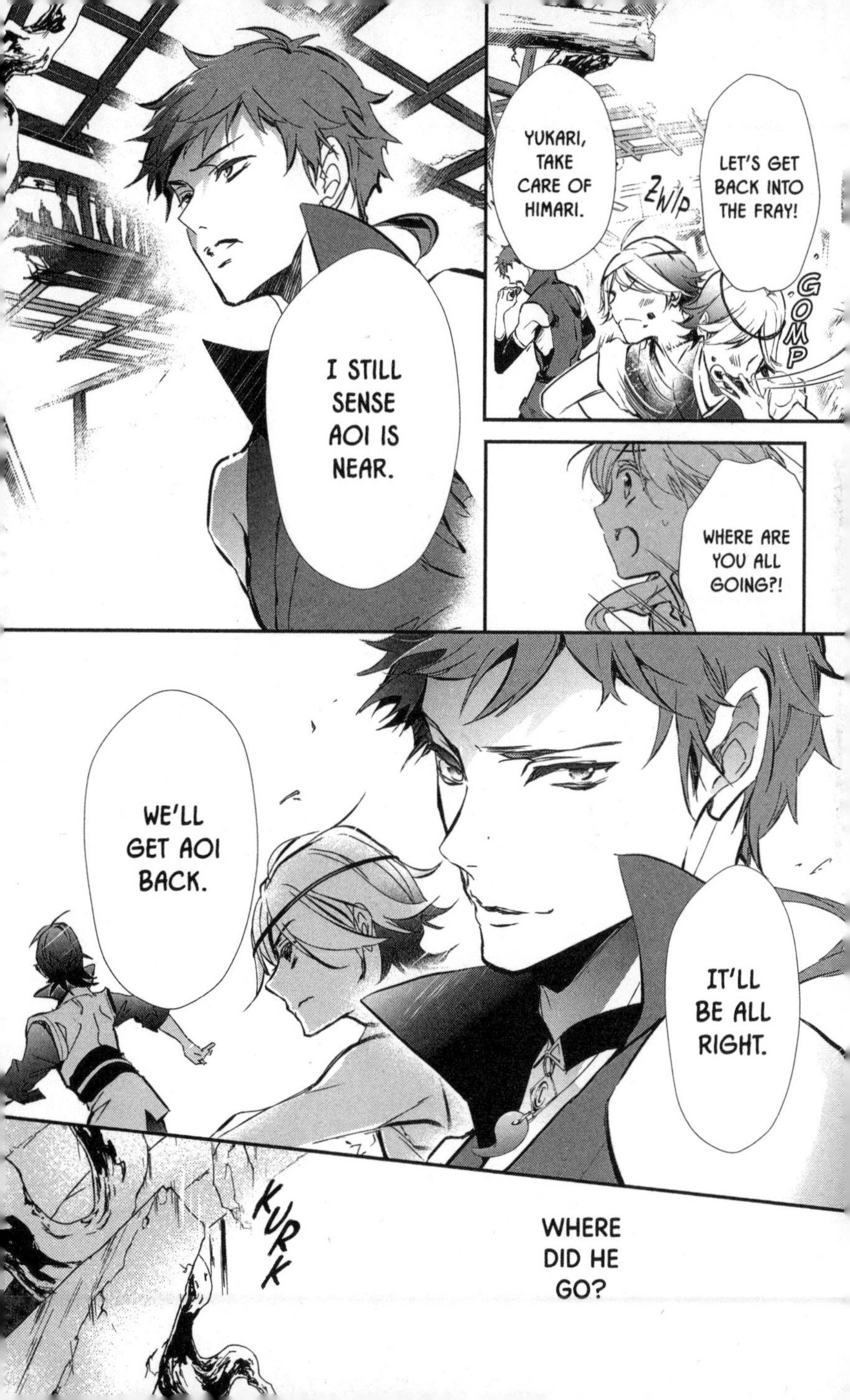
LET'S GET BACK INTO THE FRAY!
YUKARI, TAKE CARE OF HIMARI.
ZWIP
GOMP
WHERE ARE YOU ALL GOING?!
I STILL SENSE AOI IS NEAR.
IT'LL BE ALL RIGHT.
WE'LL GET AOI BACK.
WHERE DID HE GO?
KURK

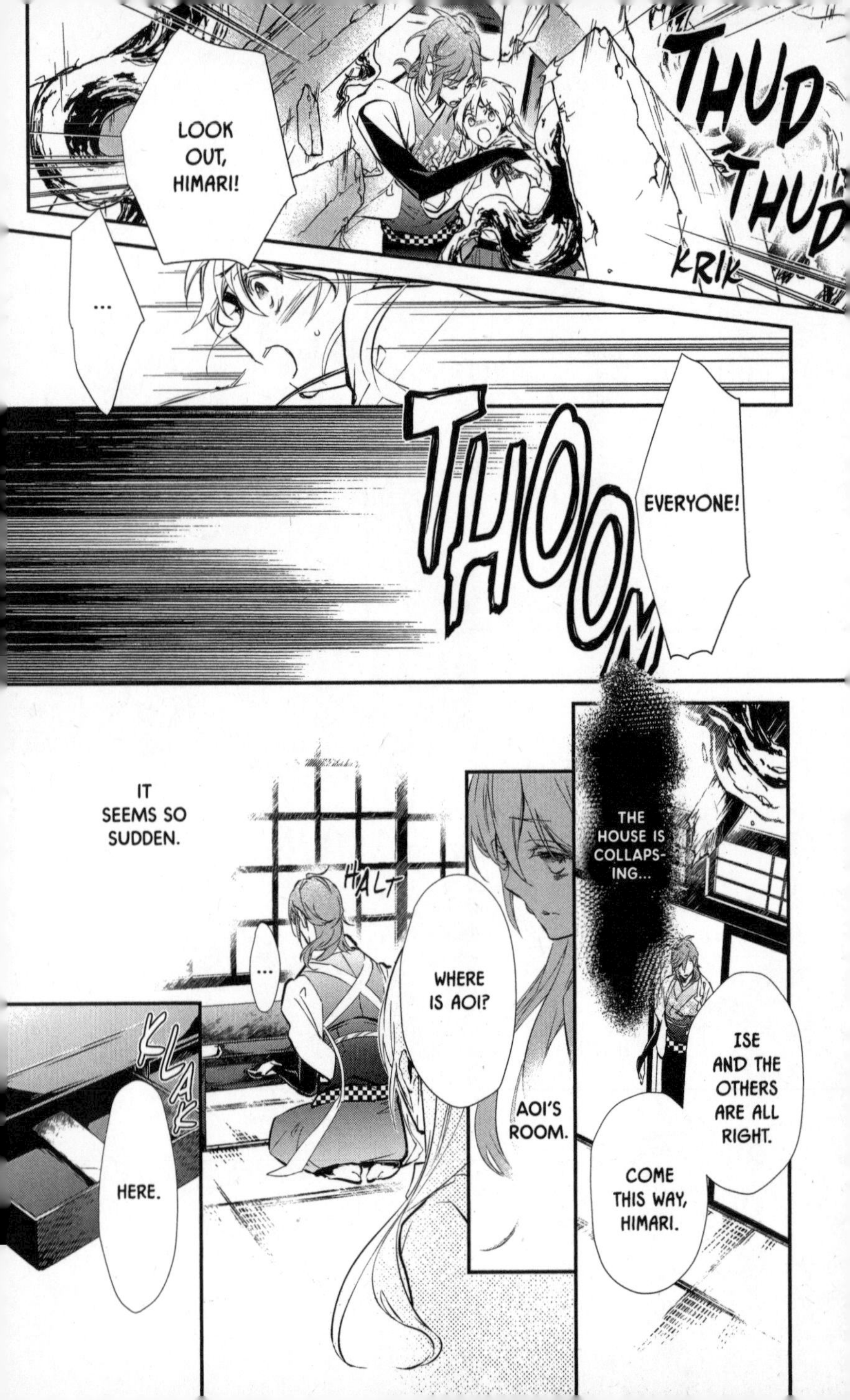
THUD
THUD
LOOK OUT, HIMARI!
KRIK
...
EVERYONE!
THOOM
THE HOUSE IS COLLAPSING...
ISE AND THE OTHERS ARE ALL RIGHT.
COME THIS WAY, HIMARI.
WHERE IS AOI?
AOI'S ROOM.
IT SEEMS SO SUDDEN.
HALT
...
KLAK
HERE.

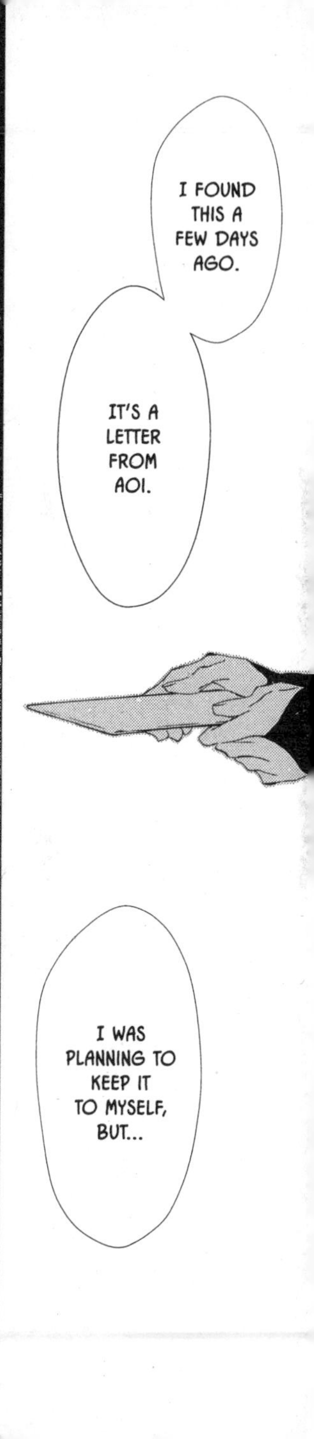
I FOUND THIS A FEW DAYS AGO.
IT'S A LETTER FROM AOI.
I WAS PLANNING TO KEEP IT TO MYSELF, BUT...

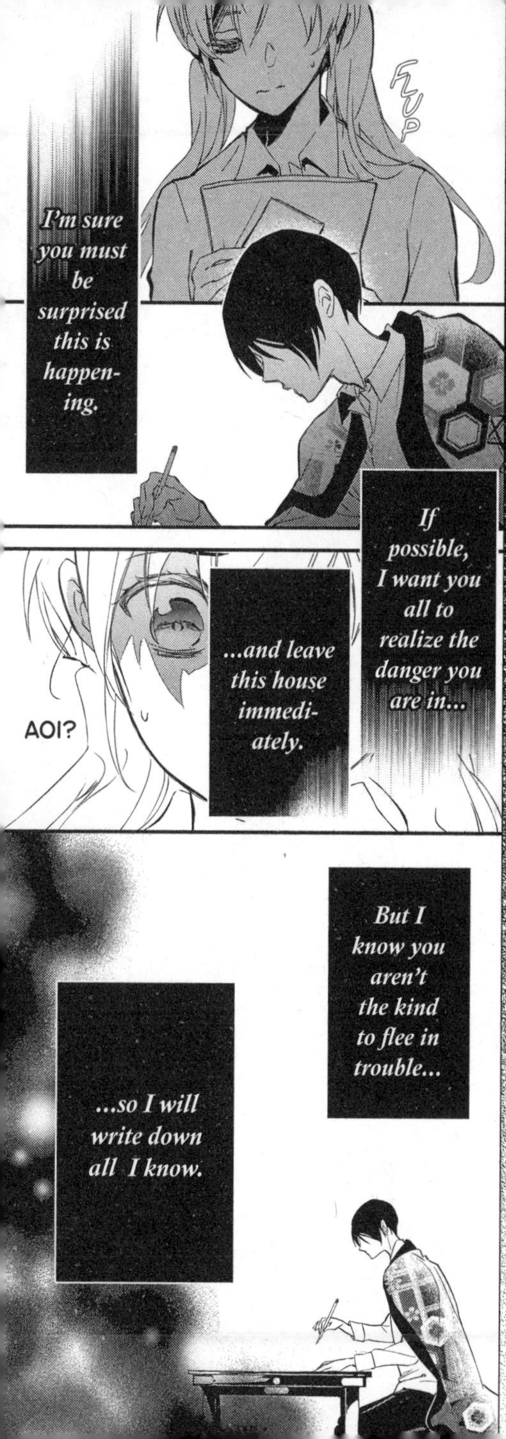
FLUP
I'm sure you must be surprised this is happen-ing.
If possible, I want you all to realize the danger you are in...
...and leave this house immedi-ately.
AOI?
But I know you aren't the kind to flee in trouble...
...so I will write down all I know.

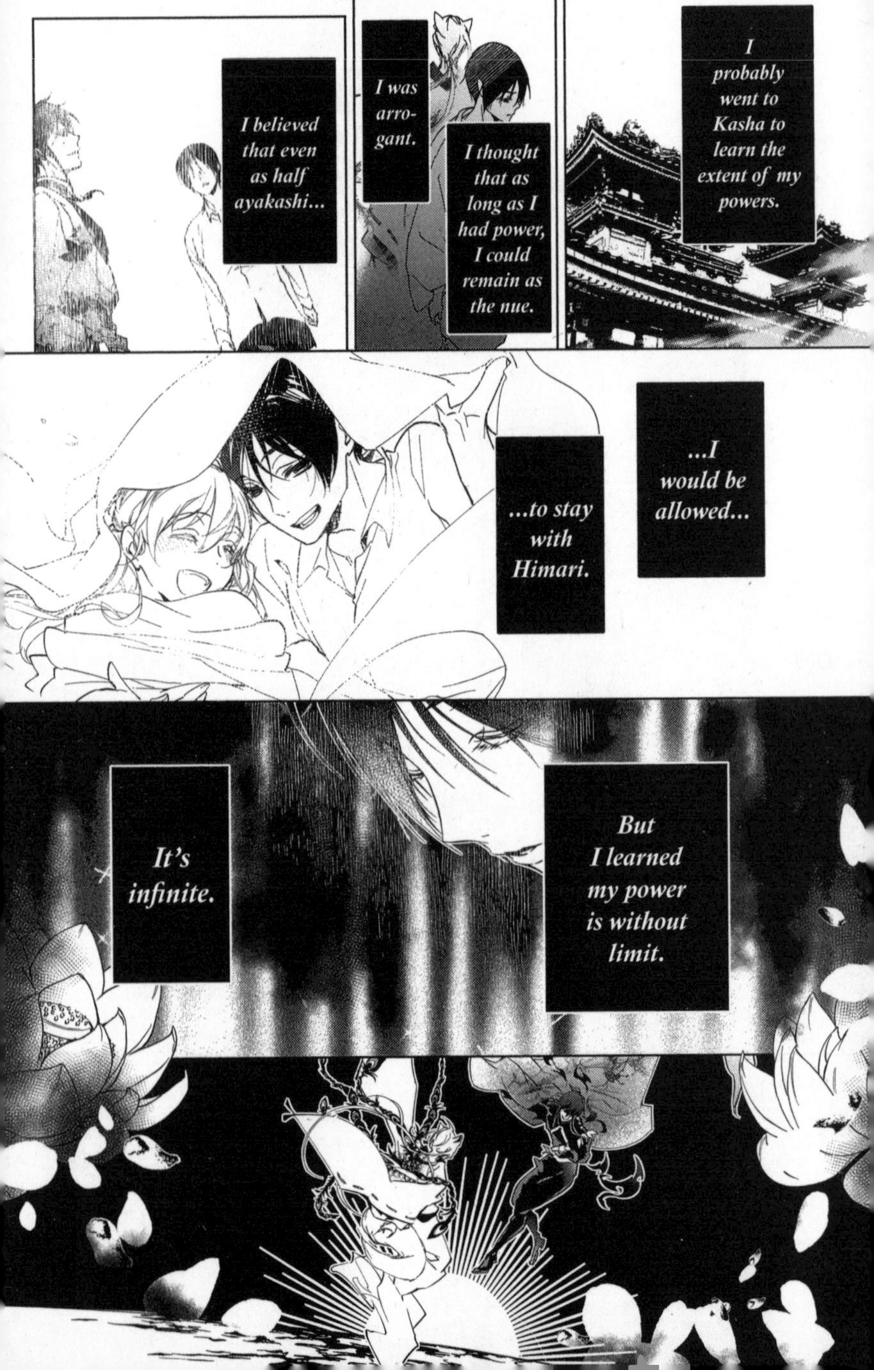
I probably went to Kasha to learn the extent of my powers.
I was arro-gant.
I thought that as long as I had power, I could remain as the nue.
I believed that even as half ayakashi...
...I would be allowed...
...to stay with Himari.
But I learned my power is without limit.
It's infinite.

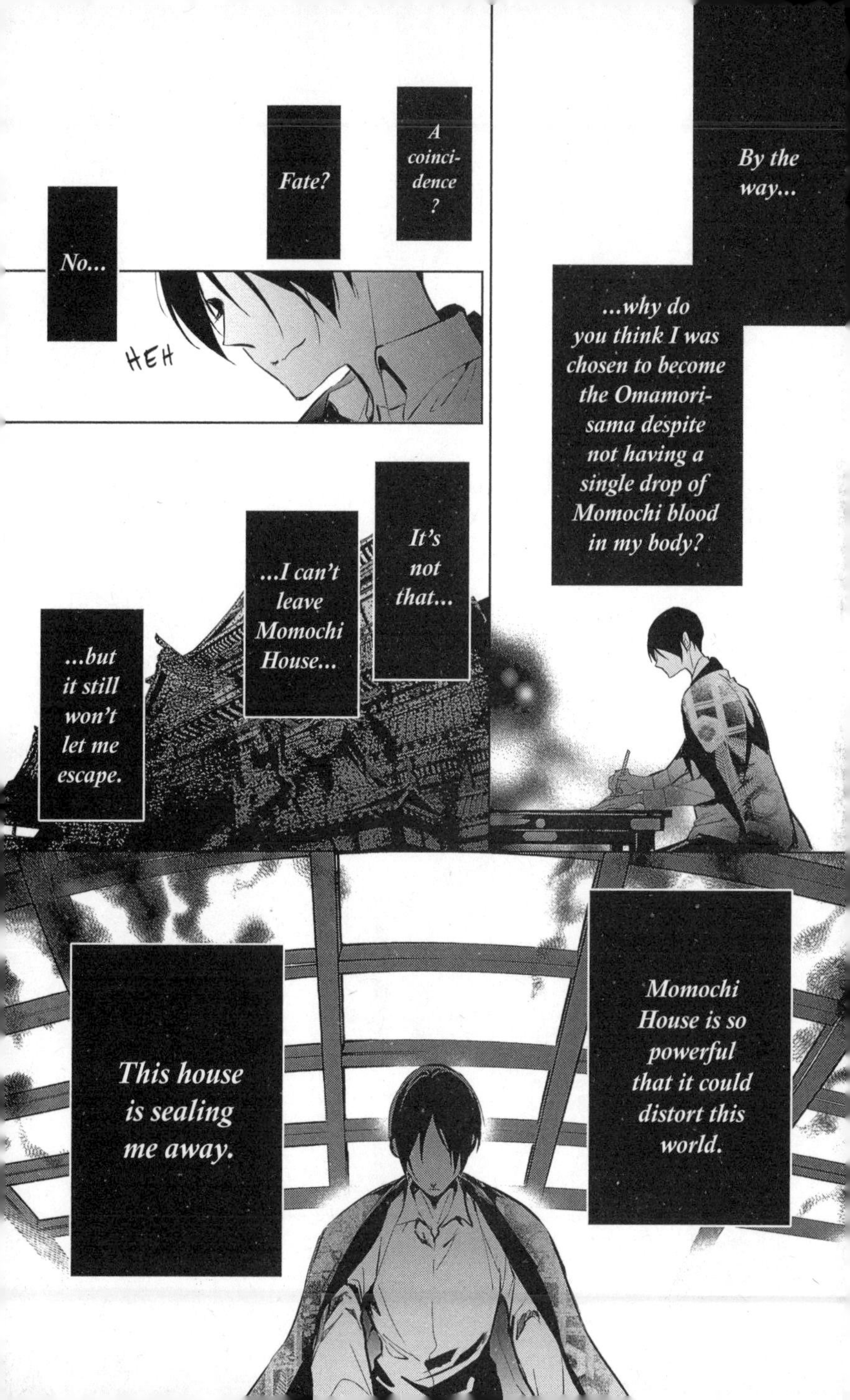
By the way...
...why do you think I was chosen to become the Omamori-sama despite not having a single drop of Momochi blood in my body?
A coinci-dence?
Fate?
No...
HEH
It's not that...
...I can't leave Momochi House...
...but it still won't let me escape.
Momochi House is so powerful that it could distort this world.
This house is sealing me away.

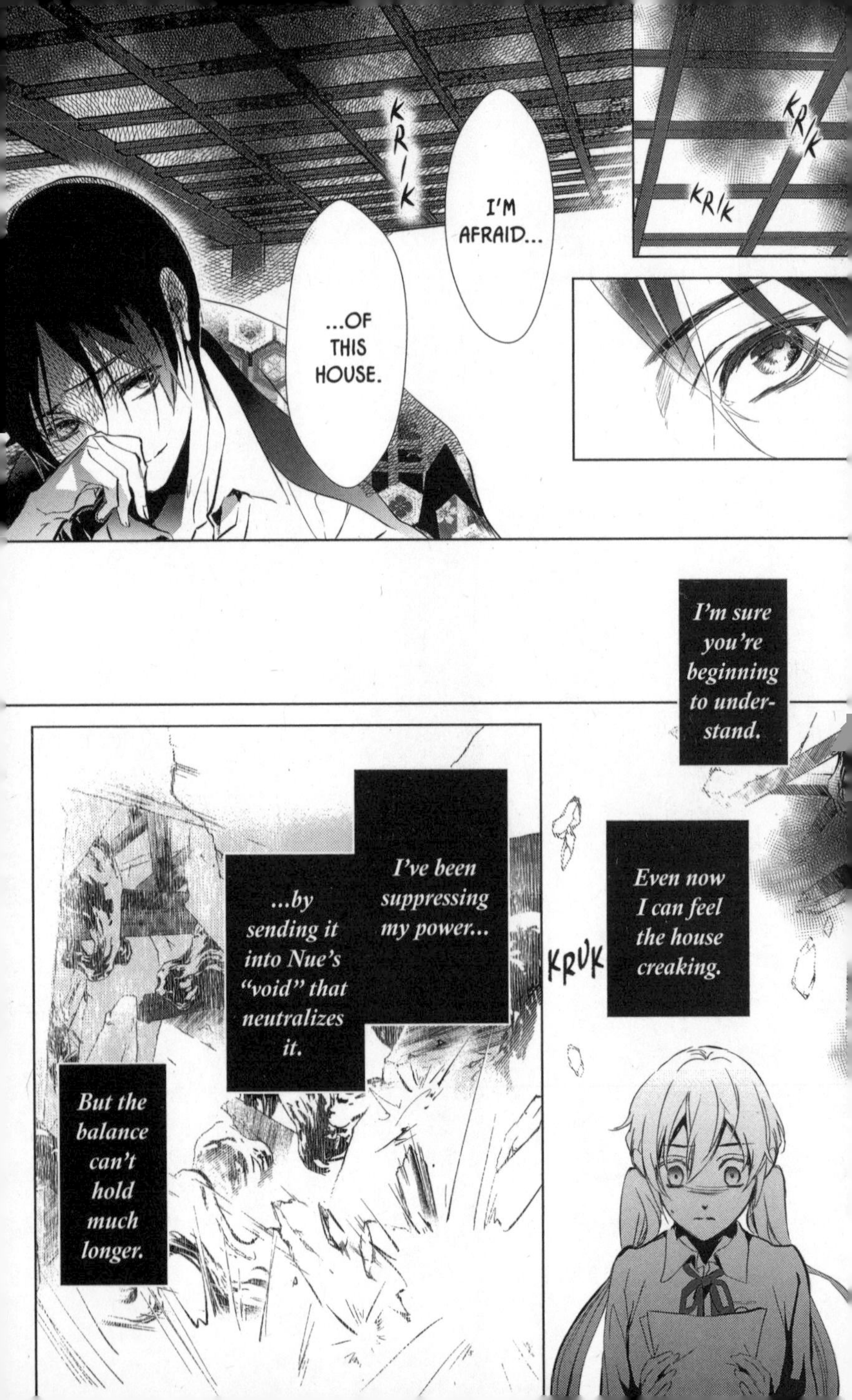
KRIK
KRIK
KRIK
I'M AFRAID...
...OF THIS HOUSE.
I'm sure you're beginning to under- stand.
Even now I can feel the house creaking.
KRUK
I've been suppressing my power...
...by sending it into Nue's "void" that neutralizes it.
But the balance can't hold much longer.

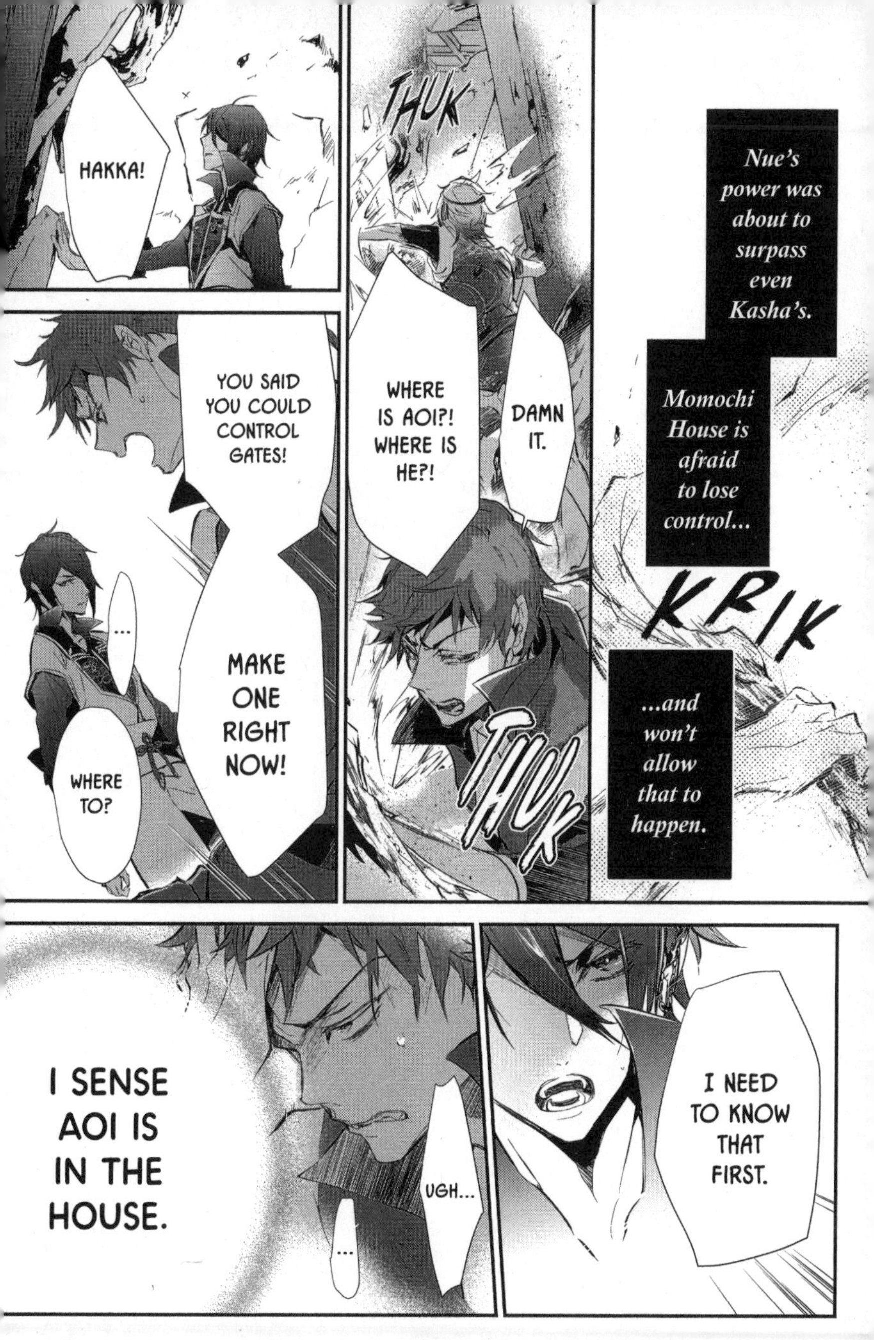
Nue's power was about to surpass even Kasha's.
Momochi House is afraid to lose control...
KRIK
...and won't allow that to happen.
THUK
DAMN IT.
WHERE IS AOI?! WHERE IS HE?!
THUK
HAKKA!
YOU SAID YOU COULD CONTROL GATES!
MAKE ONE RIGHT NOW!
...
WHERE TO?
I NEED TO KNOW THAT FIRST.
UGH...
...
I SENSE AOI IS IN THE HOUSE.

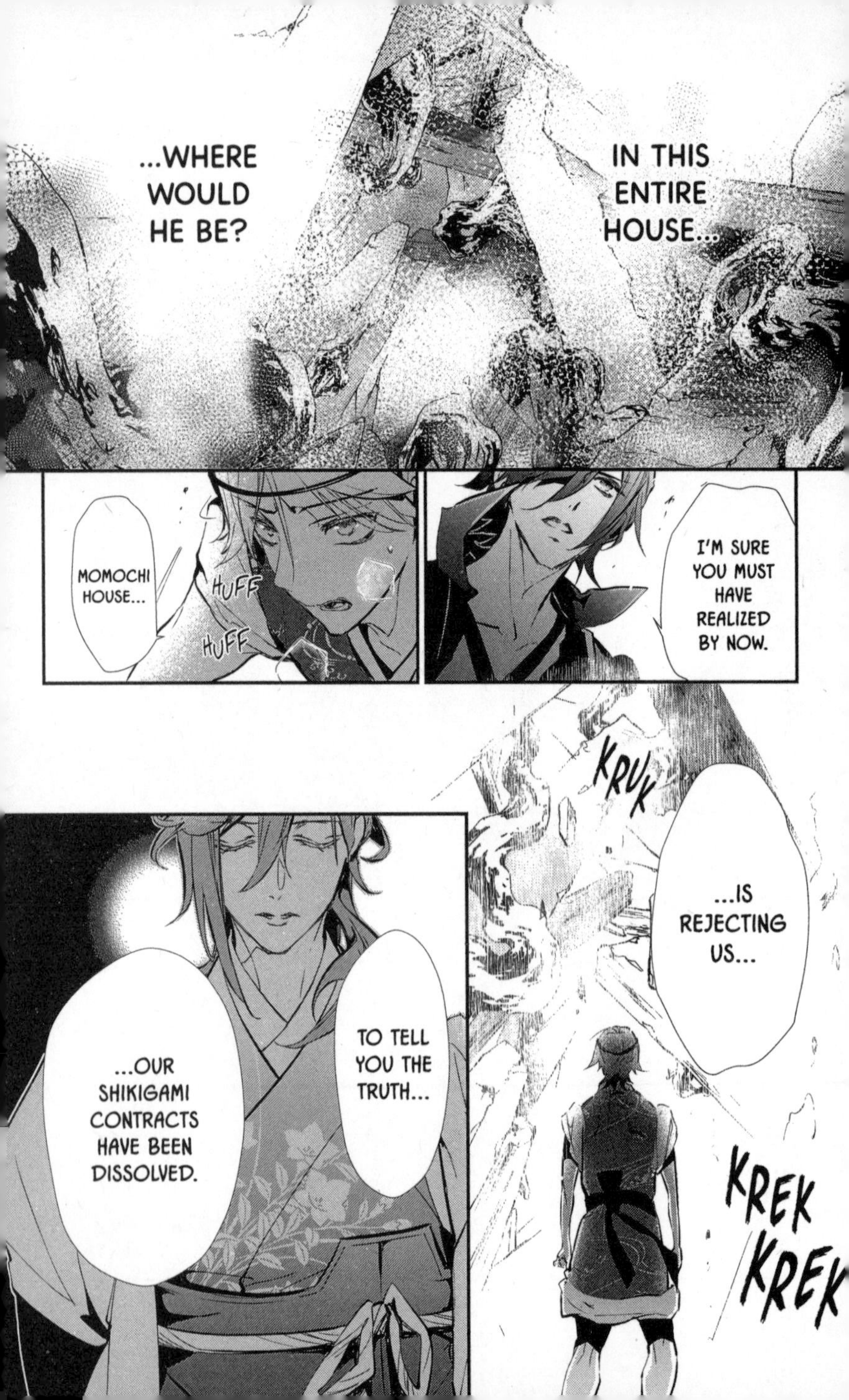
IN THIS ENTIRE HOUSE...
...WHERE WOULD HE BE?
I'M SURE YOU MUST HAVE REALIZED BY NOW.
MOMOCHI HOUSE...
HUFF
HUFF
KRUK
...IS REJECTING US...
KREK
KREK
TO TELL YOU THE TRUTH...
...OUR SHIKIGAMI CONTRACTS HAVE BEEN DISSOLVED.

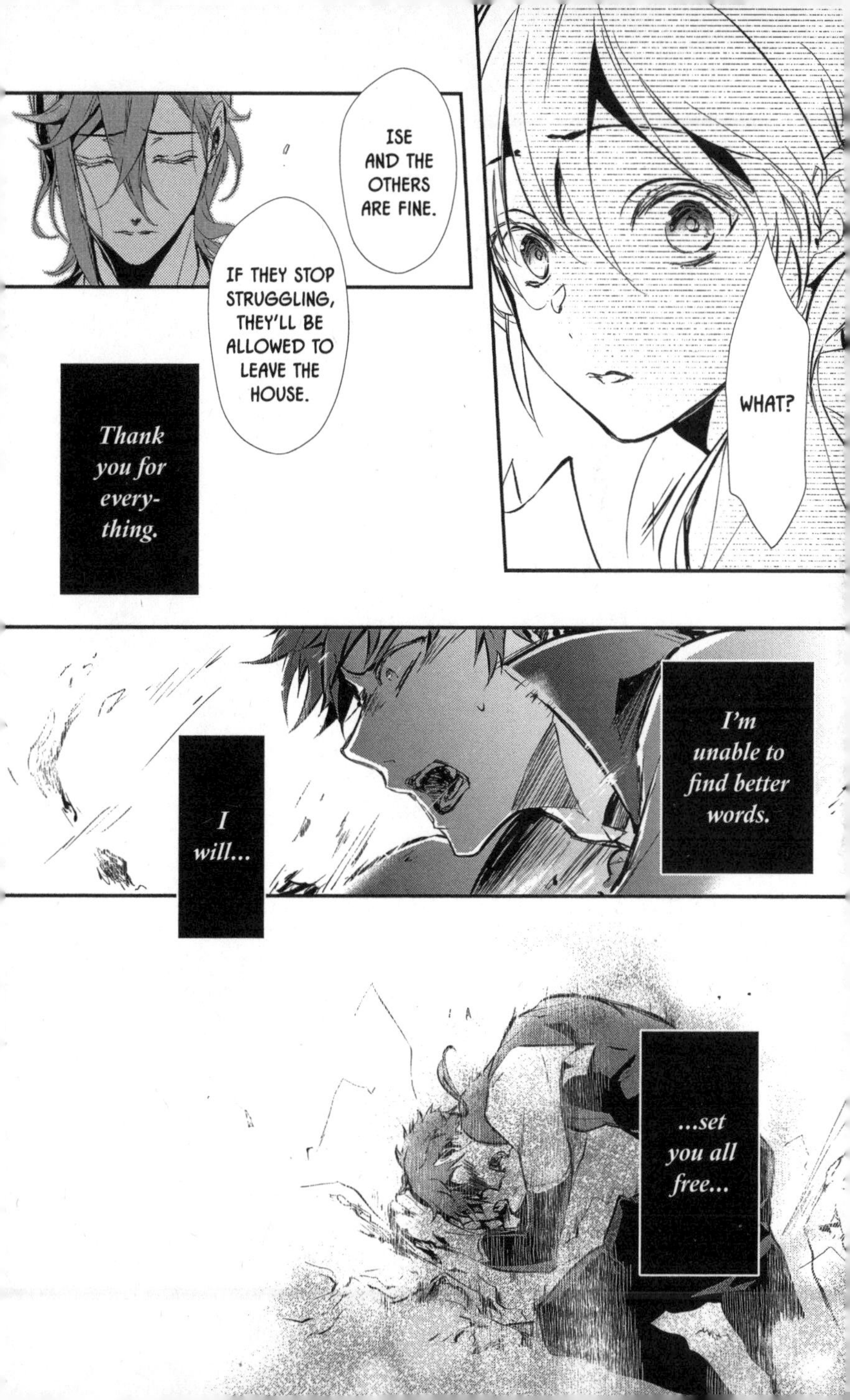
WHAT?
ISE AND THE OTHERS ARE FINE.
IF THEY STOP STRUGGLING, THEY'LL BE ALLOWED TO LEAVE THE HOUSE.
Thank you for every-thing.
I'm unable to find better words.
I will...
...set you all free...

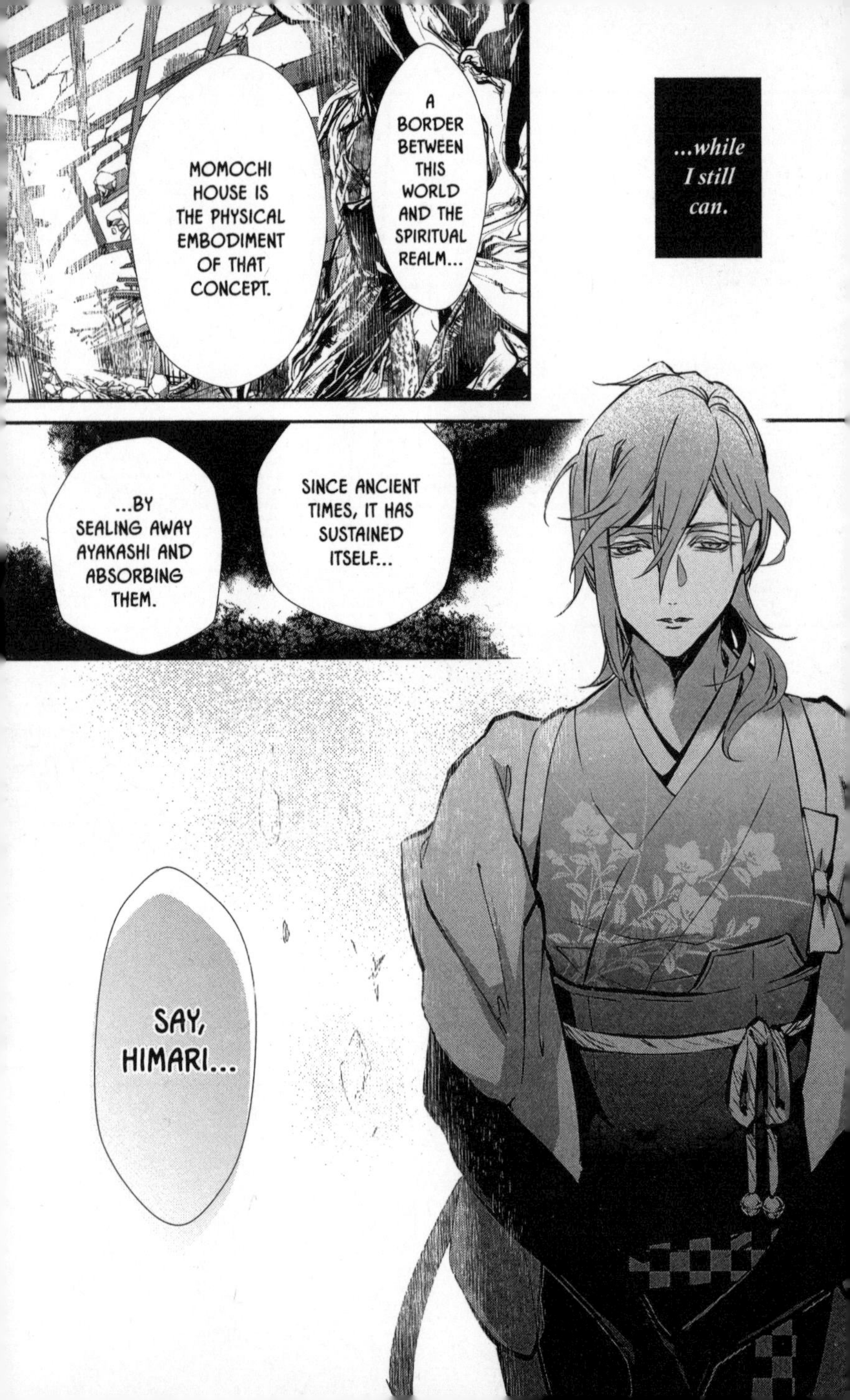
...while I still can.
A BORDER BETWEEN THIS WORLD AND THE SPIRITUAL REALM...
MOMOCHI HOUSE IS THE PHYSICAL EMBODIMENT OF THAT CONCEPT.
SINCE ANCIENT TIMES, IT HAS SUSTAINED ITSELF...
...BY SEALING AWAY AYAKASHI AND ABSORBING THEM.
SAY, HIMARI...

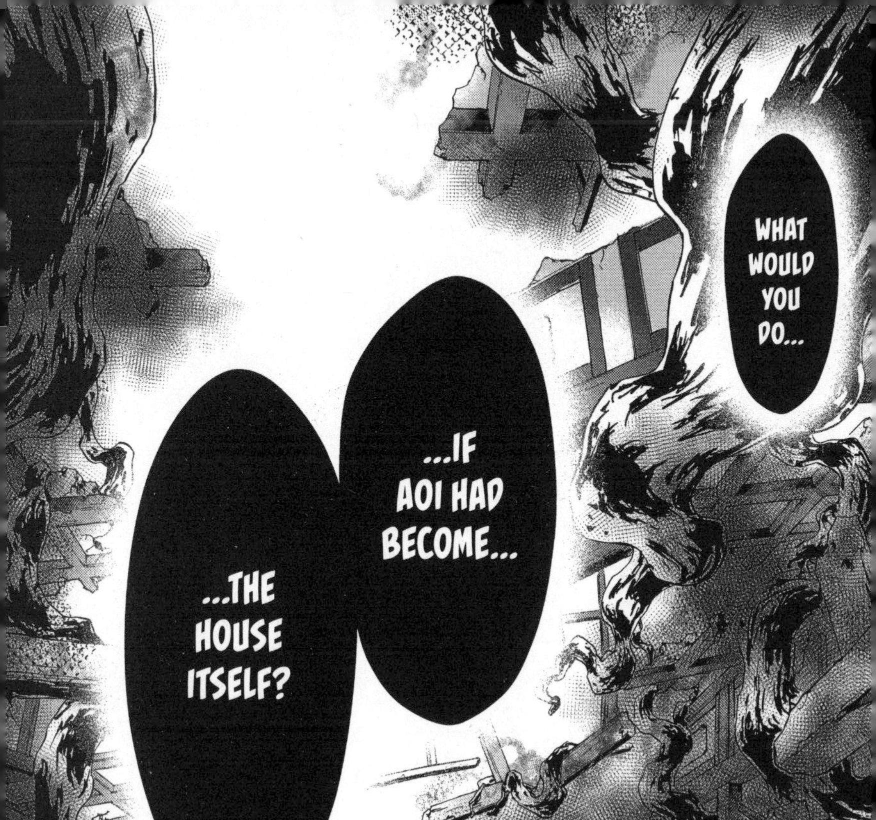
WHAT WOULD YOU DO...
...IF AOI HAD BECOME...
...THE HOUSE ITSELF?
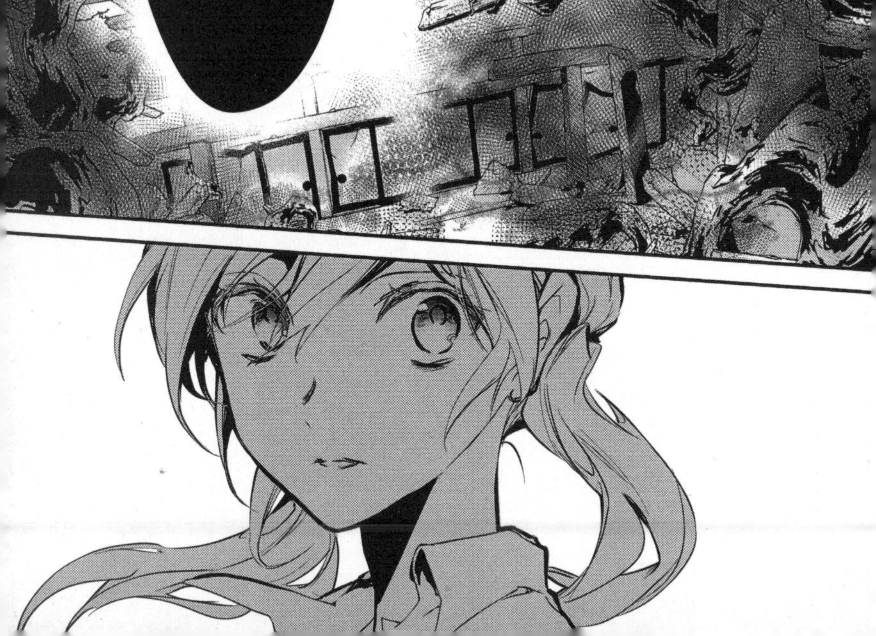

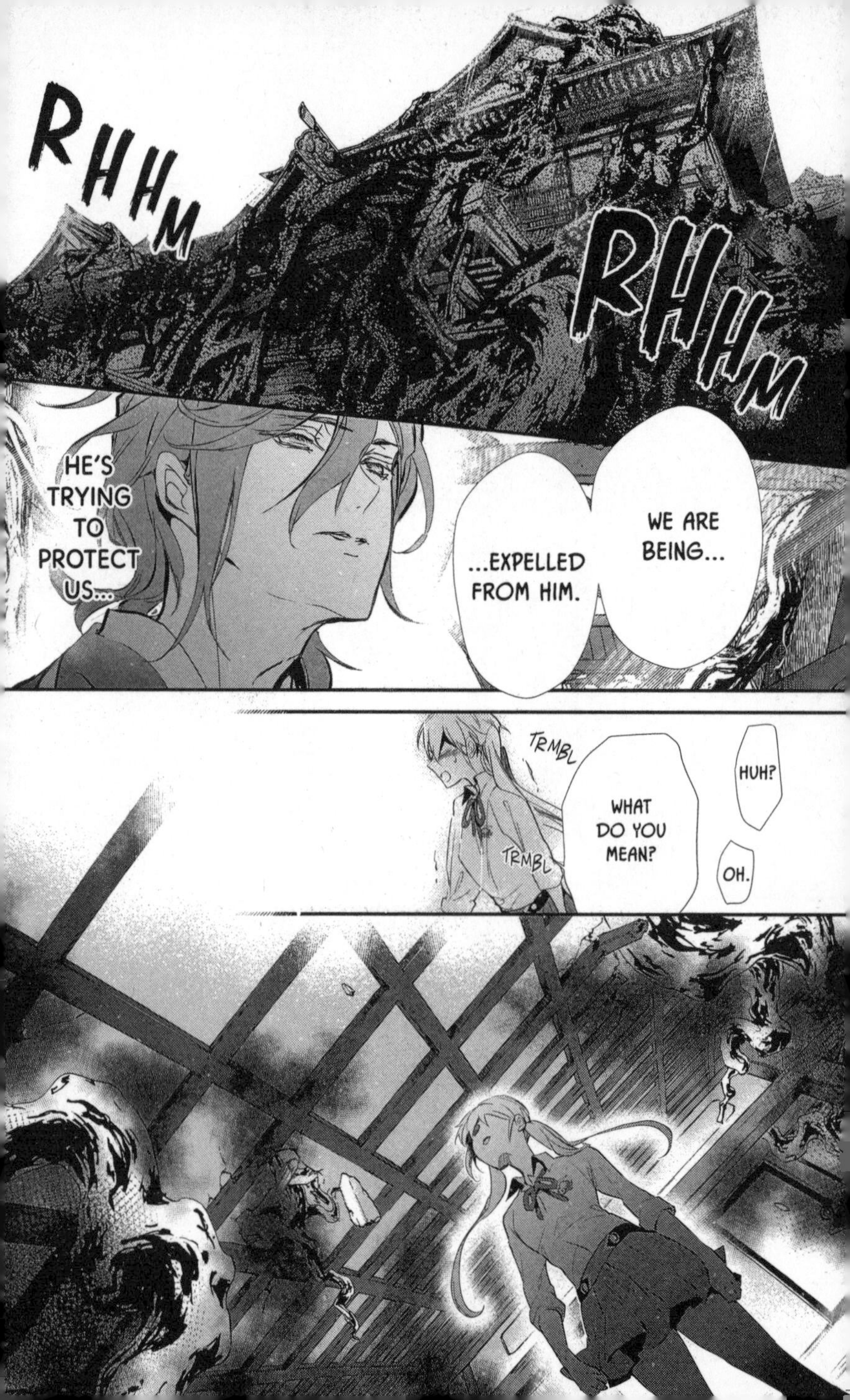
RHHM
RHHM
WE ARE BEING...
...EXPELLED FROM HIM.
HE'S TRYING TO PROTECT US...
HUH?
OH.
WHAT DO YOU MEAN?
TRMBL
TRMBL

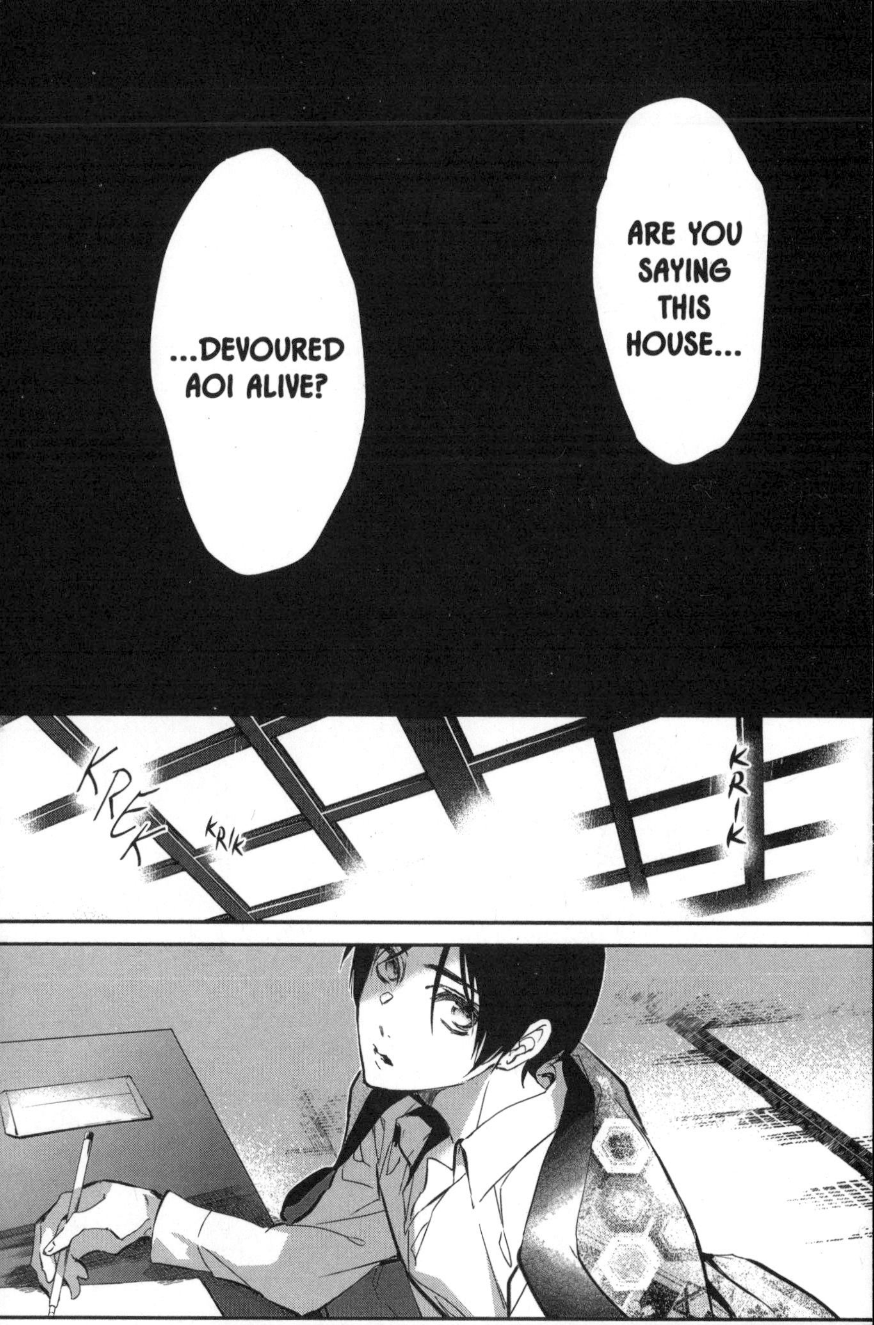
ARE YOU SAYING THIS HOUSE...
...DEVOURED AOI ALIVE?
KRIK
KRIK
KRECK

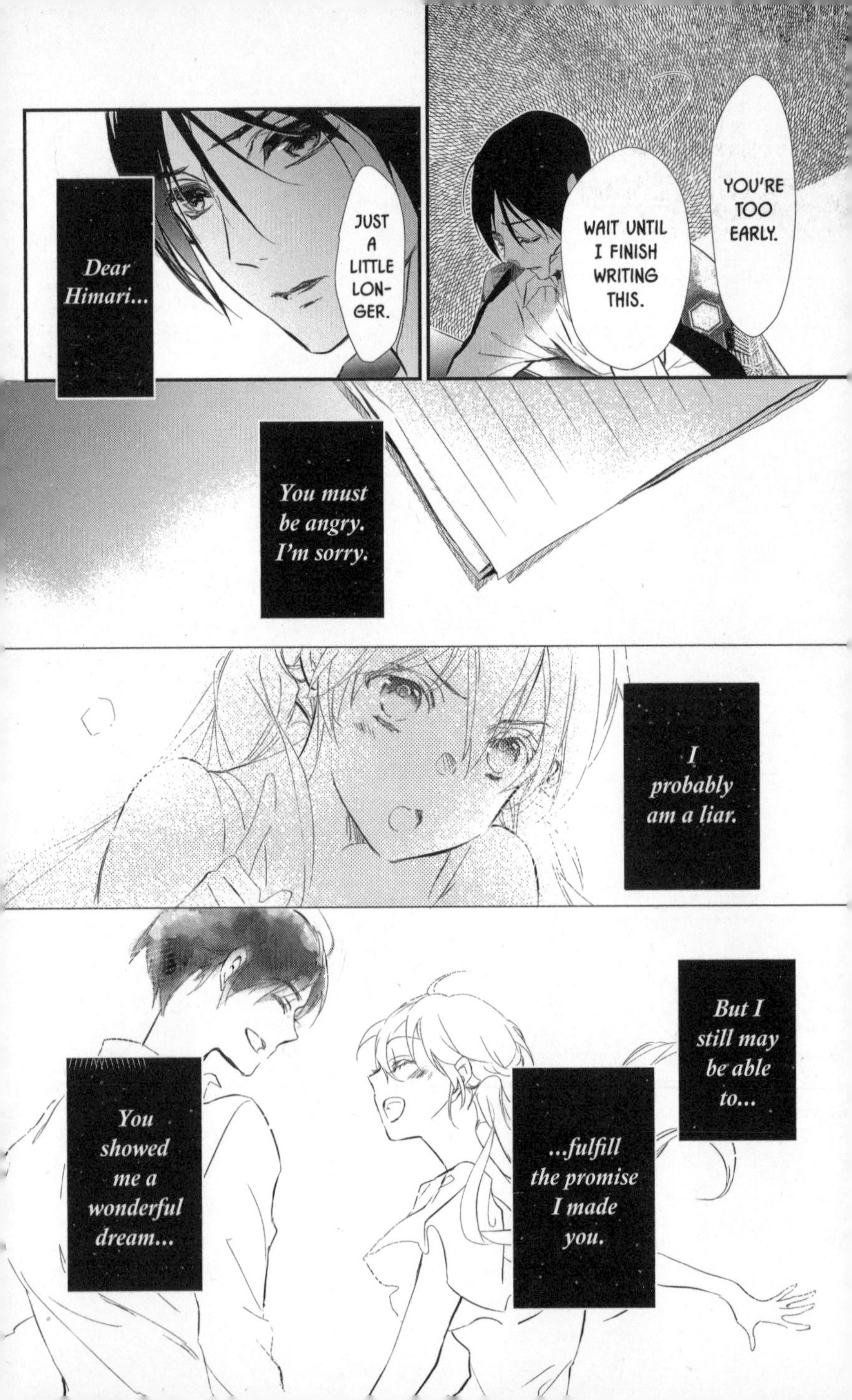
YOU'RE TOO EARLY.
WAIT UNTIL I FINISH WRITING THIS.
JUST A LITTLE LONGER.
Dear Himari...
You must be angry. I'm sorry.
I probably am a liar.
But I still may be able to...
...fulfill the promise I made you.
You showed me a wonderful dream...

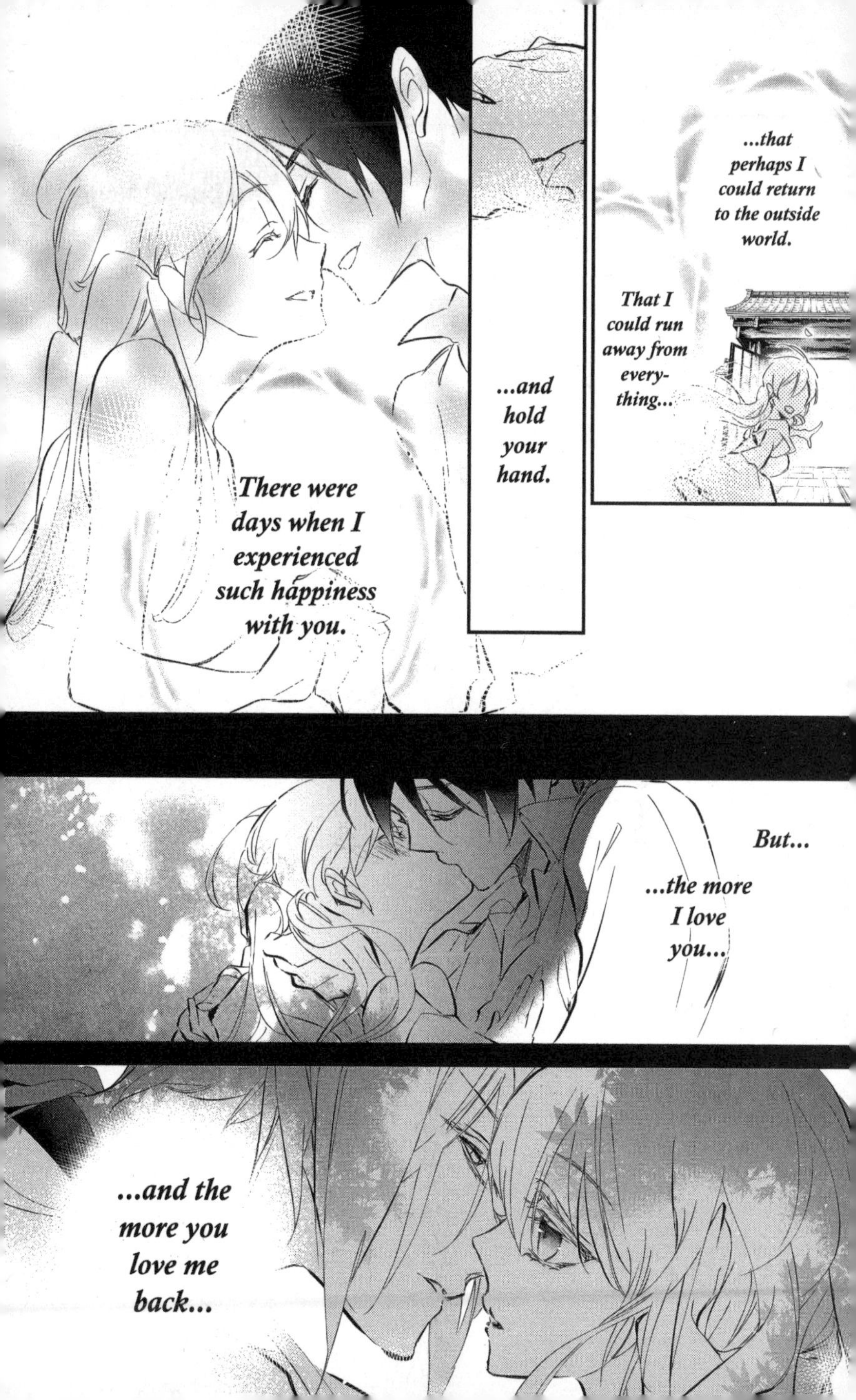
...that perhaps I could return to the outside world.
That I could run away from every- thing...
...and hold your hand.
There were days when I experienced such happiness with you.
But...
...the more I love you...
...and the more you love me back...

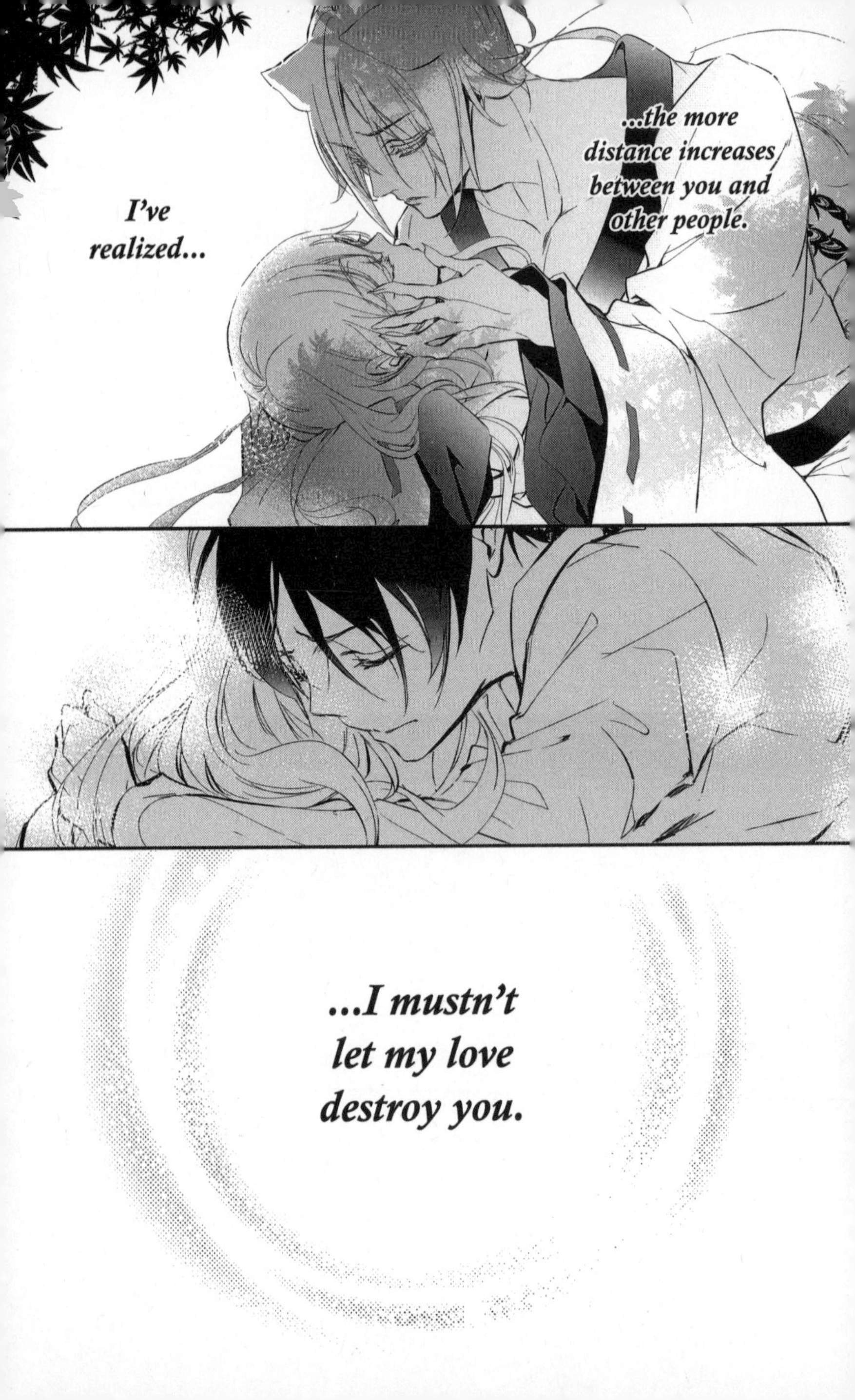
...the more distance increases between you and other people.
I've realized...
...I mustn't let my love destroy you.

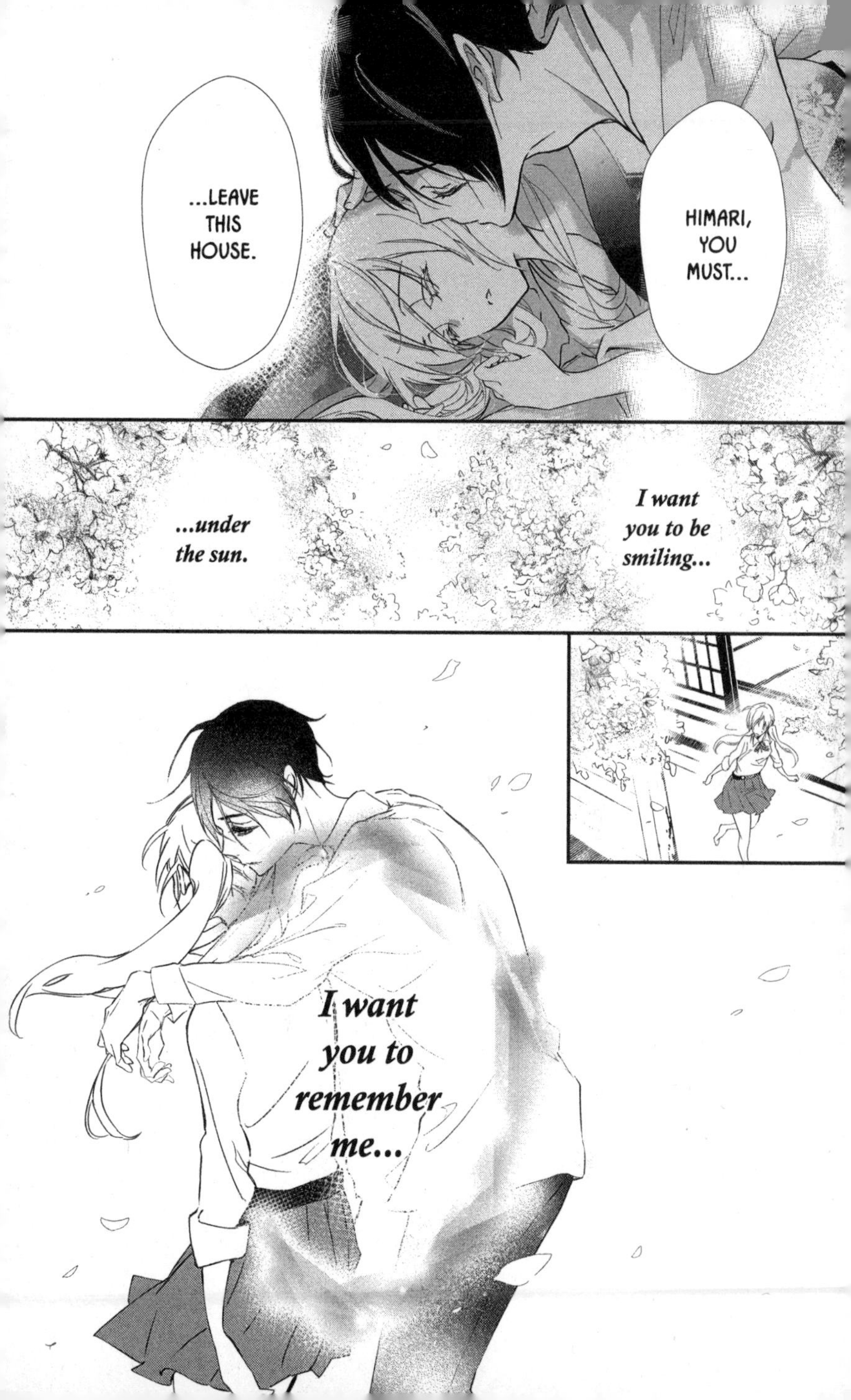
HIMARI, YOU MUST...
...LEAVE THIS HOUSE.
I want you to be smiling...
...under the sun.
I want you to remember me...

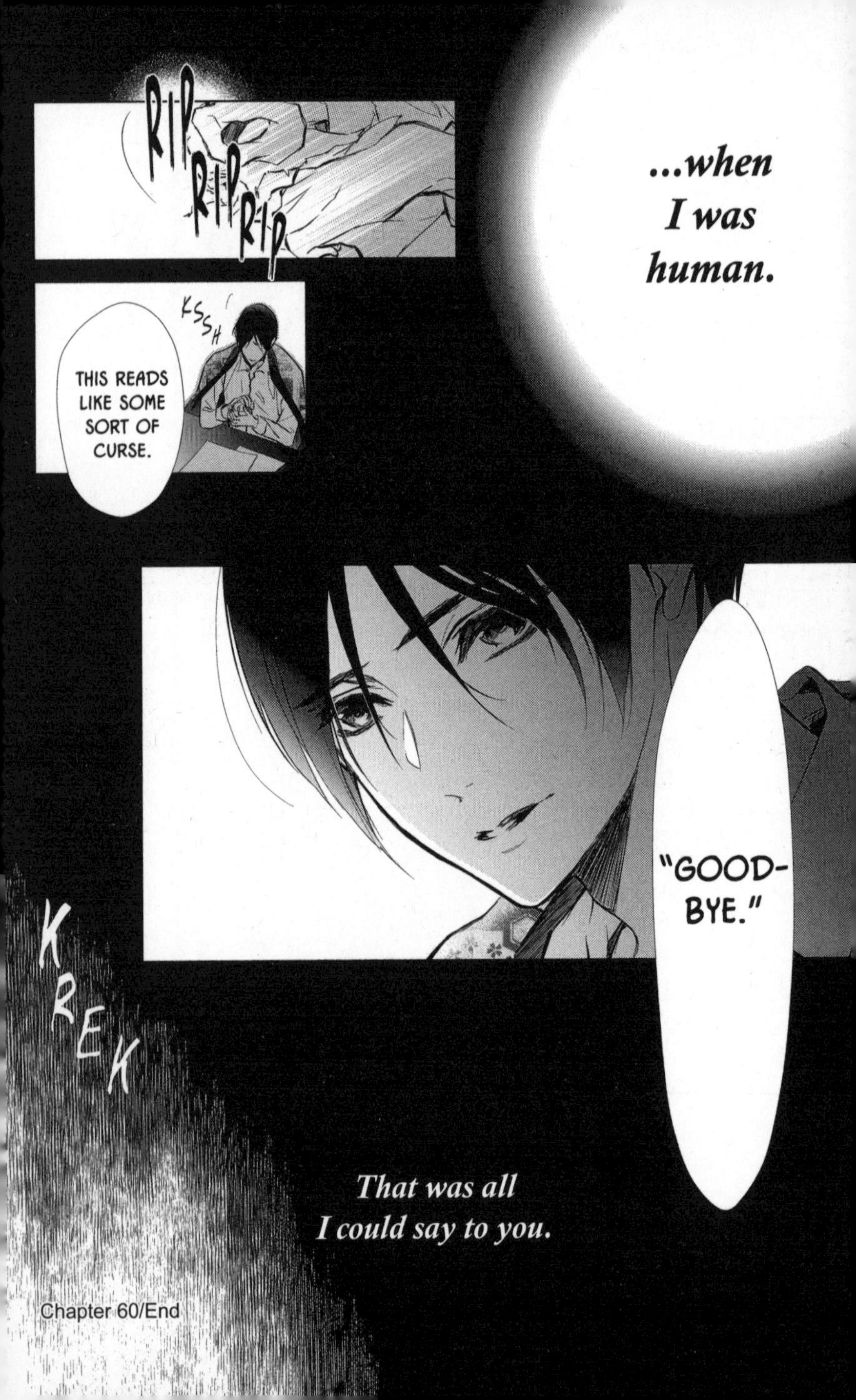
...when I was human.
RIP RIP RIP RIP
KSSH
THIS READS LIKE SOME SORT OF CURSE.
"GOOD-BYE."
KREK
That was all I could say to you.

Chapter 60/End

The DEMON PRINCE of MOMOCHI HOUSE

I'm glad to have spent so much time with *Momochi House*. I've entrusted Aoi to express my many feelings on the cover. Will you accept them? The next volume is the final one.

-*Aya Shouoto*

Aya Shouoto was born on December 25. Her hobbies are traveling, staying at hotels, sewing and daydreaming. She currently lives in Tokyo and enjoys listening to J-pop anime theme songs while she works.

The Demon Prince of Momochi House

Volume 15
Shojo Beat Edition

Story and Art by Aya Shouoto

Translation JN Productions
Touch-Up Art & Lettering Inori Fukuda Trant
Design Jodie Yoshioka
Editor Nancy Thistlethwaite

MOMOCHISANCHI NO AYAKASHI OUJI Volume 15
© Aya Shouoto 2019
First published in Japan in 2019 by KADOKAWA CORPORATION, Tokyo.
English translation rights arranged with KADOKAWA CORPORATION, Tokyo.

Printed in the U.S.A.

Published by VIZ Media, LLC
P.O. Box 77010
San Francisco, CA 94107

10 9 8 7 6 5 4 3 2 1
First printing, March 2020

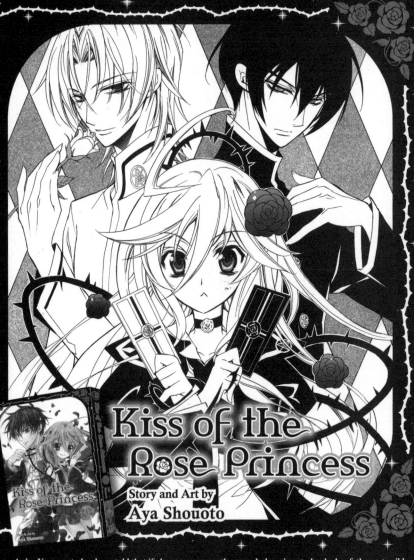

Kiss of the Rose Princess
Story and Art by
Aya Shouoto

Anise Yamamoto has been told that if she ever removes the rose choker given to her by her father, a terrible punishment will befall her. Unfortunately she loses that choker when a bat-like being named Ninufa falls from the sky and hits her. Ninufa gives Anise four cards representing four knights whom she can summon with a kiss. But now that she has these gorgeous men at her beck and call, what exactly is her quest?!

Shojo Beat

RATED T FOR TEEN

viz media
viz.com

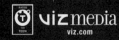

"Bloody" Mary, a vampire with a death wish, has spent the past 400 years chasing down a modern-day exorcist named Maria who is thought to have inherited "The Blood of Maria" and is the only one who can kill Mary. To Mary's dismay, Maria doesn't know how to kill vampires. Desperate to die, Mary agrees to become Maria's bodyguard until Maria can find a way to kill him.

Bloody † Mary

Story and Art by
akaza samamiya

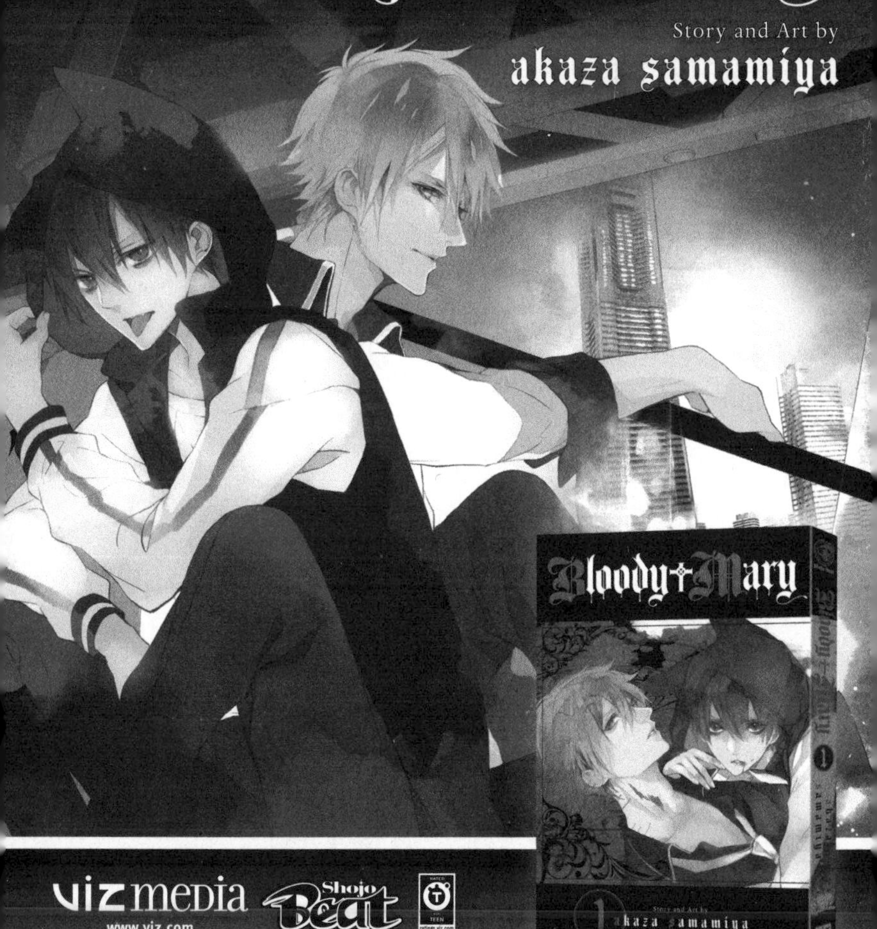

BLOODY MARY Volume 1 © Akaza SAMAMIYA 2014

Ao Haru Ride

STORY AND ART BY
IO SAKISAKA

Futaba Yoshioka thought all boys were loud
and obnoxious until she met Kou Tanaka in
junior high. But as soon as she realized she
really liked him, he had already moved away
because of family issues. Now, in high school,
Kou has reappeared, but is he still the
same boy she fell in love with?

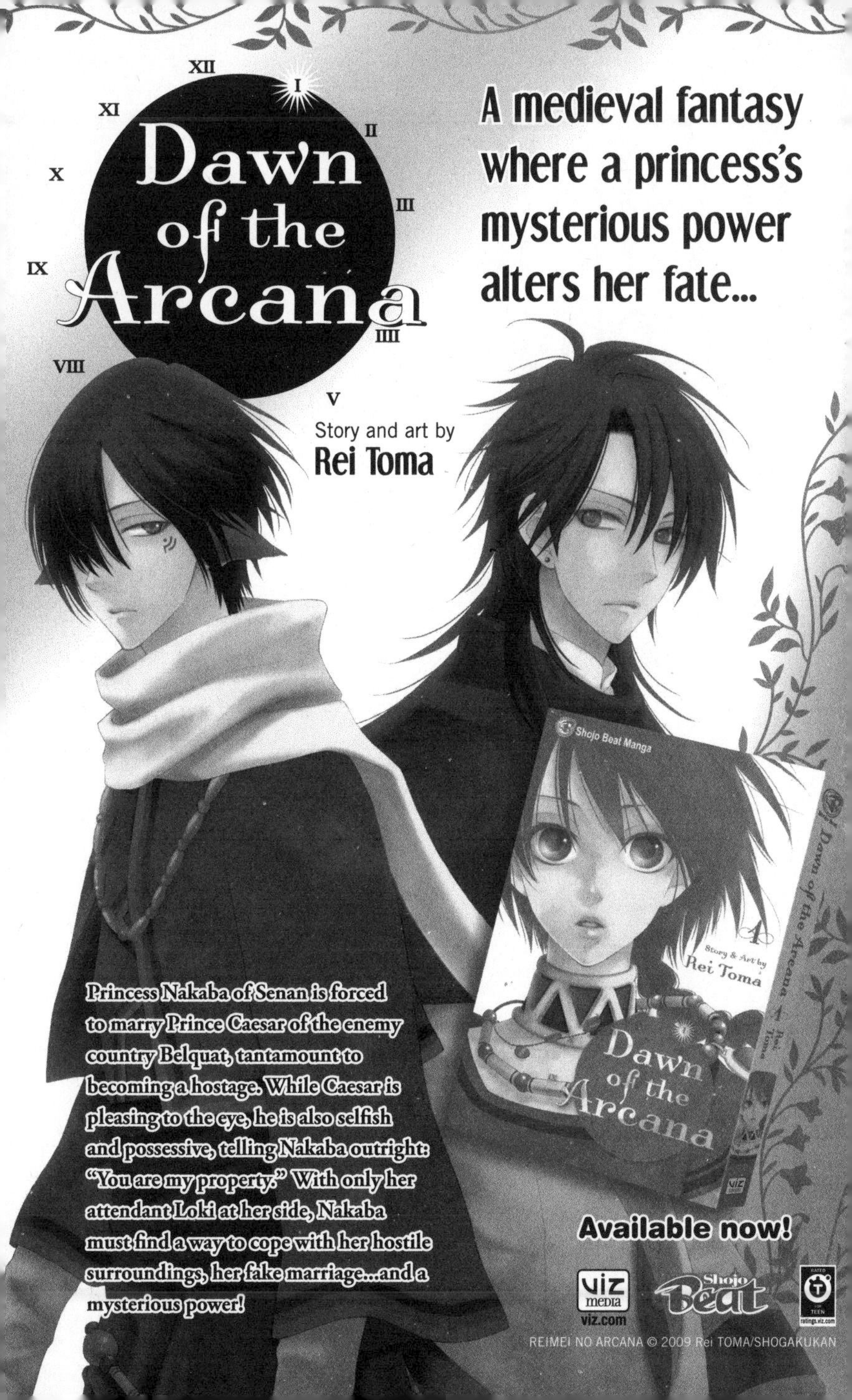
XII
I
II
III
IIII
V
VIII
IX
X
XI
Dawn of the Arcana
A medieval fantasy where a princess's mysterious power alters her fate...
Story and art by
Rei Toma
Shojo Beat Manga
1
Story & Art by
Rei Toma
Dawn of the Arcana
Princess Nakaba of Senan is forced to marry Prince Caesar of the enemy country Belquat, tantamount to becoming a hostage. While Caesar is pleasing to the eye, he is also selfish and possessive, telling Nakaba outright: "You are my property." With only her attendant Loki at her side, Nakaba must find a way to cope with her hostile surroundings, her fake marriage...and a mysterious power!
Available now!
viz media
viz.com
Shojo Beat
RATED T FOR TEEN
ratings.viz.com
REIMEI NO ARCANA © 2009 Rei TOMA/SHOGAKUKAN

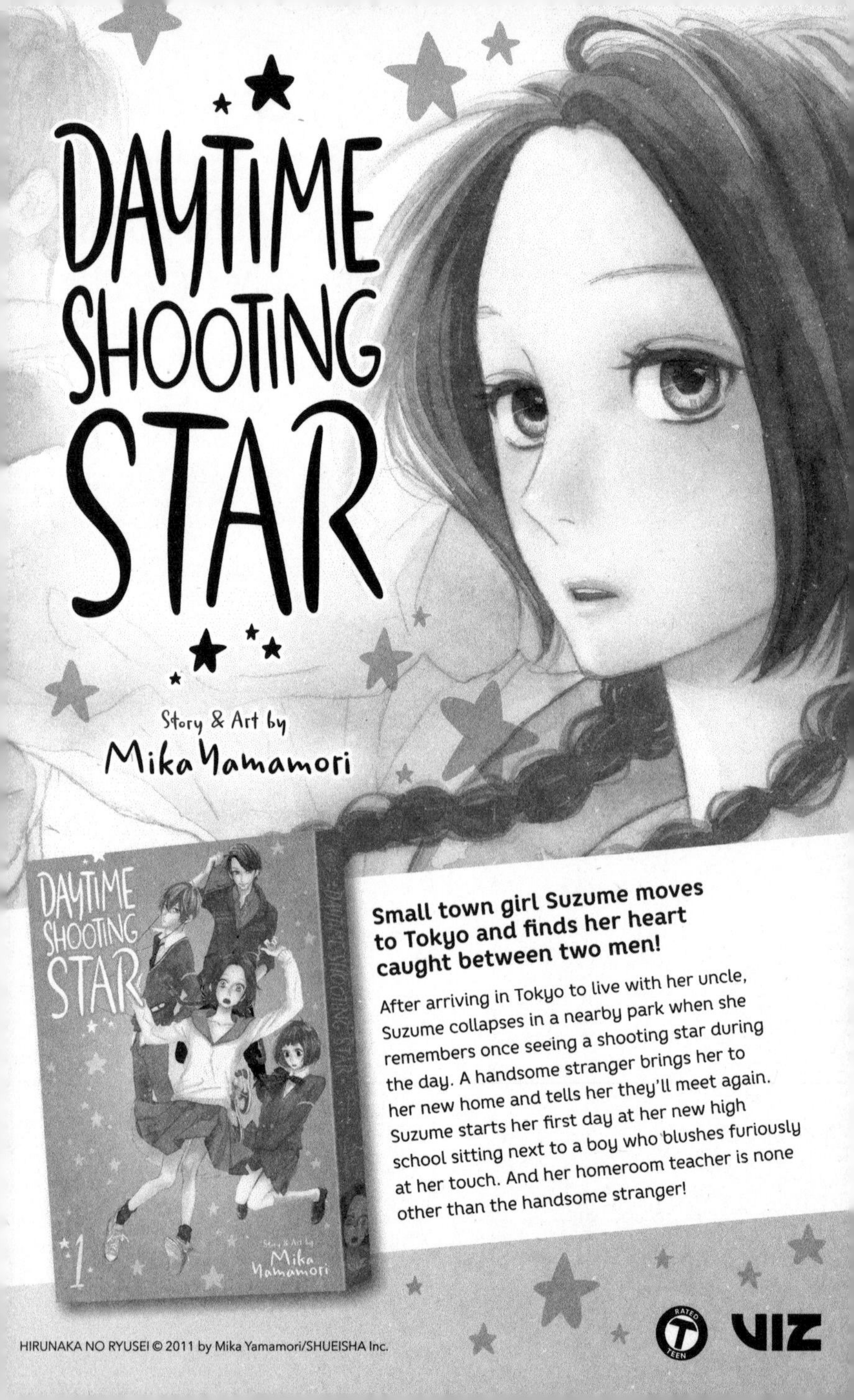
DAYTIME SHOOTING STAR
Story & Art by
Mika Yamamori
DAYTIME SHOOTING STAR
1
Story & Art by Mika Yamamori
Small town girl Suzume moves to Tokyo and finds her heart caught between two men!
After arriving in Tokyo to live with her uncle, Suzume collapses in a nearby park when she remembers once seeing a shooting star during the day. A handsome stranger brings her to her new home and tells her they'll meet again. Suzume starts her first day at her new high school sitting next to a boy who blushes furiously at her touch. And her homeroom teacher is none other than the handsome stranger!
HIRUNAKA NO RYUSEI © 2011 by Mika Yamamori/SHUEISHA Inc.
RATED T TEEN
VIZ

QQ sweeper

Story & Art by
Kyousuke Motomi

By the creator of *Dengeki Daisy* and *Beast Master*!

One day, Kyutaro Horikita, the tall, dark and handsome cleaning expert of Kurokado High, comes across a sleeping maiden named Fumi Nishioka at school... Unfortunately, their meeting is anything but a fairy-tale encounter! It turns out Kyutaro is a "Sweeper" who cleans away negative energy from people's hearts—and Fumi is about to become his apprentice!

QQ sweeper

1

Story & Art by KYOUSUKE MOTOMI

viz.com

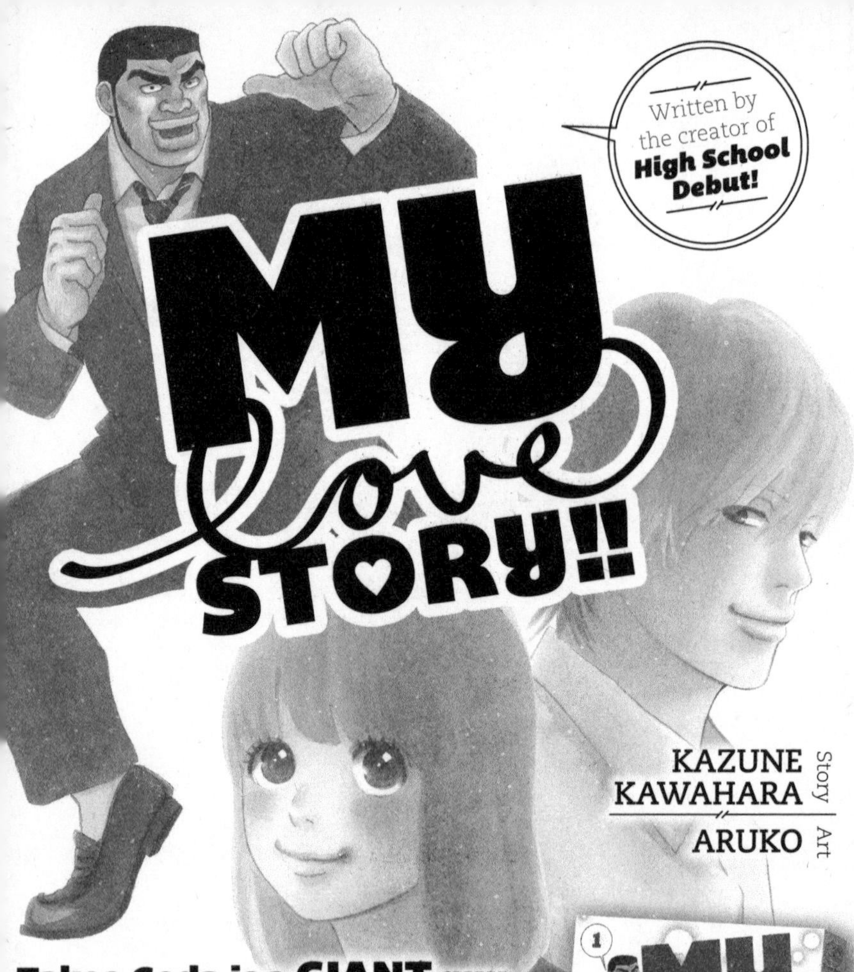
Written by the creator of High School Debut!
MY love STORY!!
KAZUNE KAWAHARA Story
ARUKO Art

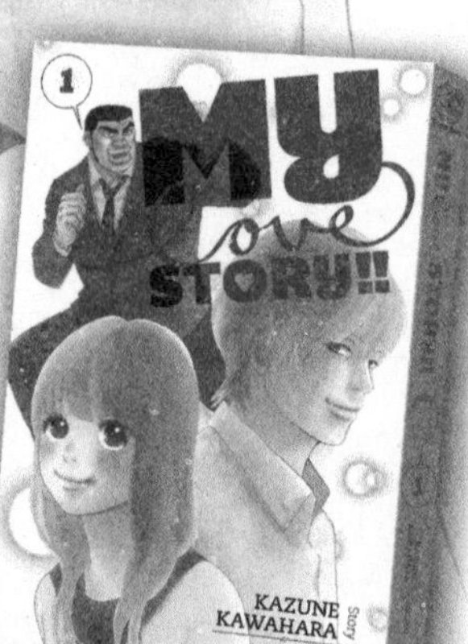
1
MY love STORY!!
KAZUNE KAWAHARA Story
ARUKO Art

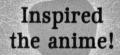

Stop

You may be reading the WRONG WAY!!

IT'S TRUE: In keeping with the original Japanese comic format, this book reads from right to left—so action, sound effects and word balloons are completely reversed. This preserves the orientation of the original artwork—plus, it's fun! Check out the diagram shown here to get the hang of things, and then turn to the other side of the book to get started!

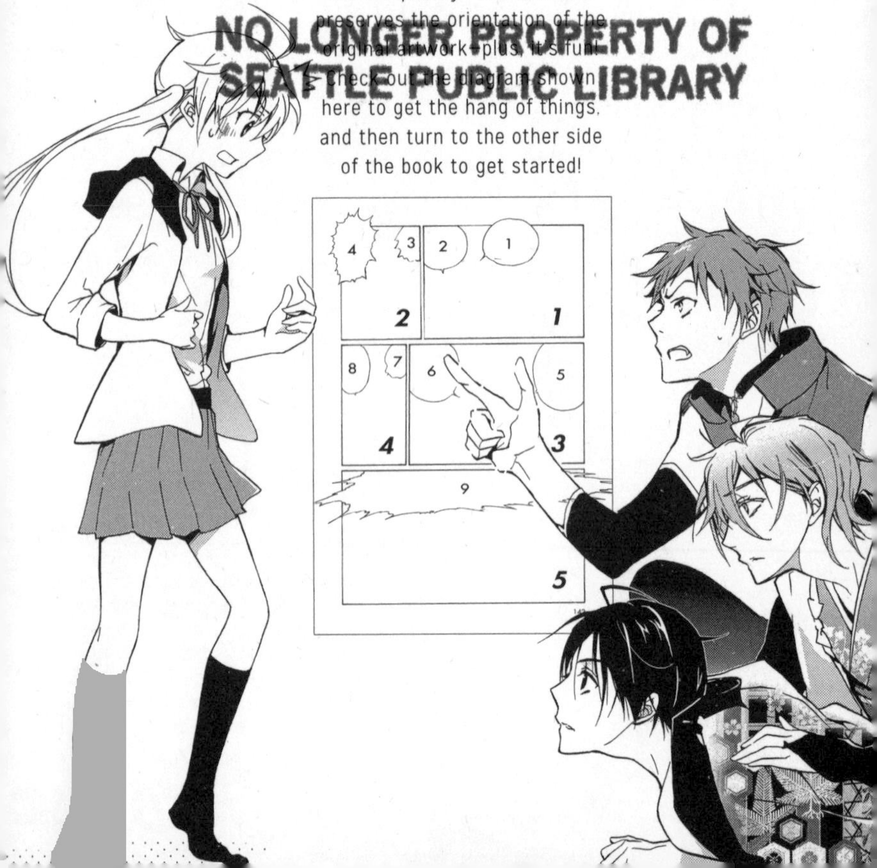
1
2
3
4
1
2
5
6
7
8
3
4
9
5